CAVE
PASSAGES

Roaming the Underground Wilderness

MICHAEL RAY TAYLOR

SCRIBNER

SCRIBNER
1230 Avenue of the Americas
New York, NY 10020

Copyright © 1996 by Michael Ray Taylor

DESIGNED BY ERICH HOBBING

Text set in Electra

Manufactured in the United States of America

10 9 8 7 6 5 4 3 2 1

Library of Congress Cataloging-in-Publication Data
Taylor, Michael Ray, 1959–
Cave passages: roaming the underground wilderness/Michael Ray Taylor.
p.   cm.
Includes index.
1. Caving. 2. Taylor, Michael Ray, 1959– .
3. Spelunkers—United States—Biography.   I. Title.
GV200.62.T37   1996
796.5'25—dc20   95–26266   CIP

ISBN 0-684-81854-X

ACKNOWLEDGMENTS

This book could not have been written without the dedicated work of the individual volunteers who make up the National Speleological Society and the Cave Research Foundation, and it is to these cavers—not just the few mentioned in the text but the many who labor continually for cave conservation, education, and exploration—that I owe my greatest thanks. I am especially indebted to the members of the Florida State Cave Club (which has recently evolved into the Flint River Grotto) and the Northern New Jersey Grotto for my training as a caver and for the many role models and lifetime friends these clubs provided. And I thank Ron Kerbo for always choosing the higher path.

I am also grateful to the organizations that funded many of the expeditions described in this book: CRF, Discovery Communications, the National Audubon Society, the National Geographic Society, *The New Yorker*, the NSS International Exploration Committee, the Smithsonian Institution, *Sports Illustrated*, and Whittle Communications.

Much of the prose was originally shaped under the guidance of several magazine editors. I wish to thank specifically Chris Hunt, Gary Soucie, Gary Parker, Ron King, Rob Fleder, and Bill Beuttler for thoughtful commentary.

I appreciate the diligent work of my primary reader, Lea Ann Alexander, who graciously offered her time to help me through early drafts. Thanks also to Carl Miller and Kathy Taylor for their willingness to read chapters on short notice. Jennifer Chen, Hamilton Cain's assistant at Scribner, helped the book along in a thousand small but essential ways, for which I remain grateful. My gratitude also to Angella J. Baker and Jack Lynch who are surely the sharpest-eyed copy editors ever to scan a page. And thanks to Emily Davis Mobley for always knowing exactly where to find (and always sharing) anything ever written on caves.

Finally, I can never fully express my gratitude to my agent, Esther Newberg, or my editor, Hamilton Cain, for steering me through my first book with wisdom, aplomb, and dead-on publishing savvy.

For
SHECK EXLEY
1949–1994

CONTENTS

10 • Contents

CAVE————

PASSAGES

PREFACE

The great mountains have been climbed, the vast deserts crossed, the long rivers run. Every corner of the planet has been mapped and analyzed, studied by satellite. As the global community shrinks, any explorer who would be the first to set foot on unknown land is left with three choices: fly into space, descend to the ocean floor, or head underground. Of the three, caving remains the choice most reasonably open to the individual.

Some cave for science, some for sport, still others for reasons that they never quite explain. Membership in the National Speleological Society topped 12,000 in 1995. That's more people scrabbling around underground than ever before, but odds are you would never recognize any of them. And it's even more unlikely that you have heard of more than one or two of the thousands of wild American caves through which they travel. That's because, as the outdoor writer Tim Cahill puts it, "Cavers are by and large a closemouthed, introverted, even slightly hostile group." With reason.

Caving is unique in the way it destroys its own environment. A careless nudge can obliterate a crystal latticework thousands of years old. The oil from the touch of a human hand can permanently halt the growth of a forty-foot stalactite. Even the layered mud of a virgin floor is noticeably changed by a single caver's crossing. Cavers continually discover new land. Most of us are driven (some would say obsessed) with preserving that land in its pristine condition. We gate it, purchase it, lie about its location or even its existence, do almost anything but stop caving through it.

And the word is *caving*, not *spelunking*—crossword puzzles not withstanding. The latter term, from the Latin noun *spelunca*, was coined in 1937 by Roger Johnson, a bookseller and caver living in Springfield, Massachusetts. After a friend of his used it in several newspaper articles, *Life* and *The Saturday Evening Post* picked it up in the 1940s. Lexicographers loved it, but "spelunking" never really caught on with practitioners, who had been "caving" for decades. The verb *cave*, meaning to explore subterranean passages, and the related noun *caver* have been in use since 1865, according to *The Oxford English Dictionary*. (Other terms from the caving lexicon are defined in the glossary beginning on page 269.)

By any name, caving—along with cave diving, a far more dangerous offshoot—is in the midst of a golden age of discovery, comparable to the jungle penetrations of the last century or the mountain conquests of Hillary's day. The greatest caverns are presently being explored for the first time. Since I began in 1979, enormous cave systems have been discovered on the island of Borneo, in the jungles of Belize, beneath the ice of central Alaska, and below a desert plateau in the Sultanate of Oman.

I've been lucky enough to have met a few of the explorers who find the great caves. I have joined them in Mexico, Jamaica, China, and throughout the United States. This book is their story, and it's my own. But mostly it's about the caves themselves. It is the story of a hidden realm of delicate beauty, of a wilderness that deserves our understanding and our protection, of a surprising universe that lies just beneath the surface of the world.

PEBBLES

Until the spring of 1994, I had never been on a trip where someone died. I had always known that caving could be dangerous and that cave diving *was* dangerous. And it was a diver who had died, the world's most experienced cave diver, in fact, and he had died while operating in the most extreme conditions imaginable. But such knowledge in the abstract amounts to very little. So two weeks after Sheck Exley drowned in Mexico, I'm sitting in my office in Arkansas, trying to reconcile knowledge and experience.

The phone rings. A picture editor at *Sports Illustrated* wants my help in locating underwater portraits taken during Sheck's earlier expeditions. I am writing an article about his life and death. I say I will try.

I dial the number of a noted cave diver who is also a professional photographer and explain what I want.

He is quiet for a moment, then says, "So you've decided to make some money off of Sheck's death, have you?"

After a few seconds, I manage to stammer that I joined the expedition strictly at the request of its leader, Sheck's partner Jim Bowden. I had traveled to a training dive the previous December, I remind him, had helped the project find financial support. The world needs to know what kind of a man Sheck Exley was, I say. I tell the caver—a recognized expert whom I have accompanied underground on several occasions—that he's full of crap.

He backs down, says he hadn't realized that I was there as

an actual member of the team. "I was just yanking your chain," he says.

It was a good yank.

He suggests some names for the kind of photos the magazine wants, and we hang up. For a while, I stare out my office window at the Garrison Quadrangle of Henderson State University, where I teach journalism. Students toss Frisbees in the Arkansas sunshine. The window, shaped in the familiar oblong proportions of the big screen, takes up most of one wall. Through it, I have followed the march of summer thunderheads, studied the rare winter snowfall as it slowly shut down the campus.

As I look out the window, I absently fish around in my top desk drawer until my fingers brush something hard. I lift a small black rock to the light. It is cool to the touch, smooth as though polished in a tumbler. Here is tangible proof of some dark place I have been. I rub it like a lucky rabbit's foot, a talisman against the ordinary.

I pull out other pebbles to hold them in my palm. I roll them around like Bogart with his ball bearings in *The Caine Mutiny*. These bits of polished chert and limestone bear the marks of lost rivers, of powerful forces working underground.

So do I.

I found one amid a jumble of boulders the size of Winnebagos, at the bottom of a 750-foot pit in central Mexico, in 1989. I remember that I was the seventh person to descend the pit. Another, an irregular marble of red brick, lay for decades on a gravel bank inside an abandoned water tunnel beneath Spanish Harlem, in upper Manhattan. It was two or three in the morning when I crawled upon it. Two friends and I had just rappelled the hollow, 100-foot-tall stone supports of an aqueduct bridge built over the Harlem River in 1843. We were passing through a valve chamber en route to a crumbling exit shaft located in the Bronx.

I plucked a third pebble from a ledge somewhere inside a mountain of northern Guangdong Province. The same two friends and I were rigging a short pit at the back of a cave when the black oval caught my eye. Something made me drop it into my pack before I stepped into unexplored space and rappelled a hundred feet in the general direction of Arkansas. Throughout the long course of geologic history, the three of us are probably the only sentient beings who will ever stand in the white, crystal-lined room at the base of that otherwise unremarkable shaft. We brought light where no light had been. We left footprints which should remain undisturbed throughout the lives of my great-grandchildren. As we climbed out, we sang the Monty Python song "Sit on My Face and Tell Me That You Love Me."

I was a caver who came to writing, not the other way around. I always try to emphasize safety and conservation in my work, to avoid the gee-whiz, Indiana Jones approach. And now Sheck Exley is dead in a gee-whiz, Indiana Jones sort of accident, and I'm writing about it. My justifications for the article are exactly as I explained them to Sheck's grieving friend. But I know that he and most cavers—including Sheck—have always shunned publicity, with good reason.

Stories on the dangers of caving and cave diving make landowners jittery about lawsuits, leading them to close entrances. Accounts of bejeweled chambers may inspire underground traffic by beginners, who are prone to damage rare formations and suffer needless—and often highly publicized—injuries. And he was right: Sheck is dead, and I'm getting paid. The article, like my teaching career, my writing, and much of my adult life, will come to exist because of what began as a teenage hobby.

I'm a thirty-four-year-old assistant professor. With the exception of these pebbles, I've always followed the caver's creed: "Take nothing but pictures, leave nothing but footprints, kill nothing but time." Slipping little rocks into my pocket never felt like vandalism, in the way that collecting a gypsum flower or a crystallized bat skeleton certainly would.

Sooner or later, I know that erosion will carry off the loose rocks, the gypsum flowers, the stalactites, the land overhead, and my own decayed remains. Like mountains and continents, caves are permanent structures only when considered from the human perspective. Still, out of deference to that perspective—geologically negligible though it is—and out of respect for the beauty of the caves themselves, I have taken from them nothing but these pebbles and the permissible pictures.

On the wall before me is a diploma from Florida State, another from South Carolina. They look insignificant beside the pictures. In the poster hanging over my desk, for instance, sunlight streams through an oval shaft to illuminate a sandy cavern.

Whenever visitors comment on the photo, I ask them to find the person. "You have to stand close," I say.

Beneath the shaft, atop a smooth rubble pile that looks like an anthill, stands a human figure a quarter inch tall.

Everyone says the same thing: "Wow. That's not real, is it?"

It is real. The picture was taken during a National Speleological Society expedition to the Sultanate of Oman in 1988. The tiny person is an American caver named John Ganter, who is actually over six feet tall. I wasn't there. The photographer, Kevin Downey, gave me the poster in 1990, when he visited me in New Jersey, which is where I used to live. Kevin had come to discuss a planned expedition to Lechuguilla and to photograph the old aqueduct in New York.

A few weeks ago, *Sports Illustrated* hired Kevin to take pictures of a world-record scuba attempt by Sheck Exley and Jim Bowden. We shared a rental car from Tampico to the remote dive site. I shuffle through my desk and pull out a page of manuscript. Here's Kevin, using his telephoto lens to spot Mary Ellen Eckoff, treading water in the sinkhole below us. Again I hear the way he says "Oh my" when he sees her tear-streaked face. Again I look away from the immense sadness in his eyes as he passes the camera to me.

A black-and-white print hangs to my left, across from the window. Hazy light filters from a distant entrance into an irregular passage with a sloping roof. The chamber appears roughly 30 feet tall by 50 feet wide. Two figures face each other in silhouette. One stands in a dry streambed at bottom right, the other atop a ten-foot boulder to the left. I'm the guy on the boulder. The guy in the streambed is Tom Stockert. The photographer is Ian Baren. It was around two in the afternoon, halfway through a 1990 scouting trip in southern China. We were heading into Swallow Cave. After the photo was taken, the three of us stayed underground all night, mapping several enormous rooms before we hiked out to the village of Ru Yuan for a pepper omelet and *cha*.

Beside Swallow Cave hangs a small color print clipped from a 1991 caving calendar. It shows a room called the Great Hall, a vast arched chamber reminiscent of the nave of a Gothic cathedral—except that it lists thirty degrees to the left. Four explorers in orange coveralls work their way toward the far end of the slanted corridor, backs to the camera. The figures are evenly spaced, shrinking in perspective as they scramble over rocks and along ledges, striking macho poses. All of them are me. The multiple exposure was taken by Ron Simmons in 1987, during a difficult trip to a cave called Great Expectations, beneath the Bighorn Mountains of Wyoming.

The shot was carefully lit, with no ghost images. I look like four different people. I lean into the print. I can see no evidence of Jeb Blakely, who hid behind boulders, firing large, old-fashioned flashbulbs to paint the tunnel with light. I can see no zigzag yellow trails left by my helmet-mounted lamp, because Ron hung a handkerchief over the open lens each time we changed positions.

I can't see a lot of things: Me sweating in the full wet suit I wore beneath the coveralls, the quarter inch of neoprene I had donned as protection against the icy water I knew lay ahead. The other five shots we tried that weren't quite as good. The way I'd overheat in the wet suit during the long climb out, dehydrating to the point that I'd start vomiting near the entrance. How I'd remain sick in camp for the next two days, while Ron and stronger cavers shot roll after roll of subterranean waterfalls, rapids, and crawlways for a *National Geographic* story that eventually ran in *Sports Illustrated*.

The pebbles rattle.

Over the past few years, I've gradually begun to avoid big expeditions in favor of fatherhood, a regular job, home repair—all the insidious trappings of normalcy. Before my trip to Tampico, six months, maybe a year, had passed without my talking to another caver. In the year before that, I went caving exactly twice, two weekend tourist trips that didn't amount to much. I remember Kevin Downey calling in 1993 with a lovely opportunity to inspect Neanderthal art in a secret cave in Romania. A couple of months ago he called about a cave expedition to a previously uncharted corner of Borneo's Sarawak region. I cringed a little as I turned down both projects. Since Alex and the twins were born, I explained, since I became an assistant professor, I can't just vanish for weeks at a time. Not anymore.

The stones feel like misshapen dice. The places and events they represent have grown so different from my surface life that they seem a part of someone else, personal metaphors whose meaning has gone fuzzy. My department chair and I play racquetball twice a week. I put the kids to bed, grade papers, have cookouts with the neighbors. I host poker nights. I've achieved such distance from my long obsession that here, sitting in my comfortable office, looking at my pages on the death of a true explorer, I am at last tempted to ask the question my wife and mother and friends have been asking for fifteen years: Why do it? Why risk life and limb to go underground?

What have I gained, besides photos on the wall and a handful of rocks?

2

Down to a Sunless Sea

Caves and blue springs dot the cactus-covered limestone plains of east-central Mexico. Here the rivers flow underground, gathering heat and minerals, boring tunnels under the desert. Above the teeming aquifer a flat, rocky scrub stretches from the El Abra Mountains in the west to the Gulf of Mexico, thirty miles to the east. Home to snakes, scorpions, and a few scraggly cows, the baked plain is blasted by el viento del norte, *a hot northern wind that comes often. When it comes, it lingers for days.*

April 6, 1994

At high noon the *norte* rages. I stand with a handful of reporters and ranchers above an enormous water-filled sinkhole called Zacatón. We stare down 70 feet at the surface of a warm thermal spring. White plumes of sulfur swirl through the water like milk. The sinkhole's diameter is greater than the length of a football field; its contours define a natural arena gouged from stone. We stalk the perimeter of the hole, straining for a glimpse of two men who should soon rise from a world scuba depth record, achieved in absolute darkness over 1,000 feet below the water's surface.

Hot wind snatches hats from our heads and words from our mouths. Bright circles of floating saw grass, 10 to 30 feet in diameter, bounce across the water like slow-motion billiard balls. I try to comprehend the spring's impossible depth. If the Empire State Building sank to the bottom, I could step onto its main observation deck from where I stand. We amble like tourists. Hands in pockets, cameras dangling from straps, we wait for something to happen.

Somewhere down in the water is Sheck Exley, a high school calculus teacher and karate expert from Live Oak, Florida. Exley, forty-five, is also the undisputed master of deep scuba, which is practiced mostly in cave pools and flooded pits. He has logged more than 4,000 successful cave dives, far more than anyone else. It is Exley's own depth record of 867 feet, set in 1989 at another Mexican cave spring called Nacimiento Mante, that he and a colleague, Jim Bowden, have set out to break this morning.

Bowden is a fifty-two-year-old adventurer and dive instructor from Austin. Five years ago, he discovered Zacatón after more than a decade spent searching the springs and caves of Mexico and Central America for deep places where no human had been. Under Exley's tutelage, Bowden has trained for the past year for this moment. He poured thousands of dollars into the equipment needed to make a record descent. He recovered from a case of the bends—suffered on a training dive at Zacatón in November—that would have retired, if not killed, other cave divers.

Closer to the surface, yet hidden from us by the suspended sulfur, three support divers hover, waiting to assist in an anticipated ten-hour decompression. A 1,000-foot descent packs nitrogen into the blood like bubbles in beer; rising too fast would rip joints and muscles from within. The hours of slow ascent, while they breathe precise mixtures of oxygen, helium, and nitrogen at prescribed levels, will let the divers properly outgas, or shed, the excess nitrogen.

Parallel ropes, 25 feet apart, are tied to rocks at the water's edge. They dangle halfway down the pit's plumbed depth— 1,085 feet at this side. (No other soundings along the perimeter have been taken.) The twin ropes hold more than two dozen dive tanks that are to bring Bowden and Exley back to air. Two hours ago the explorers entered the sinkhole by swimming through a 600-foot-long horizontal cave, thus avoiding a difficult rappel down the cliff face. Hidden 30 feet below the floating grass, this natural tunnel carries currents that rise from the depths of Zacatón to spill from a nearby spring.

At last two of the support divers surface. The wind gusts so strongly that none of us above can hear what they are saying. But we can see. We see a woman in a wet suit grabbing the shoulders of another woman, holding her, placating her. We see bubbles, as regular as breath, plopping up near one of the ropes. We see the other rope hanging in water that is chillingly still.

The sun beats down. The hot wind blows. A few others gather at the edge of Zacatón, among them Marcus Gary, who at twenty-three is by far the youngest member of the expedition. "What's going on?" Gary yells to the figures treading water 70 feet below. They don't answer. Perhaps the wind has kept them from hearing.

The third support diver surfaces to join the other two. Beside them, bubbles rise from one line only.

Two photographers use their telephoto lenses to close in on the women in the water. What they see makes them stop snapping frames. "Oh my," one of them says, his voice barely audible in a lapse between gusts.

Gary moves closer to the edge, leaning precariously from a gnarled tree. "What?" he shouts. Again, louder: "Hey! What! Happened!"

The photographer silently lowers his camera and passes it to me. I bring into sharp focus the tear-streaked face of my friend Mary Ellen Eckoff, who once held the women's world scuba depth record and is the longtime companion of Sheck Exley. Just then she looks up and screams, "No!"

The shout echoes from the limestone walls and dies in a sob that the wind carries to us all.

Each year, an avarage of 600 people are certified as cave divers by the National Speleological Society Cave Diving Section, located in Branford, Florida. According to Joe Odom, chairman of the society, there are now more than 14,000 certified cave divers, compared with just a 1,000 in 1984. Yet from rank novices to those on the cutting edge of discovery, all cave divers are continually faced with their own mortality.

The sport is to open-water scuba as flying an F-16 is to piloting a Cessna. The difference is that the weekend pilot can't grab the stick of a fighter, while Joe Scuba needs only to find an underwater hole and swim in. It is a sport in which nearly all errors are fatal. Most cave divers with more than five years' experience have participated in at least one body recovery. Sheck Exley made a total of thirty-six recoveries.

The dead are usually open-water divers, sometimes even dive instructors, unaware of the special hazards of submerged caves: loose ceilings; silt that rises from the floor of disturbed passages to darken water that was transparent going in; vertigo induced by huge irregular chambers, confusing some to the point that they literally cannot tell up from down; mind-numbing cold and depth; flashlights that won't operate below shallow depths, or, believe it or not, no light source at all. Bodies have been found within ten feet of a silt-obscured entrance, fingers scraped raw from a last, desperate attempt to claw through solid rock. Sometimes untrained cave divers panic and drown for no discernible reason. At least four died in the past decade with more than thirty minutes of air left in their tanks and an easy way out.

Odom reminds his students: "When you've reached your maximum penetration"—by definition, when a cave diver has used one-third of his air reserves—"you are farther from breathable air than a space shuttle astronaut. NASA could scrub a shuttle mission, de-orbit, and land quicker than you could exit a cave. Your technology needs to be at least as redundant as theirs."

Those who make it through proper cave training and certification enjoy a safety record far better than that of open-water divers. *Basic Cave Diving: A Blueprint for Survival*, published by the NSS-CDS, is one of the first manuals to be read by prospective cave divers. To bring home the danger of the sport, each chapter begins with a terse accident account, illustrating how the flouting of a particular safety procedure needlessly cost a life (or several). Such reading can make even the laziest student suddenly attentive.

The author of this and six other cave-diving texts, and hundreds of published cave-diving articles, is Sheck Exley.

JUNE 29, 1968

Saturday. Wakulla Springs, Florida. Children laugh on the beach. Teenagers jackknife and cannonball from the high dive. Smells of grilled chicken mix with Coppertone and cabbage palms. Somewhere, Jim Morrison sings "Hello, I Love You" on a transistor radio. The 72-degree water hums with the pinging motor of a glass-bottomed boat. Tourists pass over the powerful boil, gawking at the great cave 120 feet below. The water carries another sound too, something distant, metallic, rhythmic: *Hiss. Bubble. Hiss. Bubble.*

Pure water, stuff so clear and clean that it will one day spawn an industry, flows under the whole of North Florida, carving up hard white limestone that rings like a bell, chuckling forth at hundreds of great blue springs, of which Wakulla is the greatest. Today, once again, its deep water has lured the Exley boys, nineteen-year-old Sheck and sixteen-year-old Edward, all the way from Jacksonville.

Irby Sheck Exley, Jr., home from the University of Georgia, dives every weekend, paying for equipment and compressed air with a summer job in the parts department of his father's Volkswagen dealership. In the five years since he took a basic scuba certification course at a YMCA pool, he's gained a reputation among the slow-talking southern boys who hang out at the Panhandle's dive shops. They say Sheck can make a tank of air last longer than it ought to, can keep a calm head at depths that should knock him woozy with nitrogen. Maybe it's the mental discipline of karate—he's only months away from a black belt—that lets him slow his heart and lungs by sheer will, allows him to think straight at 300 feet below. Maybe it's his obsession with gear, the way he rebuilds half the things he buys, finds and corrects potential flaws in regulators designed by naval engineers.

Sheck takes after his father, Irby, in his compact, muscular build and chiseled good looks, in his ability to stare a stranger in the eye and win his trust in an instant. It's as if Sheck inherited along with the face the *confidence* of the man who survived two and half years of infantry service all over the European theater; who walked out of the swamps of Clyo, Georgia, to finish a college education; who worked his way to the top of a Ford tractor dealership before starting his own shop. But put the boys together and Edward's the one who looks the natural athlete. Sixteen and already six feet tall, he's tan as Tab Hunter, good with a basketball. Edward's the one the girls watch from their beach towels as the brothers walk over the sand, carrying their masks and fins into Wakulla.

Sheck might go all afternoon without saying two words.

Edward has the old man's gift of gab, always the center of attention. He flirts at the water's edge. There's an easy and almost infectious wildness about him. Back when ten-year-old Sheck was cataloging—by sex, size, and species—the snakes that lived in the swamp across the street from their suburban home, seven-year-old Edward was slipping them down girls' dresses.

Tanks and regulators sit in the back of Sheck's Beetle, ready for another spring the two plan to visit on the way home. Signs in the Wakulla parking lot prohibit scuba. Old Mr. Ball, of the Du Pont clan, owns the springs and half of Wakulla County. He hasn't let anyone don scuba gear on the property since the 1950s. But Wakulla is a great place for free diving, for the brothers to see how long they can hold their breath and how far they can push the needle on Sheck's new depth gauge. They swim effortlessly out to the deep water, where they take turns strapping the stainless-steel dial on their wrists.

Over and over again they hyperventilate and head for the bottom, waiting until the last possible second to turn and point their bursting lungs toward the Florida sun. Edward pushes the needle to 40 feet. Sheck takes it to 45. Edward makes 52. Sheck focuses his mind, relaxes, and hits 60 feet. Edward laughs and sucks in mighty gusts, hyperventilating to the edge of consciousness. Sheck watches his brother plunge to 60 feet and keep going, swimming deeper than either of them has gone without scuba. He watches Edward start to turn and suddenly go limp. He watches Edward begin to float slowly downward.

Sheck hyperventilates and kicks with everything he's got. It's not enough: The bottom is so very far away. Edward grows smaller in the distance. After three fruitless efforts, Sheck climbs out of the water, shouting for help. He runs to his car for the air tanks, but another swimmer, a certified diver, convinces Sheck that he's too exhausted and panicked to dive. This man straps on the tank, running back down the beach as seconds tick by. He enters the water and pumps his fins. *Bubble. Hiss. Bubble. Hiss.* Risking the bends, the swimmer pulls Edward from the sandy bottom and up to the beach. Before a panicked crowd, Sheck pounds blood-tinged water from his brother's lungs, willing him to live, calmly and correctly breathing life into him. Just life enough to place Edward into an ambulance and onto a machine. Late that night, with his parents standing by the bed, with Sheck and his younger sister Beth nearby, the machine is turned off.

Edward is gone.

June 8, 1972

After Edward's death, Sheck turns his grief into a drive for perfection underwater, for safety and technique, for achievement without mishap. He begins diving with Ned DeLoach, the most experienced cave diver of that time. By 1970, he holds world records for both linear distance traveled and depth achieved in a cave dive. His gear designs and safety procedures are adopted by much older, more experienced divers.

People pay attention to Sheck Exley, pay him compliments. Sheck always turns the compliments around, praising the speaker: *Nonsense, I didn't do anything special. I'm sure you could have done the same. Probably a lot better. The important thing is that we had a safe dive.*

He confides to a friend, "I can't stop diving, but I can make it safer. I've got to. I can't put my parents through that kind of pain again."

Sheck makes his black belt, spends hours a day in exercise. He eliminates every ounce of body fat. He writes, reads poetry, plays the piano, toys with differential equations, listens to Beethoven.

Today he has come home with his business degree. The swamp across the street has been drained, has begun to fill with increasingly prosperous-looking homes. The walls of his father's office have been covered with plaques and certificates, all testifying to a community pillar: head of the Jacksonville Chamber of Commerce, chairman of the annual United Way drive, Sunday school teacher at the Ortega Methodist Church. Sheck sits across from the desk, waiting for his father to come home.

Irby closes the door and sits down. "You wanted to talk?"

"Dad, I'd like a job."

The older man nods. "All right. I've got a question to ask." He looks his son in the eye. "Do you want a job, or do you want a career?"

"What's the difference?"

"Son, a job is coming in at eight, punching the clock, and at five o'clock you punch the clock and leave. If you want to develop a career, you come in at eight o'clock, punch the clock, and at five o'clock, if the business needs you there to do something, you stay and do it for the good of the company. If you want to sit in my chair at my desk, you've got to earn the right. If it's a Friday afternoon, and you see that there's a company need for you to come in the next day, you come in the next day. Even if you have a diving project planned. Now, that is the difference between having a job and developing a career."

"Well, I want that. That's fine."

They shake hands.

APRIL 21, 1980

By the time Sheck has worked his way through parts, sales, and accounting to assume the position of general manager of Westside Volkswagen, I'm a twenty-year-old senior at Florida State University. With two college roommates, I have begun to climb and crawl into the air-filled caverns dotting the Florida Panhandle, crystal-lined tunnels scoured by the springs of a previous geologic age. We have joined a university cave club, progressing to the complex passages of Climax Cave, an eight-mile labyrinth in nearby South Georgia.

The muddy rooms of Climax are punctuated with sumps, or cave pools, some of them leading to known tunnels flooded in the 1950s, when construction of a dam thirty miles away raised the area water table. Our club suspects that other sumps lead to virgin territory. This weekend, five cave divers and fifty cave sherpas—volunteer labor to hump tanks and gear—have gathered at Climax for a major underwater push. My roommates and I are sherpas. Support teams work ten-hour shifts, hauling gear to and from three distant in-cave sites, unlikely blue holes opening amid muck and limestone.

My job is to lower heavy air tanks down a 30-foot entrance pit and then ferry them, one at a time, through a twisted 300-foot crawlway, a sandy tube punctuated by tight squeezes. Other sherpas move tanks from the end of the crawls to the widely separated pools. We work well in advance of the divers, who are to arrive "fresh" for the penetration effort.

I'm eating a tuna sandwich on the far side of the crawls when the divers begin to trickle in. Several stop to rest, and to check the schedule with the caver in charge of the event. The divers boast varied backgrounds. There's a clean-cut aero-space engineer and a long-haired, tie-dyed Southerner whose main source of income is his own plasma. Yet they all seem pretty much alike. I expected a little macho swaggering—after all, hundreds of volunteer man-hours support this effort. All I see is quiet determination. They joke about the difficul-ties of the crawl, but each is detail oriented, picky. I watch two of them unpack (each carries three or four large duffels) and gear up for a sump. It is impossible to observe such a highly regimented routine without thinking of a preflight check.

One of the quietest in that group is Sheck Exley, intro-duced to me as "the grand old man of Florida cave diving." He is thirty years old. Of medium height, powerfully built, he looks as if he's stepped from a turn-of-the-century boxing poster: thick mustache balanced on a sharp face; grooved dimples cutting toward an angular jaw; short, wavy brown hair; muscular chest and arms; skin as pale as a shark's belly.

Exley asks my roommate to lead him on to his appointed sump, in the room called Batman's Den. There's no question-ing the calm authority in his voice. They push on.

Later I learn that my friend took Exley down a wrong fork. They spent four hours lost, eventually finding their way from the maze of passages to Batman's Den. Exley, fatigued from the difficult caving, decided to call the dive, saying a primary safety rule was to never dive when tired. The other two teams dive without incident, finding only a few hundred feet of new passage.

The haul out proves as long and difficult as the haul in. As I shove an unused tank back through the crawls, a protective valve cover malfunctions. Nudged by the tunnel wall, the valve twists open, spewing air and sand in my face. The sud-den wind extinguishes my carbide miner's lamp and shoots sand down my coveralls. I can't reach the valve, so I lie in darkness for the few minutes it takes the tank to empty, eyes shut tight against the grit.

I imagine myself as a diver, the crawlway as a water-filled

sump, and this tank as my last. I picture escaping air pooling into bubbles in the ceiling. In water, the sand I lie in would become a brown, enveloping fog. I would float upside down, my face pressed to the roof, and breathe for the five or ten minutes it would take the loose air to retreat into tiny channels in the rock. If I were very near dry cave, I would hyperventilate, then swim for it. If not, I'd have time to compose a few last words for my dive log.

The tank expires with a hiss. I light my lamp and resume the schlepp out of Climax, resolving never, under any circumstances, to go cave diving.

Diving for depth increases underwater danger geometrically. The tremendous pressure reduces body volume by up to a third, leaving divers swimming inside suddenly huge wet suits. Descent on compressed air can cause nitrogen narcosis (also called rapture of the deep), a dangerous light-headedness that can lead to fatal errors of judgment. Simple tasks become confusing; divers may feel something similar to a drug-induced euphoria. Meanwhile, oxygen becomes increasingly toxic. Dive tanks empty quickly. At extreme depths some of the gases commonly mixed with oxygen—usually helium and nitrogen—themselves become toxic.

As divers push below 600 feet, they are exposed to perhaps the greatest danger of all: high-pressure nervous syndrome (HPNS), a neurological reaction to rapidly increasing pressure. The eyes shrink, causing divers to see flashing auras around people and objects. Accurately depicted in the science-fiction film *The Abyss*, HPNS can cause violent body tremors, convulsions, hallucinations, and death. Naval and oil company divers successfully battle the syndrome by descending slowly, inside submersible habitats—expensive steel capsules that would be impossible to transport into most caves.

Divers with COMEX, a French petroleum firm, have worked successfully below 2,400 feet. But such divers descend in fully equipped habitats over a period of days, acclimating to the depth while watching videos and eating TV dinners. After spending days at the bottom, conducting short dives between long rests, the slow rise to the surface may take weeks. "Open-circuit" divers, with no habitat to retreat to and only minutes of breathing time on their backs, face a near certainty of HPNS from deep descents. The syndrome often hits in combination with a condition called "compression arthralgia," known to navy divers as "no joint juice" because it feels as if their knees, elbows, and wrists have suddenly rusted solid.

DECEMBER 17, 1989

I sit in my office and dial a Florida number. "I can tell you everything you need to know about Sheck Exley in four letters," says the voice on the line, an easygoing drawl reminiscent of Chuck Yeager. "All you need to know is u-g-l-y."

I've called to ask about joining his surface team on the next Mante effort, and to try to talk the publicity-shy diver into letting a known writer hang around him for a few days. Although I haven't seen Exley since that day in Climax Cave, I've followed his career in the pages of the *National Speleological Society News*. I know that in the mid-1980s, he became intrigued with research on scuba and rapid decompression. He studied a series of rapid submarine dives made two decades earlier by Hans Keller, a pioneer in mixed-gas diving. The deepest point Keller reached in his sub was 305 meters. The diver who accompanied him (a journalist of limited underwater experience) panicked at the bottom and swam away from the habitat until he passed out and died.

Exley had located a number of very deep water-filled caves in Mexico; rapid descent on mixed gas seemed to be the only way to see where they went. He began diving with Jochen Hasenmeyer, a German who had taken away Exley's early depth record in the 1970s. Hasenmeyer had recently set a seemingly unassailable open-circuit (as opposed to a dive aided by submersible habitat) scuba mark of 656 feet.

The deep work involved travel to France, Mexico, the

Caribbean, and elsewhere, and travel involved time spent away from the family business. In 1985, Exley resigned as a full partner in his father's dealership and began teaching advanced algebra and calculus at rural Suwanee High School in Live Oak, Florida. He bought Cathedral Canyon, a long and complex underwater cave near Live Oak. A house trailer at the entrance became his home. He established the school's karate club and began leading teenagers in strenuous work-outs after school. On weekends, school holidays, and during the summer, he was free to travel to deep sites.

The years Exley spent training advanced divers have helped him develop a passion for teaching. He is popular at the high school, known for drawing smiley faces in his pie charts on the blackboard. When a student misses an answer, "Mr. X" will roll his eyes and say "Noooooo" in a way that puts the class in hysterics. He writes his home number on the board, labels it "Mr. X's Fabulous Hotline." "Call me day or night if this stuff gives you trouble," he says. Many call with troubles that have nothing to do with differential equations. Exley makes personal projects of wild sixteen-year-old boys who've had a brush with the law or are on the verge of dropping out. One by one, he pulls them into the karate club. He teaches them to avoid danger through physical and mental discipline, to take control of their lives by thinking.

One by one, he calmly breathes life into them.

In January 1989, Exley had established the longest distance traveled in a single cave dive, 10,450 feet, going in and out the same route, solo, in his backyard cave. By the time he emerged, he had been submerged for fourteen hours, a third of that in decompression—also a world duration record. That April, in Nacimiento Mante, he surpassed Hasenmeyer's record with a dive to 868 feet.

Unlike other cave divers at the highest levels of achievement—notably, Bill Stone and Wes Skiles—Exley made these record dives without fanfare. He didn't seek support from National Geographic or the BBC. After the Mante dive, *Good*

Morning America called to invite him on the show. So did *Today*. Exley turned them down.

One cave diver who stopped by Exley's camp at Mante was Jim Bowden. Like Exley, Bowden had labored for years in a successful family business—an Austin photo studio—and then gave it up for what he called "the old Star Trek syndrome": going where no one has gone before. Traveling through Mexico and Belize on a shoestring, often alone or with only two or three friends, Bowden had discovered and explored more underwater passage than many huge, well-funded expeditions. In 1986, he and a few other divers had formed a small organization called the Proyecto Espeleológico de Buceo Sierra Madre Oriental, through which they solicited official recognition and support from government agencies and corporate sponsors.

Bowden and Exley hit it off. Both loved exploration for its own sake. Both were dive instructors who sought to instill confidence and a dedication to safety in their students. Both had studied literature and loved to quote romantic poetry. And both knew the secret locations of very deep holes that no divers had entered. Sitting in camp at Mante, they arranged to teach a cave-diving class together that summer, and to develop plans for deep dives.

After setting world length and depth records earlier in the year, in October Exley returned to Wakulla Springs, the site of Edward's death, as a member of a National Geographic team. He helped map nearly five miles of underwater cave passage, spending several days camped in a submersible habitat at the cave's entrance. Pulled behind an electric scooter, he glided silently over the bones of drowned Ice Age animals.

We talk for a while. "You don't really want to write about me, do you? Nobody would read it. I mean, I guess you can come on down here if you want, but I don't think you'll see anything very interesting. Just ugly."

We agree to meet at Mante in March, should he decide to go. Several days later he calls to say that Hasenmeyer, the German who is Exley's only possible competition in the depth record, has been paralyzed during a faulty decompression. Details are sketchy, but Exley will put off any Mante attempt until Hasenmeyer's accident has been carefully analyzed—until 1991, at the earliest. If then.

But he plans some work at a Florida cave, yet another Panhandle spring that might eventually yield a new distance record. If I want to come watch, he guesses it's okay.

FEBRUARY 22, 1990

The Florida sunset spreads out in pastel bands, orange sherbet reaching into pale turquoise. Two metal sheds sit beside Exley's modular home. In front of one shed is a battered Ford cargo van, side and rear doors open. Mexican tourist stickers dot the windshield. I see Exley loading tanks into the back of the van. He walks up to me and says, "Hey there, you must be Mike," as if I am the one person on the planet he most wants to see. "We need to go get some air. Then I thought maybe we could meet M.E. for dinner."

M.E. is Mary Ellen Eckoff, the world's most experienced woman cave diver. A tanned, good-looking woman with a strong southern accent, Eckoff is a grant writer for Florida school boards and has trained over a hundred cave divers, logging more than a thousand dives in the process. In 1987, at Nacimiento Mante, she set a women's depth record of 400 feet.

Eckoff and Exley met in 1977 and were married in 1983. The marriage lasted only three years, but the diving relationship and love have somehow endured.

She and Sheck's usual partner, Paul DeLoach (no relation to Ned), will take part in the coming two-day dive effort. We climb into the van and head down winding blacktop through scrub pine. The console is cluttered with hand tools and cassette tapes: Rachmaninoff, Brahms, and the sound track from *South Pacific*. There are also a couple of swollen, water-warped paperbacks, cheap science fiction with the pages glued together. These Exley uses to pass the time during long decompressions. He can't finish a novel on the surface, after it dries, but next time down, the pages will become pliable once more.

"What's your motivation in going to Mante?" I ask. "Why do such deep dives?"

"I held both the world depth and distance records in 1970," Exley says. "I thought it would be nice to hold them both again before I retire. It just took me nearly twenty years to do it." He pauses before adding, "I'm not sure I'll go back to Mante. I had wanted to reach a thousand feet. It's a nice round number. But that might be pushing it. I'm going to have to hang up my tanks—at least from that sort of thing— pretty soon. I guess the real reason I'm doing it is I just want to know what's down there."

After stopping at a dive shop to fill air tanks and talk with some local cave divers, we drive to a Live Oak barbecue house to meet Mary Ellen. As she and Exley share diving tales over heaping plates of ribs, both display playful sides I've missed from watching divers only in caves. Eckoff describes the small pranks Exley and Paul DeLoach have pulled on each other during decompression. There was, for instance, that time at Cathedral Canyon.

Exley's backyard cave is entered via a flooded pit, 130 feet deep. Twenty feet below the surface, a small ledge cluttered with rotting logs, concrete blocks, and other debris makes a convenient decompression stop after long dives. Once, as DeLoach sat on a log, lightly dozing through the wait, Exley tapped him on the shoulder.

DeLoach looked up to see his partner standing at the edge, a cinder block in his hands. Exley gestured with the block, as if to call it to DeLoach's attention. DeLoach shrugged. Exley shook the block a couple of times. DeLoach shrugged again. Exley grinned around his mouthpiece, then tossed the hunk of cement over the cliff.

Only then did DeLoach notice that the cinder block was tied to a coil of nylon line. Rapidly uncoiling nylon line. While he had napped, Exley had looped the other end around DeLoach's manifold. Water slowed the block's fall to the skewed gravity of a Roadrunner cartoon. DeLoach had just enough time to draw his knife and cut the line before it yanked him over the cliff. Exley blew out great bubbles of laughter.

As Eckoff tells the story, Exley turns a vivid red, grinning behind his mustache.

APRIL 6, 1994

I stand in the hot wind, pointing a telephoto lens into Zacatón. I see Eckoff's face, and I put down the camera. The message is conveyed. The details, I know, will come later.

Bowden's rapid descent went smoothly, but his bottom gas mix—the tank for the deepest portion of his dive—began to run out faster than he anticipated. At the 925-foot-mark on his line, he began his ascent. (His two digital depth gauges later read maximum depths of 915 and 924 feet; a third gauge malfunctioned.) He didn't see Exley, but visibility was poor, and he assumed Exley had continued down to 1,000 feet. As Bowden made his first decompression stops, he realized that he was using gas faster than expected and that he might not be able to put in all the required decompression time.

Hundreds of feet above him waited support divers Karen Hohle and Ann Kristovich. (Kristovich, the team's medical officer, broke Eckoff's depth record with a 554-foot dive in Zacatón in September.) The two women saw Bowden's bubbles and knew he had begun ascent, but there was nothing on Exley's line. Eckoff, who had just entered the sinkhole from the tunnel, saw worried looks on the faces of Hohle and Kristovich.

Where's Sheck? Kristovich asked on her underwater slate.

Eckoff descended to 279 feet, the border of light and darkness. As she stared at Exley's vanishing line, she saw two tiny white squares drifting up toward her. Suddenly, she realized they were the laminated pages of his dive profile, something he would never let go of alive. Somehow, she made it to the surface. More than an hour later, she heads out of the cave.

Bowden is not out of the water yet. He cut seven minutes off one decompression stop because of inadequate gas reserves; at another stop, a free-flowing regulator dumped out several minutes more. At about 250 feet, Bowden realized that he had still not seen Exley. Only then did he understand what that meant. At about 100 feet, Hohle used sign language to confirm the worst. For the next several hours, he will continue his decompression in terrible knowledge.

When he finally emerges in the night, after an extra hour spent on pure oxygen at ten feet, Bowden will suffer his second case of the bends. Using a controversial French technique which proved effective with the first case, Kristovich will treat him with massive intravenous steroids, anticoagulants, and painkillers. By the next morning, Bowden will be on his feet. After a period of reflection and mourning, he will continue deep diving, in Zacatón and elsewhere. Having reached at least 915 feet, Jim Bowden now holds the world open-circuit scuba depth record.

All of this will happen later. Long before Bowden leaves the water, I'm driving Mary Ellen the two hours to Tampico. She needs to talk to Sheck's parents. She needs to make arrangements for Paul DeLoach to fly in and help her drive the van home. She needs to buy a spare tire. She needs to be away from Zacatón.

The battered Econoline bounces over the highway, and I don't know what to say or do. Sheck's wallet and glasses lie on the console where he left them, along with tapes of Beethoven, Brahms, and several Broadway musicals.

I don't say it, but I assume—and I suspect Mary Ellen assumes—that Sheck's body will never be recovered, that he continued sinking from the point where the trouble occurred, whatever that trouble was. Zacatón will have to be a fitting tomb for the world's greatest cave diver.

I am wrong. Three days later, when the dive team begins to

pull up Exley's unused decompression tanks, they discover him entangled in the guideline. His single depth gauge reads 904 feet. Whether he was conscious when he became entangled or merely drifted into the line later is unknown. In 4,000 cave dives, Exley had certainly become entangled in dive lines before, but had never experienced trouble in extricating himself.

The exact cause of death is unknown. There are several reasonable guesses, high among them drowning as a result of HPNS, but they will remain only guesses. With help from Sergio Zambrano, a celebrated Mexican cave diver, Irby Exley is able to cut through international red tape. He claims his son's body and has it cremated within just twenty-one hours.

APRIL 12, 1994

I join divers from around the world at the Ortega Methodist Church in Jacksonville, Florida. The church bulletin contains an excerpt from Samuel Taylor Coleridge's "Kubla Khan," one of Exley's favorite poems. "Through caverns measureless to man / Down to a sunless sea," read the famous lines. The week before Exley and Eckoff drove to Mexico, Exley's publisher had called to say that his latest book, his memoirs, had gone to the printer. The book's title: *Caverns Measureless to Man.*

After the service, Don Jacobs, a twenty-year-old who studied karate with Exley for seven years, progressing from beginner to black belt under his instruction, sees me taking notes.

"I want you to write this down exactly," he tells me. He thinks for a long minute before saying, "The man taught us to love and respect every individual no matter what race, religion, whatever, the way he loved each of us. He treated us like his own kids. Sheck Exley was the best friend I ever had."

I write it down, exactly like he says.

In 1991, the National Speleological Society presented Exley with its Stephenson Award for lifetime service—the highest honor in American cave exploration. Exley asked his friend Wayne Marshall to introduce him at the ceremony. Before an audience of 2,000, which included Irby and Victoria Exley, Marshall said, "We honor Sheck as an explorer, as a man who set fifteen world depth and distance records. But we also honor him as a guide and a teacher. This man has done more to promote safe cave diving than any living person. His ideas, books, and personal instruction have saved hundreds if not thousands of lives."

Marshall's is a sentiment I hear echoed dozens of times as I phone cave divers around the country in the days following the memorial service. More than one tells me how Sheck literally saved their lives in past underwater mishaps.

Four days before the fatal dive, as Exley and Eckoff set out on I-10 toward Texas and the Pan-American Highway, she asked him, "Is diving to a thousand feet worth dying over?"

Mr. X rolled his eyes as if she were a slow algebra student. "Nooooo," he said. "Of course not. No dive is worth dying over." The date was April 1, 1994—his forty-fifth birthday.

Two days before the fatal dive, as he, Bowden, and the rest of the team placed the decompression bottles in advance of their attempt, Sheck Exley set his last world record: He descended to 422 feet on compressed air, surfacing with no ill effects. The deepest previous dive on compressed air had been to 410 feet. Underwater, he grinned at Eckoff and pointed to his depth gauge.

She read the numbers and wrote on her slate, "You're crazy."

The morning of his last dive, I watched Exley kit up at his van, which was parked beside the concrete dock at the spring leading into Zacatón. A strong breeze carried the scent of barbecue from across the water. Local villagers, many of whom had befriended team members during earlier expeditions, were preparing a fiesta to celebrate the world record dive. Mante, Karen Hohle's exuberant husky, splashed in and out of the water, barking playfully at cows on the other side.

I walked over to Sheck. He was stuffing into a net bag plastic tubes full of colorful liquid, the sort of children's treat commonly frozen for after-school snacking. I knew that during the long decompression he needed to drink plenty of fluids in order to ward off dehydration. Sheck had hit upon a well-packaged, inexpensive, and flavorful alternative to the specialty fare available from custom dive shops.

I waited until he had closed the bag and clipped it onto his harness before I asked the question that had just occurred to me. "What do your high school students think of cave diving?"

"I don't let them know about it," he said. "Those kids look up to me, and I wouldn't want one of them to try to make some macho point, prove his manhood or something, trying to copy me."

Ten minutes later, Sheck Exley walked over to the spring and stepped in. He grinned and pushed away from us on the shore, kicking with his back to the current and the *norte*. He swam slowly, back to the breeze, a smile on his face. He grew smaller and vanished underwater.

3

TRUTH IS STRANGE

It is a commonplace of caving to meet someone on a trip, say to West Virginia, and later run into the same caver in Alabama or Montana. For instance, I first met Jack Kehoe, a Maryland caver, in Jamaica. I saw him a year later in the Dallas–Fort Worth Airport, where we waited for separate connecting flights to separate expeditions in Mexico. On my way back from China in 1988, I ran into Karen Witte at Tokyo's Narita Airport. She had been president of the Florida State Cave Club when I was a member; now she flew 747s for Northwest Airlines. A few months after that I met Craig White, an NBC journalist, underground in Lechuguilla Cave. He was shooting a segment for the *Today* show. It turned out we lived in bordering New Jersey suburbs and frequented the same small diner.

And I tried for weeks in 1986 to locate Pete Shifflett, a caver who could get me into Great Expectations, an extremely difficult Wyoming cave. Shifflett had moved from the Virginia address the NSS recorded. No one I talked to seemed to know where he'd gone. I gave up. Days later, I was visiting friends in the English department at the University of South Carolina and wound up in a poker game with Shifflett's brother. Andy Shifflett, a new graduate student, had Pete's phone number in his pocket.

My life has been punctuated with odd little coincidences of this sort, things that shouldn't happen outside of Dickens but

43

do. The difference between life and fiction is that in a novel the coincidence generally amounts to something, ties loose ends together, gives the story meaning. When unlikely connections bubble up in the real world, as they do from time to time, you just look at them and say, "Huh, that's strange." Then you go on doing whatever you were doing.

Perhaps I'm like a caveman alone on a clear night, seeing lions and bears in the stars because I need to see *something*. Or the guide in a tourist cavern who christens one group of stalagmites "The Fairy City" and another "Madonna and Child." Humans—especially writers—tend to see patterns where there are none, to "give airy nothing a local habitation and a name." I know that bizarre but verifiable coincidences have attached themselves to all the cave stories I've written. I don't know what to make of them, collectively or individually. All I can do is toss off the facts and ask in my best Rod Serling voice, "Is it coincidence, or *something more*? You be the judge."

Consider, if you will, the means by which I met Jim Bowden.

The first magazine to send me caving was *America: The Nissan Student Travel Magazine*, given away twice a year to over two million college students. Readers were expected to enjoy the adventure travel articles it contained and thus, presumably, to pay attention to the Nissan ads spaced among them. *America* was one of several single-advertiser magazines created by the media wunderkind Chris Whittle. During the four years that I was a contributor, from 1987 to 1991, a succession of *America* editors sent me caving in Jamaica, kayaking in Baja, mountain climbing in the Pacific Northwest, traveling by rail to Ulan Bator, and on several other amazingly fun trips. After a brief incarnation as *Student Traveler*, in 1991 the magazine—like many Whittle titles—was permanently shut down, its personnel transferred to Whittle's more lucrative video and educational divisions.

But in early 1989 it was one of the world's most widely read college publications. Sometime that February, editor Ginny Hostetter called to say she was interested in assigning an article on low-cost adventures in Mexico. "Ideally," she said, "I'd like you to accompany a group of college students to some ruins in Mexico over spring break."

I was always up for Mexico. And in this case, the timing couldn't have been better. Some friends of mine had been invited to join a March expedition to Cueva de Borbollón, near San Luis Potosí. According to the Mexican cavers who had just discovered it, the cave contained an unexplored pit more than 700 feet deep. And I knew that Sheck Exley had planned another deep dive at Mante sometime in the spring; I wanted to pitch a story on his effort to *Sports Illustrated*. I reasoned that if *America* could send me to Mexico, I might hook up with one or both cave expeditions before I returned home.

My only problem was that Ginny didn't have any *particular* college students in mind. The subject was merely one that a focus group had suggested would go over with *America*'s budget-conscious, adventure-loving readers. "The question is," she said, "how do we go about finding ruin-bound college students?"

I suggested checking under the tables of any beer joint.

"Seriously. The thing is, this has to be a real, existing trip to Mexico. We can't create an artificial one just for the sake of a story."

I thought for a minute. "When I was at Florida State, I remember the student activity board used to set up all sorts of adventure travel. One time I almost signed up for a rafting trip with them. Maybe if I started calling counterparts in the Texas colleges, I'd find somebody driving to Mexico."

The idea sounded reasonable to Ginny. "Give it a shot and get back to me tomorrow," she said.

I figured I might as well try the biggest first. Austin information gave me the number of the student activities office at the University of Texas. I called and explained what I wanted. The student worker on the line had one trip that might fit my bill: She said that some students enrolled in a recreational scuba course were taking a bus into the Sierra Madre Oriental over spring break. They planned to camp out and take their final certification dives in several mountain springs. The student worker believed that the dive instructor had said something about visiting ruins while they were there. She gave me his number.

When I reached the guy on the phone, he described the campgrounds and dive sites as "beautiful, unspoiled Mexico, as far from the tourist trail as you can get." He added that he usually visited one or two ruins on these trips, and tried to include hiking and perhaps even some caving in his itinerary. This sounded like exactly what Ginny had in mind. When he mentioned one of his planned destinations, I perked up.

"Did you say Nacimiento Mante?" I asked.

"Yes, I did. Mante has a great campground. Nice swimming hole. And there's a little pit above the water where I might give a rappelling lesson."

"What did you say your name was?"

"Bowden," the man said. "Jim Bowden."

A month later, I was snorkeling in Mante, staring down at the hole where Sheck had set several world scuba depth records. He had met Jim Bowden here the year before, while setting a record of 770 feet. In two weeks, as I hung underground at Cueva de Borbollón, firing flashbulbs 750 feet above the floor of a rocky chamber, Sheck Exley would quietly set another record here, descending 867 feet below the surface on mixed gases. I would hear about the dive only after I returned to the States.

It wasn't Sheck who invited me to Zacatón in the fall of 1993. It was Jim. He didn't normally encourage publicity, he said, but he'd always liked the article I wrote about the small trip he led in 1989, when he'd loaded his old school bus with a group of dive students from the University of Texas, a group I had found with a random phone call.

Coincidence? Or something more? Consider Edward Exley.

After Sheck's death, I flew to Florida for the memorial service and the toughest interview I've ever done. I had a tight deadline from *Sports Illustrated*. To meet it, I would have to talk with Irby and Virginia Exley, Sheck's parents. After the service, they invited the many cave divers and friends who had attended to come to their home and share the food relatives and neighbors had delivered. The Exleys spent more than two hours entertaining Sheck's friends, then graciously led me down to Irby's study, built into the basement of the home where Sheck grew up. They talked for half an hour about his childhood, about his brother Edward, about a dozen other details which no reporter had a right to probe in their time of grief, but which they seemed genuinely glad to share with me.

I wrote my story that night in an anonymous motel room. The air-conditioning was out, I remember. I finished the last paragraph around three in the morning, the window open, tears on my face. I was dressed in my underwear, surrounded by empty room-service coffeepots and beer cans. (When I described the scene to my editor, Chris Hunt, he said, "That's the way most of our writers on deadline work.")

Everything I wrote about Edward's death at Wakulla Springs came from my interview with the Exleys. Unlike other episodes of Sheck's life, I had nothing else with which to verify my version of the facts. During the weeks of editing and waiting that followed, I tried to hunt down a contemporary newspaper account, with no luck. *The Florida Times-Union* had nothing relevant from that summer of 1968, nor did the *Tallahassee Democrat*. I knew that some source would have to be consulted by the magazine's fact checkers before my story could be published. Reluctantly, I added the Exleys' telephone number to my fact-check list. I hoped that Mr. and Mrs. Exley would be willing to tell their sad tale yet again, to yet another nosy stranger.

That July I vacationed in Florida with my parents. On the way home to Arkansas, my wife, Kathy, and I spent the night with Lee and Sharon Pearson, a caving couple we first met when we were dating in the early 1980s. Lee and Sharon have long been among our closest friends. In 1994, they lived in Monroe, Louisiana. (They have since moved back to Tennessee, where they had lived the summer of 1982, when Lee and I explored new pits and caves each weekend.) I've never done the math, but I feel reasonably certain that I've spent more time underground with Lee than with any other human.

These days, Sharon and Kathy would as soon visit a mall as virgin passage. Our kids love to play with their kids. Most visits, Lee and I armchair-cave more than anything else, surrounding ourselves with topographic maps and carbide lamps the way some men my age pull out yellowing playbooks and sweat-stained jerseys. This trip, we were spending only one night in Monroe, so all we did was go to dinner.

Lee knew about Sheck's many achievements and recent death, of course, most cavers did, but he didn't think he'd ever met the man. At dinner, I described events in Mexico and the article I had written. I talked about how hard it had been—how cruel and intrusive I felt—to force nice, ordinary people to describe at length the two sons they lost in similar accidents.

"Two sons?" Lee asked.

I told him Edward's story.

"This happened at Wakulla Springs, in June of 1968?" Lee stared into my eyes with sudden emotion. His was a look I've seen when a baby is born, when someone dies, in those rare moments when I'm prone to believe a soul and not a person is talking to me. "On a Saturday?"

"Yes," I said.

He shook his head. "I was there. It was a family picnic. I was twelve years old, and it was my first experience of death. God, I'll never forget that day as long as I live."

Lee began to talk about what he had seen. I realized that I had gotten one important detail wrong. I thought it was Sheck, not another diver, who actually pulled Edward from the water. "The older brother—I never knew his name until now—tried to put on the tank. The other guy talked him out of it. The older brother was so upset, no one thought he could survive the dive."

Wakulla has always been a popular picnic spot, after all. Lee's family did live in Florida. But I couldn't shake the strangeness of our conversation.

"We've known each other for years," I said, "and we've never mentioned Sheck Exley or Wakulla Springs, right?"

"Not that I remember."

"But between us, we watched Sheck and his brother die."

"We sure did," said Lee. "Huh, that's strange."

We went on with our meal.

4

COLD FEAR, GREAT EXPECTATIONS

Imagine a clear alpine stream rushing through a beautiful, primitive mountain range, the sort of icy, frothing scene you see in a beer commercial. Now picture a two-foot hole opening in the streambed, an unexpected rip in the mountain's white limestone skin that sucks the stream under like bathwater rushing down a drain. Seven miles away, 1,800 vertical feet nearer to sea level, just as unexpectedly the stream reappears, shooting out of a mossy rock wall with the power of an open city hydrant. Finally, put yourself somewhere beneath those seven missing miles of streambed, slithering along in the near-freezing water, snatching desperate breaths from the few inches of air space between you and the thousands of tons of rock overhead.

That should give you a pretty good idea of where I am.

Ahead of me in the two-foot-diameter tunnel are the boots of Sheri Engler, thirty-eight, a caver from Illinois. I assume that the rest of Engler is attached to the boots, and that Ron Simmons and Keith Goggin are still in the passage ahead of her. But that's pretty much guesswork: The carbide miner's lamp mounted on my helmet has just been put out by a wave. Somewhere beyond the cavers are silent, enormous chambers, sparkling waterfalls, and coal-black fossils that the stream has passed on its way to dousing my lamp.

The water seems a living, angry thing. It wants me *out*. If I let go of the submerged cracks and stone nubs my numb fingers cling to, I'll shoot backward, losing the hundred feet of crawl I've gained. The surrounding rock is brilliant white dolomite, a limestone containing large amounts of magnesium, the main ingredient of the mythological philosopher's stone and of laxatives. The dolomite also holds thousands of wormlike fossils, the ancient burrows of tiny sea creatures. These fossils protrude from the floor and walls like so many straight razors, forming a surface cavers call "Velcro" because of the way it snags and rips any clothing or skin that touches it.

The stream forms bizarre peaks and dips over this gleaming rock meringue. I can breathe well enough by turning my head sideways. But breathing is not the only issue. Although this is one of the country's deepest caves in relation to the surface overhead, I am still 7,500 feet above sea level, where the snow-fed current remains a constant 39° F. Unless I move soon, the giddiness of hypothermia will set in, quickly followed by oppressive fatigue and a sleepy death. Pete Shifflett, the world-class caver who—with thirteen crossings—knows this passage better than anyone, has warned: "If you stop in there, you die. Period." So I stare at Engler's immobile boots by the dim light of a lithium-powered backup lamp, wondering what has caused them to become immobile. There's no point in trying to shout over the roar of water. Already cold seeps into my wet suit.

This passage—seen by only fifteen people since its 1980 discovery—is called the Grim Crawl of Death. The name makes it sound entirely too pleasant. It is a 1,000-foot tube located in Wyoming's Bighorn Mountains, in a cave called Great Expectations, and I am here by choice.

Somewhere in the back of every caver's mind is a little kid watching a Saturday matinee. Modern cave explorers scoff at the clichés of the typical Hollywood cavern—flesh-eating monsters, lost cities, bats tangled in some blonde's hair—but what lies beyond the next crawlway or at the bottom of a new-found pit still tantalizes them. The world's highest mountains, wildest rapids, and steepest ski slopes are visible, but the deepest, most challenging caves—like the fastest runner or the highest jumper—are never absolute; they remain forever open to historical revision. I've heard Ron Simmons say, "I don't do this 'because it's there.' I do this because of what's *not* there—yet."

Gaining access to what's not there can be a delicate matter. Most caves are located on privately owned land. Given American society's litigious mood, many cave owners would rather not know about an underground wilderness on their property. Some would sooner bulldoze an entrance shut than risk a day in court with the survivors of some careless spelunker who perished beneath their alfalfa crop. Cavers carefully cultivate landowner relationships, keeping names and exact locations of the most spectacular—and potentially dangerous—caves secret from the general public. Not infrequently, the caves are kept secret even from other cavers. Most NSS chapters, called grottoes, maintain one or two "sacrificial" caverns for novices and the public, revealing more exciting and delicate caves to new members only after months of proven dedication and gained experience.

Such secrecy can have more personal motives, however. Genuine frontiers exist underground—unknown miles of passage to be mapped, vaulted chambers to be named. Cavers become protective of "going leads," passages that promise larger virgin finds to come. For many, the sport's greatest thrill is stepping into subterranean halls, rivers, and canyons never before seen, shining the first beam of light on new land. The quiet competition among top cavers is made all the more fierce by the way it is uniformly denied to exist.

Caving etiquette requires a new passage to be surveyed as soon as it's found. Underground points of reference are vague at best. Twisting, tortuous routes can confuse anyone's sense of direction. By noting subtle changes in rock color or composition and by simply looking over their shoulders at major intersections, experienced cavers have developed the ability to find their way out of even complex, multilevel systems. But accurately describing where they have been—surveying—

requires tape, compass, and inclinometer. To overlook this nicety, to plunge hell-bent through virgin passages and crawls, particularly on a going lead provided by someone else, is known as "scooping booty." He who develops a reputation for scooping booty quickly finds himself anathema in the caving community. Plunging boldly on is not a decision to be made lightly.

A case in point involves Great Expectations, or Great X as cavers call it. The upper cave's entrance—a vertical slot dubbed Crisco Crack, which was once so tight that cavers had to strip out of coveralls and wet suits to wriggle through—sits in a dolomite hollow just above the point where the surface stream vanishes into the western flank of the Bighorn Mountains. The nine-inch squeeze was first negotiated in the summer of 1977 by a group of cavers from the area, led by Jerry Elkins of Sheridan, Wyoming. Elkins went on to survey several hundred feet of tall, narrow fissures, a cobbly streambed winding beneath a five-foot ceiling, and a few unimpressive, mazelike crawls. Word of the cave filtered through the Rocky Mountain region, and in August 1978, local caver Andy Flurkey invited John Scheltens, a principal explorer of 52-mile-long Wind Cave in South Dakota, to join him on what he said would be "a two-hour survey of a little cave in the Bighorns."

While Flurkey and two others mapped easier walking passage, Scheltens, his wife, Pat, Dave Springhetti and his wife, Carole, were sent to survey a network of convoluted crawl-ways. Scheltens, who later became president of the NSS, recalls the trip: "The stuff we were in was cold, damp, and tight, and it didn't seem to be going anywhere. The cave just meandered through breakdown [a jumble of loose boulders]. Dave had crawled ahead, and I was sitting between a couple of slabs of breakdown, about fed up with the place, when I noticed a little slot three feet over my head."

Scheltens carefully climbed the chimney, and was surprised to pop into a dry upper-level passage. A tunnel 15 feet in diameter reached into the darkness. No previous footprints marked the sandy floor. Expecting nothing more than a short, circular loop (several of which had been found elsewhere), Scheltens and Springhetti left their wives in the crawls below while they examined the find. They followed 100 yards of unremarkable passage before they rounded a corner and saw the stuff of every caver's dreams: a 100-foot-high borehole, stretching ahead as far as they could see.

The two men ran through a quarter mile of the huge trunk passage, climbing and sliding over a dozen steep, dusty hills of fallen rubble, the gleaming magnesium-white ceiling far overhead, before returning for their wives, who by then had waited more than an hour in the crawls. The four explored the borehole—which they christened the Great Hall—to a length of 2,000 feet. At the end of the enormous room the rocky floor rose almost to the ceiling before dropping away into a pit. They had brought no rope or climbing gear with them, so they began the tedious, sixteen-hour process of mapping their way out.

The discovery soon flashed through the caving community: The Bighorns had a big one going. On a later trip, Scheltens and Springhetti found a narrow side canyon a quarter mile beyond the 20-foot drop that had ended exploration earlier. This passage, which they named the Lunchroom, led them to a 100-foot rappel into a roaring, white-water stream they dubbed the Lost Worland River. The two were stopped by a series of waterfalls, but the sporting river passage promised miles of cave yet to come.

During the following two summers, survey groups—which expanded in size and experience to include a dozen top cavers—mapped almost two miles along the Lost Worland River, working their way down Gonzo Falls, B52 Falls, Lover's Leap, and other waterfalls no one took the time to name; swimming and splashing through rapids; and rigging slippery traverses above silent, swirling pools. Survey trips became increasingly arduous, lasting twenty hours or more. Cavers contemplated an overnight camp along the river, but no one could find a ledge large or dry enough for a safe night's sleep—even in full wet suit.

✻   ✻   ✻

The biggest discoveries often come aboveground, when a freshly drawn map of what's beneath the surface is compared with surface topography to suggest a likely passage trend. The lines of the canyon above Great X led explorers to search for another entrance closer to the new finds. Hiking in difficult terrain far below the known extent of Great X, an inquisitive caver followed a hunch: He found a stream bubbling from an impenetrable slot in a rockface seven miles down-canyon from the Crisco Crack. Another explorer stumbled upon a small cave, which he appropriately named Dumb Luck, on the floor of the same canyon, but two miles closer to Crisco Crack. If either of these two openings could be shown to connect with Great X, the change in elevation would guarantee a new U.S. depth record. Thus the stage was set for what many consider the greatest single trip in the history of American caving—and one of the most infamous.

Tom Miller and Pete Shifflett, who had joined the Great X survey on the strength of previous international discoveries, carried a full complement of survey gear as they entered Dumb Luck on August 17, 1980. Just fifty feet into the small cave the two found rushing water and wind they were convinced could come only from Great X and the Lost Worland River. But the passage quickly deteriorated into a steep, frigid crawl. The streambed bristled with submerged Velcro.

They would struggle upstream for a few yards, their heads uncomfortably tilted so that sometimes just a single nostril could be held above the frothing water, only to hit a dead end. Then the two would backtrack and try another, equally miserable lead. The force of the stream whisked away any bit of loose gear that it touched. Surveying in such conditions, they realized, would be a nightmare. Yet the tantalizing presence of wind suggested that the water level did not reach the ceiling somewhere up ahead in this maze, although they were about to discover that it came very close.

They had decided to rename Dumb Luck as the Great Exit if they could connect with the upper cave. Only the desire for a connection urged the two forward through the excruciating current. In places, the stream was not as deep, but still unnerving. Shifflett could not shake visions of accidentally wedging his helmet between the uneven floor and the low ceiling, pinning his head facedown and drowning in three inches of water.

At one point the stream flowed to one side of the crawl, forcing the wind through a narrow, but relatively dry, natural sluiceway. To pass the squeeze, the two had to slide forward on the exhale. There was so little clearance that they had to keep not only their clothing but also their rib cages from snagging on the rough passage. This time, the cave rewarded their determination: Instead of another dead end, the crawl grew to a hands-and-knees height, then opened into a narrow fissure large enough for them to stand.

After walking several hundred yards, Miller and Shifflett reached an easy climb into a towering, canyonlike passage similar to what they had seen on trips along the Lost Worland River. They fought their way up increasingly difficult climbs through the virgin canyon, including one over an imposing 100-foot cascade series. Hours later, Miller stopped to rest. He found a narrow pocket at one side of a 15-foot rockface. It was deep enough to shield him from the spray off a crashing waterfall. As he sat there, numbly waiting for Shifflett to catch up, he suddenly recognized a crack running up the wall to the right of the falls. This was the spot where he had turned around on his longest Great X survey trip, two weeks before: He and Shifflett were standing in the deepest known cave in the United States.

Remembering what they had undergone to reach the connection, Miller convinced Shifflett to abandon the idea of surveying back out. Instead, they named the spot Connection Falls and pressed forward. Ahead of them lay several grueling climbs—one of more than 100 feet—that had been rigged with ropes by previous cavers exploring from the upper end. The two successfully free-climbed these, working their way steadily up the slick rock to the Great Hall, the crawls beyond it, and finally through the narrow Velcro chimneys to the Crisco Crack and the surface.

When they emerged after midnight to a full moon and the

heavy smell of sagebrush, they had climbed through five miles of cave and gained 1,403 feet of elevation, scooping booty most of the way. They were elated. They were pioneers of the most daring kind. And, for a while, their names were mud in the caving community.

"Tom Miller got to be a dirty word with some people," recalls Idaho caver Jeb Blakely. "Him and Pete scooping Great X pissed everybody off."

After the Miller-Shifflett connection, a few sporting through-trips were made, but the extreme difficulty of the Grim Crawl of Death continued to discourage survey of the new route. No one believed a passage could be so tough until they experienced it. Some cavers came dangerously close to hypothermia when their wet suits were slashed by Velcro. Others had lights and packs snatched away by the stream. One caver estimated that more than two thousand dollars' worth of cave gear had been sucked away in the crawlway.

John Scheltens describes his one—and only—trip through the Grim Crawl in 1980 (which would prove to be the last Great X through-trip anyone would make for five years): "It was a definition of hell. I had several holes in my wet suit, and ice water kept shooting in, ballooning the material out. Water got under my helmet and ripped it from my chin strap. I lay there in the dark, hearing the helmet go *tick, tick, tick* as the stream carried it down the passage ahead of me." Scheltens exited the crawl sharing a single fading flashlight with the four members of his group; each had entered the cave carrying three working light sources.

"If door-to-door trips become the in thing to do, Great X is going to eat someone, someone experienced," he cautions. "Under ideal conditions, the cave is horrible. I don't like body recoveries any more than the next person, but if there is a thunderstorm during a through-trip [which would raise the water level in the crawls], or if someone becomes completely hypothermic, or if someone falls during a climb, a body recovery is what you'll have. And a body recovery in that cave could kill someone."

Nevertheless, in 1985, Shifflett put together a team to finally survey the Grim Crawl of Death. It was not to be a sporting through-trip but strictly a mapping expedition, not a long ordeal but harrowing nonetheless. As Shifflett entered the crawl that summer morning on July 23, he spotted something white bobbing in the six-inch crack where the water disappeared—it was Scheltens' lost helmet, battered but still intact after five years. Shifflett's crew completed the survey. For the next two years, no one returned to Great X.

Climbing writer Jon Krakauer once made the distinction between "wanting to climb" the north face of the Eiger and "wanting to *have* climbed" it. In terms of endurance, tight squeezes, difficult climbs, and the odds of getting eaten despite all preparations, Great Expectations has become the Eiger of American caving. In 1987, I wanted very much to have done Great X. I had nightmares about actually doing it. Great X began taking on almost mythic proportions in my mind. This, despite the fact it no longer held the U.S. depth record. In 1981, several Great X explorers—purposely excluding Miller and Shifflett in retaliation for the scooped connection—dropped a shorter, more vertical cave in Wyoming's Teton Range, called Columbine Crawl. They set a new U.S. depth record of 1,550 feet.

The new record failed to dampen the allure of Great X; tremendous depth had never been the sole source of its reputation. The world's deepest cave, Réseau Jean Bernard in the French Alps, was pushed the same year to over three times Great X's depth, 5,036 vertical feet below the surface; caves in China and Mexico could soon reach depths of over a mile. Less than 2,000 feet of dolomite relief holds all of Great X— and the *100th* deepest known cave stops exactly 2,348 feet below the surface.

But Great X remained unquestionably world class. With upper and lower entrances corresponding to the cave's highest and lowest points, the depth of the through-trip was unparalleled; an explorer need not turn around and traverse the same passage twice, as in other deep caves. Since rescuing an injured caver from within would be virtually impossible, the cave became an ultimate test of skill and resolve. A sprained ankle or a stomach cramp there might well prove fatal. And with the constant change in passage type as the cave's river carved its way toward the resurgence—from climbs to crawls to waterfalls to canyons to breathtaking formation galleries—Great X presented a microcosm of everything the sport had to offer.

In 1987, Columbine Crawl's depth stood at 1,550 feet, but Great X potentially held two miles of cave between the impenetrable crack that had caught Scheltens' helmet and the still-unexplored stream resurgence farther down the canyon. The elevation change between those points (assuming a way into the presumed passage could be found) would add another 400 feet of depth to Great X, reestablishing the U.S. record. If a team could be organized for that purpose, I hoped to wangle my way onto it.

The caving community is small enough that, with perseverance and experience, almost anyone can eventually join an expedition with the living legends. I had spent enough time in TAG—the prime caving region centered where Tennessee, Alabama, and Georgia meet—to have dropped a dozen of the big ones. Along the way, I had met some well-known cavers. I figure that would get me in the door with the western cavers who had experience in Great X. But I found that in the door and into Great X are two different things.

Like Alpine skiing, expeditionary caving accommodates penniless bums who live for the sport and well-to-do techies who scarf up the latest gear—there's not much in between. Engineers, college students, and recent college dropouts make up at least half of the cavers I've met. I reasoned that if I could find some magazine to pick up part of the expense, I could probably convince Shifflett or another of the Great X veterans to organize an expedition for the summer of 1987 and let me tag along. (It had to be summer, because the road to the cave is snowed out the rest of the year.) I knew that the average caver would try almost anything for a free trip or gear, even the heroic effort of dragging a beer-bellied writer through one of the world's tightest, toughest, nastiest, most evil crawlways.

It was only after months of exchanging letters and phone calls and haggling over dates and personnel that in August I joined ten of the country's top cavers in Sheridan for a week at Great Expectations, under the sponsorship of *Sports Illustrated*. Shifflett, who had picked most of the team, had led me and a few others on a short photo reconnaissance commissioned the previous April by *National Geographic*. (We had used a helicopter to bypass the snow-covered road.) He was forced out of the August assault by an unexpected job conflict. Jeb Blakely—a bearded Great X vet who looked more like a grizzled fur trapper than the systems engineer he was—had stepped in to lead the effort. The team was rounded out by Bob and Jean Benedict of Idaho Falls, Idaho; the well-known caver Don Coons and his wife, Sheri Engler, of Rutland, Illinois (the two were divorced a few years later)—plus me; two Virginians, Keith Goggin and the photographer Ron Simmons; Jim Smith, a Tennessean who had recently set a Mexican depth record; his wife, Pam (also later divorced); and another burly Idaho caver, Steve Zeman. Most of the group had participated in at least one of the four previous Great X throughtrips. All had worked together in Mexico, Virginia, and other cave regions.

The team had settled on three goals: To seek a means of bypassing the tight, water-filled crack near the Great Exit by finding a new passage within the cave. To examine previously unexplored side passages in the middle cave. To obtain the first-ever professional photos of Great X. My personal goal was far simpler: See the cave and live to tell about it.

Shortly after the Miller-Shifflett connection was made in 1980, a local caver had blasted the flesh-peeling Crisco Crack to a comfortable width, eleven inches, in order to install the tamperproof gate that now protects the cave and unauthorized visitors from one another. The upper entrance was owned by a third-generation rancher who considered a huge cave on the spread a huge headache. He figured—livestock prices being what they were—that he had enough headaches already.

A few days before the expedition, I met Coons and Engler for the first time at the Sheridan airport. They were easy to pick out from the crowd. Both were short, wiry, and well muscled. Both were dressed in the ratty Army-surplus garb favored by cavers everywhere. The three of us drove out to the ranch to pick up the owner's key to the Crisco Crack gate.

Conversation with the rancher was an awkward amalgam of "yeps" and "nopes" and long silences. Fortunately, Coons and Engler farmed 800 acres in central Illinois, and things relaxed a bit when talk turned to U.S. farm policy. But before we left, the rancher delivered his longest utterance of the day: "First person gets hurt in there, I'll dynamite that sucker shut and be done with it." He was sizing me up when he said it.

We drove on to the Worland office of the Bureau of Land Management, which owns Great Exit and much of the canyon above the cave. With help from several NSS groups, the BLM had developed a plan to designate the canyon a wilderness area, which ensured federal protection of Great X and several other area caves. Despite the bureau's clear interest in the continued study and exploration of Great X, the BLM cave specialist's message mirrored the rancher's: Any serious accident would close the cave for good. With that thought in mind, we met the rest of the group and drove into the mountains, resolved to spend the first few days easing into the cave, via short photo trips and light exploration forays.

The western flanks of the Bighorns abound in elk and moose, deer and antelope, and the shaggy sheep that give the range its name. In the more remote canyons, hikers can still kick up loose piles of buffalo skulls, stacked like bowling balls. The upper campsite for Great X lies about a quarter mile from the Crisco Crack, in a grassy alpine meadow. Burnt-out campfires indicate that the clearing is used perhaps three times a year by cattle herders and occasional hunters. The surrounding aspen and pine produce more than enough firewood, and the clear potable water of a snow-fed creek burbles not ten yards away.

On a sunny August afternoon in such postcard surroundings, it takes a fair amount of peer pressure to force one to wriggle into a cold, grimy wet suit and head underground. Four days of hard work in the upper cave had yielded a few virgin side passages—which quickly petered out—several dozen photos, a dented lamp, leg cramps, heat exhaustion, and, for me, some sort of stomach virus. By our fifth morning at the cave, I didn't think any sort of pressure, peer or otherwise, would force me into the nasty wet suit again.

I had come prepared for the cold, but no one had warned me of the heat. Before you reach the first stream passage, long before the Lost Worland River, several cramped, dusty chimneys and crawls must be traversed. Climbing and crawling in those dry passages turns coveralls and wet suit into an instant sauna. Each squeeze through the Crisco Crack made me feel I was wearing something advertised in a supermarket tabloid: SWEAT OUT TEN POUNDS A MINUTE OR DOUBLE YOUR MONEY BACK!

It didn't help that I had always lived within fifty miles of the Atlantic. At the 8,500-foot altitude of the campsite I kept looking for a Sherpa to appear with an oxygen bottle. True to their reputations, members of the team had proved so gung ho they were at first frightening. By now, I was more disgusted than frightened. My rancid wet suit seemed more alive than its owner. The uncomfortable activity in my stomach was more alive than either of us. Still, on Day 5, I managed to hold down my dehydrated breakfast and suit up, because nine of us, everyone but Engler and Pam Smith, would be attempting the largest Great X through-trip ever tried.

The day before, we had packed an entire camp down to the lower entrance. Near the upper cave, the surface canyon was a barely discernible dip between rolling, forested ridges; as we dropped toward the Great Exit, the canyon walls grew stark and impressive. Footing was rocky and uneven. Sheer faces, topped by strange crags and spires, rose 1,500 feet to either side. During the long trek back, I had realized why it was vital that we have tents and sleeping bags in place before trying a door-to-door. The hike out was sporting under normal conditions. Late at night, after a through-trip and hauling wet cave gear, it would become a hike out of hell.

I thought about the comfortable sleeping bag waiting for me far, far below as I hung upside down in the position required to reach the awkwardly placed padlock that hangs in the Crisco Crack. Once beyond the entrance, the group spread out. Just inside Great X was a series of three Velcro-lined chimneys—each no more than a foot wide—which a caver had to descend using rock-climbing techniques to a depth 90 feet below the Crisco Crack. The opposing walls resembled the sort that, sooner or later, rumble together to crush unfortunate souls trapped in adventure movies. The walls of Great X didn't actually move, but they did manage continually to snag whichever bit of my clothing or pack was the hardest to reach at the moment.

After the chimneys came the first short plunge through water, then an hour of heavy-duty hiking, broken by occasional climbs and crawls, to reach the Great Hall. Part of the time I traveled alongside Coons, who seemed able to float past the rock without touching it. He caved effortlessly, with the fluidity of dance. He would range far ahead of the group, drop to the rear, then fall alongside someone in the middle, like a bird dog on a hunt and loving every minute of it.

Ours was not only the largest group that had ever tried a door-to-door, it was the largest group that had ever been in the cave at one time. As a result, there were long waits as other team members traversed tricky climbs and squeezes encountered along the route. Talk of other caves and cavers and debates over gear and limestone ridges filled the waits: "Damn carbide cavers, they have to stop every ten minutes to fiddle with those antiques." . . . "Oh yeah? I read where an improperly focused electric leaves a dark spot in the center of the beam that can cause severe depression, irritability, dementia, and, ultimately, death." . . . "Listen, you think you might be interested in ridge-walking in the John Crows next January? Heaviest rainfall in Jamaica, three thousand feet of limestone that's never been checked." . . . "I swear, every time I cave in one part of the world, all anyone talks about is how great some cave is somewhere else. I don't think I've *ever* heard someone talk about any cave when they were actually in it."

The talk was engrossing, but when we reached the rope drop at the end of the Great Hall, we were already two hours behind schedule. The toughest miles of climbing and crawling lay ahead. For fast, efficient progress, three to five cavers is an ideal number—any more tend to bog down. No one said it, but everyone realized that this group was simply too large.

I was keeping pace with some of the finest cavers alive, but my stomach had already suggested a couple of rumbling, unpleasant stunts it might yet pull in a waterfall climb or, worse, in the Grim Crawl of Death. Goggin, a reedy six-foot-two caving machine—but still a lowland Southerner like me—had mentioned that he too was experiencing something of an altitude problem.

Jon Krakauer turned back on the Eiger, I remembered.

Mumbling our way into it, speaking as if we each had a mouthful of hot grits, Goggin and I agreed that we should turn back. We would work our way up to the Crisco Crack, hike down the canyon, and meet the others at the Great Exit. I rationalized that rather than shake hands with the Grim Crawl while I was exhausted and desperate, my first experience of the place would occur when I was fresh, a tourist on the photo trip planned for the following day. I wished the remaining seven luck, tucked my tail up under my coveralls, and slunk out of Great X, with Goggin right behind.

So here I am, twenty-four hours later, lying in ice water that swirls past me at a velocity of several cubic feet per second. Finally, Engler's boots move again. I force my hands—more like numb paddles now—into action. Simmons and Goggin are setting up to take the first professional photos of the Grim Crawl, which means more stops ahead. It's cold. Occasionally, we hit a wide bend, and I can see several faces at once, all of them grinning as if being here wasn't a damfool thing to do.

My helmet scrapes the ceiling and I catch a mouthful of water. I try to imagine this spot the night before, as seven weary cavers struggled toward the Great Exit. Zeman and Benedict had entered Great X without the customary ballistic nylon coveralls. They paid a price for their rashness: Both were sliced by rocks in separate waterfall climbs. Zeman lost a flounder-sized fillet from his right thigh. Benedict scraped his left buttock raw.

Their injuries were aggravated by the Grim Crawl, but more damaging than the missing flesh had been the missing patches of neoprene from the two cavers' wet suits. That had left their injured skin unprotected in the 39° F water. Benedict was well on his way to hypothermia when the group reached the end of the cave at two-thirty this morning. Still, everyone made it out in good spirits, and now both Benedict and Zeman are sleeping peacefully overhead.

The short section of the Grim Crawl that I've seen so far convinces me that Scheltens was right: This cave *will* eat someone, swallow them whole, sooner or later. A lesser caver would not have made it out on his own power with a leg injury like the one Zeman suffered. And if you can't exit Great X under your own power, you won't exit it at all.

At least Zeman had been moving downstream. I'm going upstream. I fight the water for few more yards, amazed at what Pete Shifflett accomplished when he entered this passage for the first time, and, more recently, when he made a controversial solo crossing—both times against the current.

Simmons signals for a pause, and Goggin prepares a home-made waterproof flash gun, tied to his wrist to avoid loss. He will work the flash, Simmons will shoot, and Engler will model. I will wait. I stare at Engler's boots as the cold stream washes over me. My skin tingles as though I've been pumped full of novocaine. This is getting old fast.

My wet suit is a good one, but the Velcro keeps grabbing my coveralls, holding them open for the current to billow them out. A few more rips will expose the soft neoprene of my wet suit—then what? I missed my one chance to cave through this place—really cave, hell-bent for it—as the result of a prudent decision I made yesterday. Now I face another one. In a few years, I'll probably have another shot at a through-trip, provided no one gets eaten, provided the landowner and the Bureau of Land Management don't find some other reason to close Great X. For now, I can imagine nothing more embarrassing than becoming hypothermic on a short photo trip.

I grab Engler's boot to get her attention, smile, and wave good-bye. She nods and waves back. The Grim Crawl is just wide enough to let me turn around. It takes only fifteen minutes to travel out alone, water shooting through my coveralls and helmet, knocking my glasses askew.

Later in the day, Jim Smith and Jeb Blakely push a small lead near the Great Exit into 200 feet of twisting virgin passage. They follow the water noise through a dry crawlway, convinced that they've bypassed the low slot at the end of the Grim Crawl—the crack that held Scheltens' helmet—and are headed into virgin depths. Instead, they pop out in a spot they immediately recognize from the night before, and discover that they've circled 100 feet upstream from the water-filled crack. It appears that to bypass the crack will require a new entrance down-canyon. Although several of us have combed the rough terrain, no one has found one yet, and we're running out of time for the '87 expedition. The depth record will have to wait.

As night falls, the team sits on fallen logs, huddled around a campfire in a tiny clearing ten feet from the Great Exit. It has been drizzling for several hours.

When we lug our sopping backpacks up the canyon tomorrow, the drizzle will turn to rain and then hail. We'll kill a case of warm beer while breaking camp in the rain and make it off the mountain just ahead of the season's first freak snow. Our rented Suburban fishtails over the soupy roads. Coons grins and drives with the grace and speed only an Illinois dirt farmer can exhibit in such mud, scattering elk at every turn. A tribute to Elvis somehow reaches us from a distant 50,000-watt station. When we cross Snowshoe Pass, an amazing sunset will burst through the blue-black clouds.

But that's tomorrow and this is today. It's drizzling, it's dark, and we're sitting near the Great Exit, talking caves.

One at a time the through-trip survivors have come back to life. Zeman, the last of them, woke just before the gray dusk. His swollen leg is a horrible sight. As the night wears on, the cavers prepare various canned and freeze-dried dishes. They cook on backpacking stoves or over the smoky fire, passing everything around the damp circle to be shared by all. A pint flask appears and makes the rounds. Someone remembers hiding two beers under a rock when the lower camp was set up. After a brief, successful search operation, the bottles are found and they too circulate.

It is well past midnight when the group splits for the tents pitched in the minute clearings scattered about this end of the canyon. I had planned on sleeping under the stars and left my bulky dome tent at the upper camp. But there are no stars. I roam from tent to tent, seeing if anyone has room for an extra. I'm out of luck. I suppose I can make a damp bivey with plastic garbage bags, but then I remember that there *is* some soft, dry, flat ground nearby—just this side of the Grim Crawl of Death.

I pull on my helmet, fire my lamp, and lug my air mattress and bag down into the hole, along with a sheet of plastic to insulate the bag from the damp cave air. I find a fine sandy spot, in sight of the entrance. The roar of the stream—around the corner and down a short fissure—sounds like the gentle rumble of distant surf.

I make my bed, douse the light, and fall sound asleep in Great Expectations.

5

FOLLOWING THE WIND

A cool September morning in the Black Hills of South Dakota. Fog, up from the plains, obscures the presidential faces of Mount Rushmore, hugs the emerging form of Crazy Horse, and hangs in eerie flags from the Cathedral Spires. Just east of Custer, in a pine hollow a mile or so north of Calamity Peak, wood smoke curls into the fog from the chimney of Conn Cave, a stone-walled cabin tucked into the hillside. Behind the home and its simple outbuildings rise several twenty- to forty-foot fingers of granite, these also fog shrouded. From the top of the highest comes the surprising sound of flute music—Bach—each note distinct in the moist mountain air.

Wearing Army-surplus fatigues and a warm flannel jacket, seventy-year-old cave explorer Jan Conn sits cross-legged in the moss at the edge of the peak, concentrating on phrasing and intonation. It is 7:30 A.M.

"Doggone it," she says, missing a note. "That's enough for today." Jan packs the flute into its homemade corduroy quiver, which she slings over her shoulder to keep both hands free for scrambling over rocks. But she seldom needs her hands to negotiate the slopes and boulders that surround her home—"senior-citizen climbs," she calls them. Nearly fifty years have passed since she became the first woman to ascend Devil's Tower, more than thirty-five since she and her husband, Herb, established routes that climbers still follow in Wyoming's Tetons and New Hampshire's White Mountains.

But a third of a century's worth of work at Jewel Cave National Monument has kept her in shape. She moves surefooted down the granite spike and to the trail home.

Inside Conn Cave, Herb puts finishing touches on a sketch begun the night before: a promising lead beyond the Miseries, surveyed the previous weekend by caver Mike Wiles. With Herb's thick white hair, bushy eyebrows, and perpetual, unexplained grin, he resembles no one so much as the late poet Carl Sandburg. He has in fact published snippets of poetry in his and Jan's 1977 book, *The Jewel Cave Adventure*. But it is a high, narrow fissure—not free verse—that now takes shape as he guides his pencil across the transparent sheet, deftly adding two side leads and a climb-down to a crystal pocket.

Logging an incredible 15,000 hours underground, all without pay, Herb and Jan Conn have found and mapped more than sixty miles of virgin passage since they first entered Jewel Cave on September 26, 1959—a lifetime dedication that earned them a Conservation Service Award from the U.S. Department of the Interior in 1985. Because of their efforts, the total surveyed length of Jewel Cave has grown from under a mile in 1959 to more than 103 today, making it the world's fourth-longest cave, behind Kentucky's Mammoth, Russia's Peschtschera Optimistitscheskaya, and Switzerland's Hölloch. In the mid-1980s, the Conns gradually passed the survey on to a small group of younger cavers led by Wiles, a National Park Service employee currently serving as the monument's resource manager. But Herb likes to keep his map up to date. Wiles often drops by to pass along a few hundred feet of new cave.

Herb rolls the sketched passage into a tube, pulls on his boots, and heads up the hill to the Knothole, the twenty-by-thirty-five-foot pine cabin that serves the Conns as living room, workspace, and guesthouse. One inside wall is covered by a huge multicolored map of the cave, an early prototype of the one Herb drafted for display at the monument visitors' center. The cabin's remaining walls, shelves, and ceiling nooks are obscured by Jan's instruments: a massive Victorian "harp guitar," racks of chimes, two or three primitive drums, a bass fiddle, trombones, a guitarone, several flutes and fifes, a pump organ, three ukuleles, a violin, a ukolin (a many-stringed box that produces violinlike melody with a sort of ukulele accompaniment), cymbals suspended like flying saucers, sitars, mandolins, a conch trumpet, and four or five other, unidentifiable things from which Jan occasionally coaxes a tune.

A small bedroom loft sits above the tin stove at one end of the Knothole. It can be reached only by climbing the foot-thick tree trunk that supports it. The trunk "ladder's" rungs are three half-inch wooden pegs spaced evenly along its length. What more do veteran climbers need?

There is no electricity or running water in the Knothole, or anywhere else on the Conn place. There *are* two rain barrels that seldom run dry; a fine outhouse complete with library, logbook, and a view of a pleasant meadow; all sorts of carved and painted art—on the floors, hanging in the trees, every-where. "A lot of people don't like seeing us get along as simply as we do," says Jan of the life she and Herb have chosen. "It upsets them that they're out there working full-time jobs, with their color TVs and new cars every year, and we can do without all of that.

"When we first moved here in 1951, there wasn't any elec-tricity nearby. Now it runs along the south edge of our land, and our neighbors behind us have it. But we figured if we had electricity, then we'd want a washing machine. Next thing you know, we'd have to dig a well. Our needs would build and build until we'd lose everything. It's something you have to work very hard at, living simply. It takes a lot of thought and effort."

Nearly everything the Conns own reflects that thought and effort. They buy their clothing secondhand, and once a month they drive into Rapid City to purchase cases of canned food from a warehouse that sells damaged goods. The car they drive, a Renault Jan named Dimples, was purchased new, but at a discount because of hail damage. Herb and Jan do all of their cooking and heating with firewood, which the U.S. Forest Service allows them to cut from trees already downed. They have indulged in one "luxury," which they keep in the garage: a sixty-year-old gas-operated refrigerator, given to them by friends who were moving. Before the refrigerator, they kept perishables outside in the winter, underground in the fall and spring, and did without in the summer. When asked how they handle medical expenses, Jan smiles and says, "We don't get sick."

"Oh, we might eventually dig a well," Herb reflects, "but not until we need it. The few times that we've been dry here, we've always managed to get good spring water from our neighbors up the road. We've bartered for use of a washing machine in Custer, and that's worked out nicely." He grins and adds, "I don't much care for baths—if we had a well, I'd probably have to take more of them."

Herb Conn and Jan Bien were married on Valentine's Day 1944. Herb, a recent graduate of the University of Colorado with a degree in electrical engineering, was a civilian working for the Navy in Washington, D.C. Jan, a Washington native, was studying flute at Colorado. But they had known each other since childhood, when their families had vacationed together in New England, and had discovered that they shared a deep love for mountain climbing, for reaching places that no one had ever been.

While climbing with the Potomac Appalachian Trail Club in 1944, the Conns visited their first cave, West Virginia's Schoolhouse. Although they enjoyed navigating the tricky underground cliffs and complicated passageways, the trip was nothing more than a novelty—they were climbers, not cavers. At the close of World War II Herb and Jan quit work and school and began touring the country, looking for mountains to scale. To finance their summer expeditions (there were no manufacturers of Day-Glo rope or high-fashion parkas to sponsor climbers in those days), the Conns would take winter jobs at ski resorts and dude ranches: busing tables, making beds, whatever work they could find.

In 1947, they passed through South Dakota on the way to Devil's Tower in Wyoming. The U.S. National Park Service denied their request to climb the tower. Frustrated, the couple returned to the Black Hills and started looking over the Needles. What they saw amazed them. Here were hundreds of pristine pinnacles begging to be climbed. Equipped with sixty feet of manila rope, flat-soled tennis shoes, and hours of determined effort, the Conns reached peak after magnificent peak.

"When we went back to work in Arizona that year," Jan recalls, "we couldn't believe it had all happened. No place could be that nice. We decided to return the next summer to see if we had imagined it all." The next summer turned out even better. "We figured we had found enough climbs to last a lifetime. In 1949, we came back to stay."

"This was our dream of paradise," says Herb in a chapter he wrote for Paul Piana's 1983 book *Touch the Sky*, "challenging summits all about us with no tedious backpacking required to reach them. We settled into the Sylvan Lake campground and, later in the summer, we bought ten acres of land as close as we could get to the Needles." But it took another two years of resort work in other states before Herb and Jan could afford to move onto their land and into Conn Cave.

Once settled, the Conns started a mail-order leather-goods business, making belts and purses whenever the weather was too poor for climbing or their muscles were too sore. Occasionally they took other work. Jan gave music lessons and wrote *Run to Catch a Pine Cone*, a musical which was produced in regional theaters. Herb was periodically hired by the National Park Service to putty cracks in the granite of Abraham Lincoln's nose or Teddy Roosevelt's chin. Although the couple still ventured off to climbs in other states, they always returned even more excited about the Needles. They were especially interested in the Cathedral Spires group, so much so that Herb built a complex wax model depicting each jagged peak to exact scale.

Before long, climbing in South Dakota had become synonymous with the name Conn, and climbers from around the world started showing up at Conn Cave, eager to try the Needles. Herb and Jan were nearly always willing to guide them. In the summer of 1959, one such young climber appeared at their front door. He said his name was Dwight Deal, and that he was a recent college graduate working in the western Wyoming oilfields.

An energetic climber with a penchant for practical jokes, Deal spent many weekends that summer climbing with the Conns before eventually confiding to them that, nice as the Needles were, his true love was caving. He had just obtained a permit from the Park Service to explore the back reaches of Jewel Cave, but the permit required a minimum group of at least three explorers. Would Herb and Jan mind going into the cave with him? The Conns weren't very excited by the offer, but they had, after all, enjoyed their one trip to Schoolhouse over a decade earlier, so they decided to compromise: For every day Deal agreed to climb with them, they would spend a day caving.

Deal had already been to the Discovery Rooms, long corridors found during the previous year by park rangers and a few students from the South Dakota School of Mines. The new rooms had more than doubled the known length of the cave, pushing it from two thousand or so feet—surveyed by the Civilian Conservation Corps when the Park Service began administering the cave in the 1930s—to eight-tenths of a mile.

Deal tried to show the Conns every foot of it on that initial visit. As Herb puts it in *The Jewel Cave Adventure*: "It was our first trip into Jewel Cave, and we had to get used to the cave environment, to the eccentricities of our carbide lamps and to Dwight at the same time. This was a tall assignment."

"When we first went to Jewel," Jan remembers, "there was a sign at the entrance that said it was a 'small cave.' We figured that it was a good place for people who didn't know any more about caving than we did, that it would be a nice cave to start on."

As in many long caves, a strong breeze nearly always blows through Jewel as the cave's air pressure adjusts to outside conditions. In some places, it has been clocked at well over thirty miles per hour, more than enough to blow out a carbide lamp. The temperature is cool, a constant 46° F, the humidity nearly 100 percent. And with all the climbing and crawling, through crystal-coated passages which branch and intersect as though they were designed by Escher, even a short excursion into Jewel can lose an experienced caver. On their first trip, Deal took the Conns to the known "end" of the cave and a little bit beyond, into virgin passage. Then, just as they were heading back, he sat down and announced, "Okay, I led in. Why don't you lead out?"

Herb and Jan tried to take him up on it, but each passage they thought would be the right one quickly became a dead end. Finally, Deal stood and demanded in mock impatience, "What's the matter? You aren't lost, are you?"—revealing as he stood the small hole that was the only exit, which he had been blocking all along. That moment of confusion, heightened by the knowledge of the blackness that still lay beyond the point where they had turned back, had given the Conns the one thing they loved best: a challenge. Soon they began to join Deal in exploring the cave in earnest, devoting progressively smaller amounts of time to climbing. Within two years, they had found and mapped five miles of virgin passage.

"It was time for us to try something different," Jan says of those early trips. "There were so many people climbing, and we'd always been basically shy. And climbing was becoming more and more of a 'see what I've done,' macho sort of thing. Cavers were different—they weren't out to impress anyone.

"No matter how much trouble you've got, once you get into the cave it all floats up to the surface. There's no room for worries down there. With all the crawls and climbs and tight spots, it's a different world, and it commands all of your attention. There's a special feeling, a closeness, that cavers develop for each other on a long trip, even if they're the kind of people who would never associate with one another on the outside."

Most cavers also tend to have a sense of humor, she adds. "Dwight was always pulling jokes. We'd be crawling along and he'd point to a nasty spot and say, 'There's a pretty little room in there you should see.' So we'd squirm our way into something so small we could barely turn around, then as we came out he'd say, 'You'd have to agree, that's a pretty little room, isn't it?'

"Of course, we got him a few times too. Once we picked up a shopping bag from a Jewel supermarket that said 'Happier Families Shop at Jewel,' and we changed the 'h' to an 'n' and added an 'o,' so it read 'Happier Families Snoop at Jewel.' Then we stuck it way down a crawlway, which we let Dwight 'find' on our next trip."

But "snooping" at Jewel was not all fun and games. Survey work could be slow and tedious, and for every crawlway that led to open space, dozens would pinch out. Whenever the Conns did manage to follow the wind to a large room or corridor, they would carefully pick their trail so as to leave as little evidence of their passage as possible. "We always tried to walk in the same place," explains Jan, "so that if somebody wanted to come along and study the way the mud had cracked or the rocks had settled, the room would look exactly as it was before we found it." Special care had to be taken around gypsum needles, hydromagnesite balloons, helictites, and other tiny, delicate formations—a single misstep would obliterate them.

Special care had to be taken by the Conns for themselves. As the cave became increasingly complex, with exploration focusing on leads located several hours from the entrance, safety became ever more important. It would have taken days for a rescue party to remove an injured caver from more remote passages. A few crawlways were so inaccessible that a caver who couldn't exit under his own power might never exit at all. There were some close calls. Jan especially remembers a narrow, virgin chimney that nearly swallowed her a few minutes after she found it.

"I had climbed about halfway up, with my back on one side and both feet on the other, when all of a sudden I felt the crystal wall jar. Sometimes there's a gap between the crystal and the limestone—this time there had been about an inch of space behind four inches of crystal. Above me, I could see it cracking. It was all ready to come down. As long as I kept pressure on both sides, I was fine, but I didn't want to spend the rest of my life there. Herb was down below, so I yelled for him to get out of the way. I sat and planned each of my moves. As I went up, chunks of crystal came down. But I was able to get to a ledge and grab it before the whole wall collapsed."

Despite the close calls, countless scrapes and bruises, torn clothing to mend and broken gear to fix, the Conns kept coming back, even during the long dry spells, when they would work for months without finding significant passage. "When we were at twenty-three miles," Herb recalls, "we didn't have anything. No going leads at all. We looked at our rough sketch map, where we had put in all the dead leads that we hadn't surveyed, and counted up all those little odds and ends. We figured we could possibly map them and get twenty-five miles out of the cave before we gave it up. Then one of those dead-end crawls turned out to be not a dead end at all, and we were in walking passage again. That's happened so many times."

About 70 million years ago, the Black Hills were shoved up by deep volcanic action that never quite broke the surface but created instead a bulging granite blister nearly a hundred miles in diameter. The blister was covered by a thick skin of recently deposited Minnelusa sandstone, which in turn covered the 350-million-year-old Paha Sapa limestone. This sedimentary skin soon began to erode from the uplifted rock, burying the surrounding foothills to create present-day plains. Since the sandstone eroded more quickly than the limestone, the flanks of the bulge were encircled by a thin ring of exposed limestone; when limestone is exposed to the surface, caves often start to form.

For 30 million years or so, surface water flowed into the Paha Sapa, hollowing large and extensive caverns before emerging in distant valley springs. But the higher elevations of the Black Hills were still being carved by wind and rain. About 40 million years ago, during the Oligocene Epoch, a great flood of mud and sand rolled down from the peaks to mix with sediment from the Rocky Mountains and bury the limestone once again. This thick layer of sediment, called the White River Group, effectively plugged the springs that drained the caves, causing them to fill with water that remained stagnant for millions of years. Conditions were ideal for crystal growth. This is most likely the period when Jewel Cave's characteristic calcite spar was formed, slowly building up along the limestone walls until a four- to eight-inch layer coated nearly every cave surface.

Over the past 30 million years, gradual erosion of the White River Group sediments has once again exposed the ring of limestone. A minor uplift 4.5 million years ago helped to "unclog" ancient springs and drain the flooded caverns. But the older cave entrances and the streambeds that determined their location were all but obliterated by the long burial. It is only lucky coincidence that sometimes allows small connections between the present-day surface and the prehistoric emptiness below.

Jewel Cave was first discovered at the turn of the century by brothers Frank and Albert Michaud, who were prospecting for minerals in the Black Hills. One warm summer day, they were surprised by a blast of cold air that seemed to come from a clump of brush. They traced the intriguing breeze to a fourteen-inch hole in the limestone, then went home for tools and dynamite, which they used to enlarge the opening. Armed with candles and a few feet of rope, the brothers crawled gingerly into the dark tunnel, pausing whenever the wind snuffed out their flickering candles. The crawlway soon opened to an impressive domed room, its walls covered with white dogtooth spar that glittered like diamonds. Certain they were about to become rich, the Michauds immediately filed a mining claim with the Forest Service, which administered the land, calling their "mine" the Jewel Lode.

They spent the next few years enlarging passages and placing wooden ladders, while trying to seek out markets not only for the cave's unique crystals but for its chert, manganese, iron, and lithographic limestone as well. They had little luck in their enterprise. Calcite spar is too soft to be of industrial use—although they did manage to sell five tons of it from "an obscure side pocket" to decorate a religious shrine in Iowa. The other minerals could easily be obtained from less remote sources.

Undaunted, the brothers concentrated on opening the cave as a tourist attraction, but again with limited success. Nearby Wind Cave, which was much "larger" and more accessible to tourists, had been declared a national park in 1903; in 1908, Jewel Cave was proclaimed a national *monument*, a somewhat less prestigious moniker. Moreover, a citizens' group from Custer supported the idea of development but didn't trust the Michauds with the cave because of their mining bent. The end result was that Jewel Cave stayed pretty much as it was, and the brothers pursued other projects until the 1930s, when Frank Michaud's son Ira worked to reopen his father's early tours.

Ira continued to work in the cave after the Park Service took over its administration in 1933, and he helped coordinate the trail building done by the Civilian Conservation Corps. Although several Park Service rangers with an interest in exploration were placed in charge of the cave over the next three decades, few new passages were found until the Discovery Rooms were entered in 1958. Those rooms were minute compared with the discoveries that Herb and Jan Conn made soon after their first trip with Dwight Deal.

By June 1962, the cave had reached a known length of ten miles, and Herb and Jan started to consider a second entrance. They had found a series of large, well-decorated chambers that seemed to promise even larger passages to come, but the new area was so remote that it took hours of hard caving to reach it. The twisting, up-and-down route was incredibly complex, and even when following earlier survey stations (bits of plastic ribbon and carbide dots), it was common for cavers to lose their way. Herb and Jan found it difficult to imagine interested noncavers—geologists, hydrologists, park rangers, or the public—ever reaching this unique, pristine section of Jewel. They began persuading the Park Service to consider opening it up with a new entrance. It was time to share their discovery.

The Conns had several strong arguments in their favor. If a tour route was constructed in the new area, an area seen so far by five or six cavers, it would be the only cave tour in the country through true virgin passage. Visitors would see none of the broken stalactites, charcoal initials, muddy paths, and handprints common to caves that have seen heavy human traffic in less cautious times. The proposed tour loop would take up a tiny fraction of the newly discovered passages, leaving miles of wild cave available for scientific study. Moreover, the cave seemed to be trending south, toward Lithograph Canyon. It was conceivable that the Conns might find a natural connection to one of the small caves in the canyon, or that they might find a passage close enough to the surface so that only a short tunnel would have to be excavated to reach it.

Eventually, the Park Service agreed to drill a six-inch-diameter test well to find out if the new rooms were where Herb's map said they were. Herb and Jan had already named a large central chamber the Target Room with just such an experiment in mind. Herb carefully surveyed his way to the same spot in the room via sixty different routes, then averaged the differences until he could confidently point to a spot on the hillside two hundred feet overhead and say, "Drill here." The bit punched into Target Room a foot or so off—but it had wobbled back and forth nearly four feet as it worked through the solid rock. The new tour was on its way to becoming a reality.

Herb and Jan worked closely with the Park Service over the next few years, carefully planning each foot of the tour loop. Visitors had to be able to enjoy the cave in its natural state without endangering that state—or themselves. With his experience in electrical engineering, Herb was able to plan lighting placement so that no wires or bulbs would be visible and so that the cave would show only its natural colors. He wanted the Jewel tour to display none of those fluorescent blues and reds found in commercial caves that advertise along the highway: "See Amazing Wonders of the Natural World! See the Onyx Madonna! See the Crystal City!" To avoid pouring concrete paths—and thus excavating and reshaping passages—Herb planned for visitors to travel over lightweight aluminum platforms placed well *above* the mud- and rock-strewn floors, which would remain in their natural condition.

An elevator shaft was excavated to the Target Room, a modern visitors' center built atop it, and tours began in 1972. "Since then, over two million people have taken one of our three cave tours," says Park Service employee Bruce W. Bitz, who is seasonal supervisor of the national monument. "In addition to the regular tour, we give a four-hour spelunking tour, which is a general introduction to the sport of caving. It's a fairly challenging trip that allows people to see a portion of the cave as Herb and Jan first saw it." To qualify for the spelunking tour, would-be cavers must first crawl through an 8.5-inch-by-two-foot concrete tunnel in the visitors' center. Also offered is a candlelit "historic tour" of the cave near the natural entrance. (Tour guides save the candle stubs for Herb and Jan, who use them to light Conn Cave and the Knothole.)

Despite the three tours, "over ninety percent of the known cave has been visited by less than ten people," Bitz says. "Even though Jewel is the second-longest cave in the country, much less than one percent of it is accessible to the general public. It's the only true wilderness cave in the park system that is open to the public. If not for Herb and Jan's dedication, we'd probably not know about it at all. It's doubtful that the cave would have remained under Park Service management if not for their work."

The known length of the cave continues to grow. By placing anemometers, barometers, and other measuring devices near the natural entrance and in key passages, in the mid-1970s

Herb was able to calculate the cave's volume (based on air-flow) to be at least 5 billion cubic feet. Assuming an average passage size of 20 by 20 feet, that adds up to a total cave length of over *2,000 miles*. Most of that space undoubtedly lies beyond cracks and crevices too small for human penetration, but clearly a great deal of Jewel Cave remains to be found.

Yet, despite their discoveries, despite the trip to Washington for the Conservation Service Award, despite the National Speleological Society awarding them honorary life membership and declaring them "two of the best cavers this country has ever seen," Jan insists that she and Herb aren't *really* cavers. "We just got curious about where this particular mousehole went. It never stopped going."

6

NICK DANGER

I wrote "Following the Wind" on assignment to *Audubon* magazine in the Fall of 1986.

The photographer that Audubon hired to shoot the Conns at home and in Jewel Cave was Michael K. Nichols, known far and wide as Nick. One photo magazine dubs him "The Indiana Jones of Photography." Another calls him "Nick Danger." Nearly a decade earlier, Nick had partnered with adventure writer Tim Cahill, producing gonzo stories on the Amazon basin, mountain gorillas, hurricanes, volcanoes, and caves for *Rolling Stone* and *Outside*. I had been reading Cahill's stuff and thus, without knowing it, looking at Nick's photos since I first started caving at Florida State. Cahill's column in Outside was something I looked forward to every month. I had decided I wanted to be him.

A few weeks before I met Nick in South Dakota, he and Cahill had nearly killed themselves trying to hike from the lowest elevation in the continental United States—282 feet below sea level in Death Valley—to Mount Whitney, the highest point in the lower forty-eight at 14,375 feet. When their piece was published in *Rolling Stone* several months later, one photo caption read: "Two half-dead dumbshits in the desert." Cahill reprinted the article, "Fear of Frying," in his 1989 book A *Wolverine Is Eating My Leg*. It comes just before a piece called "Vertical Caving," which describes a descent the two made into Incredible Pit, a 440-foot drop in Ellison's Cave in TAG. Cahill writes:

Nick has been photographing caves for a dozen years and is well known in the speleological community. Because caves . . . are perfectly dark, it is impossible to get an idea of their dimensions with one light. Nick's genius is to illuminate the caves with light—with a combination of old-fashioned flash guns, flares, radio-controlled strobe lights, and great white-hot magnesium explosions. Cavers accompany Nick—he gets them to carry his gear—into the deepest and most inaccessible caves because he will provide them with photographs of a place they have been to but have never really seen.

This observation is true of any good cave photographer. People like Ron Simmons, Chip Clark, Ron Kerbo, and Kevin Downey had cooked up clever lighting gizmos years before Nick Nichols came on the scene. Nick's genius isn't just that he captures big, well-lit passages, but that he catches the emotions of the people in the cave. He carries with him—or, more accurately, his sherpas lug—big collapsible diffusers and reflectors, with which he lights the people in the foreground as carefully as a fashion photographer shooting Elle McPherson for the swimsuit issue. And he still gets the big room or scary pit in the background, using shadow as well as light to give the scene a sense of space and mystery.

Our first day together, Nick took a number of shots of Herb and Jan puttering about what he called "the little hobbit town" they had built around Conn Cave. Next morning, we made a long trip into Jewel to shoot the Conns amid formations and borehole. As we humped gear up chimneys and down crawlways, panting to keep up with the couple—who moved as comfortably as hobbits in their home tunnels—I pumped Nick for tips about breaking into the big time. I wanted to land the kind of assignments that editors routinely tossed to him and Cahill.

He was happy to tell me what he could, he said, but didn't seem to know quite how he'd made it himself. Nick's accent was an odd mixture of northern Alabama, where he'd grown up, and Berkeley, where he'd been living since his career took off. With his long hair and California tan, he could have passed for a rock star—a drummer, probably, with a southern band like Skynard or the Allmans. He mentioned that some airlines and travel bureaus like to encourage travel journalism. As we rested above a crystal climb, he said he had the number of an office in New York that might send me tickets to Jamaica if I showed them one or two good clips.

"Another piece of advice," he said, "is don't go anyplace where they shoot guns at you. They shot at me in Rwanda, and it wasn't fun. I told my agent, 'Man, I just don't want to get killed taking pictures.' "

Nick said his first break had come with the photos he took for a story on Ellison's Cave, which ran in the late seventies in *Geo*, a short-lived American version of Europe's leading geographic magazine. Not long after, he had hooked up with a big New York agency. Within a few years, he was globe-trotting at a day rate of $2,000.

It's July 1995, nine years after our trip to Jewel, and I'm sitting in my office looking at Nick's photos in *Audubon*. The opening two-page spread shows Jan changing carbide while Herb sketches in a survey book. They sit in front of a large irregular chamber, both intent on their work. You can see lines in their calm faces, sense their ease in the cave. The lighting is soft and natural, as if it seeps from the rock itself.

Standing on a boulder in the background, back to the camera, I hold a flash gun built from a five-cell flashlight. My body blocks the gun and the brilliant popping of an old M3b Sylvania bulb, fired a dozen times at Nick's command. I remember burning my fingertips on hot spent bulbs as I dropped them into a nylon bag at my feet.

I flip to the end of the story. Here's the view from the Conns' outhouse, door open, interesting books lined up on their cedar shelf to the right. A copy of *The Jewel Cave Adventure* is held open in the foreground, resting in Nick's hand, showing a two-page black-and-white photo of Jan, comically stuck in a crawlway with her foot near her head. The caption describes the outhouse and the circumstances of the photo in the book—taken by Herb twenty years earlier—but it doesn't identify the hand.

I didn't know it then, but at the time I assisted him in Jewel, Nick had already begun to develop what became his professional signature, since copied by dozens of the world's top photographers. It's a technique that has made Nick the darling of *National Geographic*: blurry photos.

I myself have taken blurry photos for years, beginning with the roll I shot in my parents' living room on Christmas morning 1967. But Nick's fuzziness has made him famous, while mine still produces images only a mother could love. The difference between our two lacks of focus is easy to see. By setting up perfect, studio-type lighting in exotic places, and then showing action by allowing the subject to move, or the camera to move, or both at once, Nick creates highly artistic moments that look accidental. The beauty he shows seems to exist beyond the camera's power to control it. Not that he could ever keep his subjects still anyway. Cavers on rope and foraging gorillas are equally averse to taking orders from photographers.

I set down the *Audubon* and pick up one of three issues of *National Geographic* from my desk. It's dated March 1991. Nick's first *Geographic* cover shows my good friend and sometime lead guitarist Chris Stine climbing a steep flowstone slope in Lechuguilla Cave in New Mexico. The formations are crisp and gorgeous, but Chris's face is lost in a blur of carbide flame. Cahill wrote the text, his first appearance in *Geographic*.

I met Nick for the second time in 1988, when he was at Lechuguilla working on what became a two-year project. He had moved from Berkeley to a farm in Charlottesville, Virginia— the town where Ron Simmons lives, although I don't believe the two photographers ever met each other. Nick was shooting Lechuguilla for *Smithsonian* that summer; he came back the next year with his first *Geographic* assignment. Later, he hired Chris and Neeld Messler, a young TAG caver, as sherpas; they spent as much as a week underground on each shoot.

Nick has photographed several *Geographic* stories since

Lechuguilla. The second issue of the magazine on my desk is the current one, dated July 1995. It arrived, coincidentally, a day after I found the floppy disk containing my original draft of "Following the Wind," which had lain in a cardboard box for six years. The magazine cover shows a fuzzy background and a blurry charging elephant, its eyes red from a reflected flash—exactly how my son Alex's are in a shot I took at his fourth birthday party. When I saw it in the mail I said, "There's Nick," without having to check inside for the photo credit.

I still haven't read the article, about a wildlife preserve in the Congo. But now I look at the pictures: Nick's hand swarms with ants, above a shot where a bloody leech clings to his ankle. I turn the page and find Neeld Messler, chopping at a log on a rain-soaked jungle highway, trying to clear a path for Nick's jeep. Good for you, Neeld. Glad to see another caver make it to the ranks of professional globe-trotting bum. Hang on while you can.

The third issue is dated August 1995; it came yesterday. Inside, an article compares the fictional Robert Kincaid, hero of the novel and film *The Bridges of Madison County*, with real *National Geographic* photographers. Big surprise: The real people are completely unlike the way Robert James Waller imagines them. There's a picture of Nick in the field. He hunches in submissive posture, a yard away from a 400-pound mountain gorilla. The gorilla's back is to the camera, slightly out of focus. Nick is wet, clearly afraid, eyes deliberately downcast, face hidden in his hands. His body language says: You're the boss, gorilla.

Of course, he's snapping pictures all the while. And he's not getting shot at.

7

INTO THE CITY

In March 1985, when I was a graduate student in English at the University of South Carolina, I flew to New York to interview for a *Newsweek* internship. Kathy, my wife, had been offered a managerial internship with Sony, so we already planned to live in the city for the summer. I knew that *Newsweek*'s program was designed for undergraduate journalism majors. In my application, I had argued that my qualifications, though unusual, meshed well with the duties an intern would perform.

The first question the interviewer asked was "If you were an ice-cream cone, what flavor would you be?"

"Homemade vanilla" must have been the wrong answer: I lost the job.

Since I was in New York anyway, I tried to make some editorial contacts. I had recently begun to submit magazine articles and proposals, with marginal success. The previous January, the travel editor at *McCall's* had bought a short humor piece I'd written. A few other editors had rejected me gently, encouraging me to try them with other work. An hour after the ice-cream interview, I visited the *McCall's* editor who had accepted my essay, and she took me to lunch. Before dessert, she assigned two new articles.

I was ecstatic, with the rest of an afternoon to kill. My confidence bolstered, I walked from the Helmsley Building, where *McCall's* was headquartered at the time, through the Pan Am lobby, and down into the great cavern of Grand Central Station. There, standing at a pay phone amid commuters

and panhandlers, bathed in the dusky Stieglitz light streaming from the tall windows, I called every editor who had sent
me a "friendly" rejection letter. I introduced myself and asked
whether I might drop by for a visit. Most of the people I called
were out for the day, didn't remember me, or were too busy to
be bothered. But three said "Sure, come on over."

My first stop was *Travel & Leisure*, where an editorial assistant in his twenties gave me two issues of the magazine, a
copy of its writer's guidelines, and a ten-minute tour of the
office. Then he shoved me out the door. Same thing happened at *Woman's Day*, with the minor improvement of a
senior editor in her fifties doing the giving and shoving. Last
on my list was *Audubon*, which was then located on upper
Third Avenue, a healthy walk from midtown.

The previous October, I had produced an article in praise of
bats for a writing workshop taught by William Price Fox. Bill
had said, "You know, I met a guy at a party, Gary Swiss or
Souse, something like that, worked at *Audubon*. He'd like this.
Look up his name, make sure you get it right."

The name was Gary Soucie, I discovered, and he was
Audubon's executive editor. I sent him the piece. He returned
it with two sentences scrawled over my cover letter: "Nice, but
too similar to the 'Ecopinion' piece on bats in the Sept. 84
issue. Try us again on something else."

I was not expecting much from our meeting. Only a rank
beginner would have submitted the bat article in the first
place without bothering to check whether the magazine had
covered the topic—not just in recent years but in its previous
issue. And the word "nice" barely qualified as encouraging
criticism. Still, he did have that connection to Fox. I waited
nervously in the lobby of the National Audubon Society headquarters, inspecting framed magazine covers and an original
Audubon sketch of a pelican.

When I was at last summoned to Soucie's office, I was
greeted by a tall, bearded man in a tweed sport coat. The sun
lines that creased his eyes and the fishing tackle that draped
his walls bespoke an editor whose outdoor experience was not

limited to slick pages. What had made him remember me, Soucie said, was my South Carolina return address. He had spent several months there researching a *National Geographic* article on swamps, and retained pleasant memories of the state. He was a fan of Fox's southern humor, and was interested not only in bats but in caving. He questioned me on both subjects for thirty minutes or more.

When I noticed a fishing book on his desk, Soucie's name on the spine, he launched into an hour of funny stories about what it was like to write for fishing magazines, which was something he did in his spare time. Gary Soucie was a jovial, easygoing sort who clearly loved to talk. By the time I asked how I might break into his magazine, I felt that we had become old friends.

"You know what I wish I got more of?" he said. "Essays aimed at our 'Ecopinion' slot. The point of the column is to entertain environmental arguments from unusual points of view. What most writers don't get is that this means you can take a position that would rankle the average environmentalist. You just need to have a surprising point and argue it well. I'm sick of reading the same tired call for wetlands reclamation. Too many writers are preaching to the choir."

I had an idea, one that might let me reflect on caving— something I could never do in the pages of *McCall's*. "So I could write a piece arguing that certain types of pollution can be good? That, for instance, an old car found in the woods might actually appeal to someone who loves the outdoors?"

"Give it a shot," he said. "I'd be happy to take a look."

8

A Taste for Junk

In the dense woods a few miles west of Florida Caverns State Park—a hilly, un-Florida-like place of jagged outcrops and mossy boulders—I came across the decomposing remains of a 1937 Buick. Or it might have been a '38 or '39. It was hard to tell.

A chinaberry tree grew from the open hood in place of the long-gone engine. Another tried to work its way through the cracked rear window. Preserved on the dashboard was a brown bouquet of black-eyed Susans, which had sprouted from the split leatherette, not that summer or the spring before, but perhaps in the summer before that. Likewise preserved were two or three abandoned mud-dauber nests, and the front-seat upholstery showed signs of serving as bedding for a dozen or so rodents. I didn't doubt that somewhere within the hulk were coiled two or three snakes, perhaps among the rusty bench springs, waiting for a curious mouse or pack rat.

But despite its woodsy occupants, the Buick was not of these woods, and I stood for some time wondering how on earth someone had dragged it back in there, much less why.

The 1958 U.S. Geological Survey topo map I carried showed no nearby roads, not even the faint dotted lines used to indicate the pan-gouging timber trails common to most North Florida woods. And I had a pretty good idea of where I was. I had come to the woods to help catalog new cave locations. Six of us in the Florida State Cave Club had each been given a specific corridor to walk that afternoon, to search for previously uncharted openings within the limestone bluffs.

In a month, I was scheduled to start law school. I was determined to find some virgin cave before the passages I could explore became those between stacks in the law library. Three weeks earlier, I had driven to northern Alabama and rappelled into a number of pits. A few days after that, I tried unsuccessfully to dig open what appeared to be a collapsed entrance at the base of a bluff just west of Tallahassee. The previous Saturday, a friend and I had hiked through steady rain along the spine of a malevolent, bush-covered ridge that rose in a swamp a few miles east of here, scanning for holes and kicking up sluggish snakes. I had found no caves then, and none today except for this rusting cave of Detroit sheet metal, crumbling into soil like a Mayan tomb.

If the Buick was not exactly pleasing to the eye, it was at least inoffensive. It seemed somehow to belong. It reminded me of a slide a friend had taken of a Sherman tank on Moa Island, nearly swallowed by jungle, a relic of man's Military-Industrial Age. I began circling the derelict, searching for a road hidden among the slash pines that now fenced it in. Slowly, a few feet at a time, I was able to make out a narrow depression that might once have been drivable. But for the Buick, I would have attributed the shallow trough to runoff (if I had been observant enough to spot it at all). Now, though, I was able to hike the path up a little rise to a low ridge, between white boulders the size of Volkswagens, around a live oak, and then down into an abandoned field. There I knew it could join twin ruts that eventually led to Bumpnose Road. As I slogged through the thick brush, ever mindful of snakes, the feeling began to overpower me: People had been here once.

It was a familiar feeling. Since childhood, I have been fascinated by flotsam of the past. Not beer cans and mattresses and suspicious-looking metal drums—that kind of trash and litter gives junk a bad name. What I like is honest, respectable, old-fashioned junk. The neat stuff. The excitement of stumbling upon an abandoned railroad in the middle of nowhere is close to that of discovering a pristine beaver pond or spotting a doe with her fawn.

One summer, when I was perhaps seven years old, I visited my grandfather's farm in southern Illinois. Like any town boy with a grandfather in the country, I was wide-eyed and overwhelmed by it all—tractors, woods, cornfields, snakes, knives and axes, crawdad ponds—everything. But I particularly recall a place in the woods that my grandfather took me late one afternoon, just before sunset, a clearing where a stable had stood in the mid-1800s. Beneath a tangled blanket of once tame honeysuckle lay iron harness rings, horseshoes, old-fashioned square nails, brass studs clinging to bits of rotten leather, and what I remember best of all—a two-wheeled riding plow, its iron spokes in the fast grip of a white oak's creeping root system. My grandfather explained how the plow would have been rigged behind a team of mules. He said that he had used one just like it when my mother was a little girl, then pulled away the vines so I could try out the creaking seat.

Later that night, my mother told me that she had played "farmer" with her brothers and sisters on the same old plow, that it had been stuck in the tree roots even then. "Haw! Haw, there, Sally!" she shouted, cracking an imaginary whip to show me how it was done. "Get up, there, Blue, you good-for-nothin' mule! Haw!"

I must have plowed 500 acres on that thing before my parents took me back to Florida. My romance with junk had barely begun.

A year or two later, my father bought a fiberglass boat and started taking the family on all-day trips up the Tomoka, a sluggish root-beer-colored river that emptied into the brackish Intracoastal Waterway ten miles north of our home. As we inched our way up the state-protected stream, the muddy banks would draw so close we could smell their dank odor. Rotting palm trunks hollowed by woodpeckers leaned dangerously overhead. From the twisted branches of mangroves and water oaks hung vines that I would swear were snakes. Once in a great while, they were.

My job was to sit in the front and watch the mirrored surface for floating logs, alligators, or manatees, which could leave us stranded in the jungle with a broken propeller. What a jungle it was: Everywhere I looked was vegetation and wildlife. Above us were birds I had seen only in books—herons and hawks, eagles and egrets, countless pelicans. In the scrub, we spotted deer, raccoons, and armadillos. The river brimmed with life. Besides ever-present alligators and an occasional manatee, from my vantage point I saw turtles, four-foot gars sunning themselves just below the surface, swimming cottonmouths, and once even a porpoise with her calf, headed toward Ponce Inlet and the Atlantic, thirty miles away. Actually, I heard the porpoise before I saw her, the wet clap of her blowhole rising above the outboard's gurgle only a few feet to starboard. I remember how she stared at us with an almost human eye as she escorted her youngster safely past the spinning blades.

But even as I was learning to enjoy and respect wilderness, I was developing my taste for junk. Along the Tomoka, it was hard to do otherwise. Each bend in the river seemed to take us further from the late 1960s, closer to a time when Florida was ruled by half-crazy swamp trappers and roving Seminole clans. Their evidence was everywhere. The oldest junk had been in place for centuries—oyster-shell mounds and broken conch hammers left by the Timucuans, who had lived on the river long before the Seminoles arrived from Georgia. And although the more recent human detritus had been abandoned less than forty years earlier, I often found it the most exciting.

We would sometimes leave the boat to examine two of the best caches of junk. The first stop, only an hour from the river's mouth, was a clearing that had been the set of a Johnny Weissmuller Tarzan movie filmed in the 1930s. I later heard that the director somehow managed to coax lazy Tomoka gators into assuming the roles of vicious Nile crocodiles, so that they could be convincingly wrestled by a local garage mechanic who doubled for Weissmuller. Another story had it that Weissmuller insisted on wrestling the gators by himself. Whatever happened, all that remained of the set I inspected was a collapsed hut and a tall, dead cypress tree on the bank. From the tree's highest branch hung a hemp rope, thick as a man's arm and still bearing traces of green dye: a genuine Tarzan swinging vine.

Much farther up the river—where it became so narrow that to turn around involved backing the boat thirty yards—a rotting dock marked the site of a failed turpentine operation from the turn of the century. Back behind the roofless main shed was my favorite piece of Tomoka junk: A rusted pipe stood in a low concrete basin and shot a continuous, foot-high fountain of slightly sulfurous water from its ragged mouth. A lucky well digger had punched into one of the countless underground streams coursing through the limestone aquifer and had given his customer the rare luxury of running water. The customer had gone broke, or caught fever, or become fed up with the heat, or simply walked into the swamp and vanished, but his water still gushed. I can remember the cold, wild taste of it as I gulped from the pipe before getting into the boat for our long trip home. It tasted of something hidden and magical, a potion from deep within the earth.

My quest for junk in the woods eventually turned me into an amateur historian. When you find a brass doorknob or a broken bone snuffbox, you can't help but wonder about the people who used it. By my senior year of high school I was making regular treks to East Florida's ruined indigo and sugar plantations, most of which were burned in 1836 during the Second Seminole War. One of the more accessible ruins was the John Bulow plantation. I spent hours poking about its heavy coquina blocks.

Ponce de León's men were the first in East Florida to quarry coquina, a rough reddish limestone made without benefit of geology: Its tiny shell creatures were alive in the present geologic age. Absent the millennia of compression that can transform mud into marble, it hangs together like cheap cement. If I had wanted to, I could have gouged my name into the Bulow ruins with a stick. Because coquina is such shoddy stone, and because the Florida heat can be so oppressive, early planters used blocks that were three to four feet thick. As in the sod houses of the Great Plains, the walls of the Bulow mansion retain a chill of the grave. Walking in the cool shadows cast by the relic, I couldn't help but imagine the people who had lived there, people I knew only from accounts in the county library.

Bulow was one of the wealthier planters, as the thick columns fronting his ravaged estate attest. He entertained a great many guests, among them John J. Audubon, who spent December 1831 at the plantation. In a letter to the editor of the *American Monthly Journal of Geology*, Audubon told of an ill-fated expedition he and Bulow and several hands took down Bulow Creek to the Tomoka and Halifax rivers. The letter surprised me when I found it. I knew and could picture every harrowing inch of the trip it described.

Audubon was "anxious to kill some twenty-five brown Pelicans" to enable him "to make a new drawing of an adult male bird, and to preserve the dresses of the others." The hunt was successful, but on the return trip their bark became stuck in mud shallows just as evening and the temperature began to fall. After enduring a night of harsh, nearly freezing wind, they pulled the boat through waist-deep mud to a distant marsh. From there, the exhausted men found the entrance to Bulow Creek, but they discovered that the strong wind had lowered the water level. They abandoned the bark and walked through fifteen miles of swamp to the ocean, where they were eventually rescued. Audubon penned his vivid account two days later in the warm comfort of Bulow's drawing room, none the worse for wear. But in less than five years Bulow would be lucky to escape with his life as a Seminole band methodically turned the plantation into just so much junk.

I became acquainted with the people of other plantations:

John Addison's brash Dutch overseer, who lassoed alligators from horseback; James Ormond's slave Freeport, who once bowed and humbly begged a captured thief's pardon for doing what he had been ordered to do and then "calmly blew out the fellow's brains"; an idiotic South Carolina cavalryman who tried to defend Addison's plantation from attacking Seminoles by placing a cannon on the burned kitchen roof. The first shot sent the cannon backward and burned down the rest of the house.

After reading such tales and then walking through the woods to see evidence of those who first told them—the bits of iron and stone that made the people and the stories real—I realized that junk and history are different sides of the same coin.

Once I came to college, my interest gradually shifted from history to cave exploration. The natural mazes so plentiful in the Florida Panhandle are much like ruins themselves, but are more complex and far older than anything made by man. The North Florida limestone is young as sedimentary rock goes—only 15 million years old, give or take—but it is far more substantial than coquina, supporting natural structures through which I wandered happily for hours. But now, as I threaded my way down a barely visible road, I realized that I had remained responsive to the various messages that junk offers. I began to visualize the person who had first hacked this trail from the scrub, possibly the same farmer or woodcutter who later left his broken-down Buick to pack rats and chinaberries. I guessed that the road had been built to connect the nearby field with a fork of the Chipola River, a mile or so behind me.

I stopped at the edge of the field to study the topo, to see if my theory was feasible, and noticed a small black square on the map indicating a structure over in the southwest corner. It didn't take me long to find the rough limestone foundation. The hewn blocks had supported a small barn, or maybe a sharecropper's cabin. The ground was spotted with charcoal: Whatever had been here had burned long ago.

A low rock outcrop behind the foundation stopped me cold. I saw a narrow opening at its base. I pulled the pocket flashlight from my pack and poked my head into the black circle. The light revealed a funnel-shaped cavity eight feet deep and two yards wide at the ceiling, which rose a few inches above my head. The bottom of the funnel was perhaps ten inches in diameter. The narrow, dirt-filled spout seemed to drop several more feet at the same width. The air was stale and musty, offering little hope that this tiny pit would lead to a significant find. I lowered myself into the opening so that I could quickly sketch the tiny room and add it to our survey list.

As I stood there straddling the funnel's base, holding the flashlight in my mouth while I penciled dimensions into my notebook, I caught the glint of something shiny a few feet below me. I shoved the pencil and pad into my pocket and crouched to investigate. Embedded in the mud wall of the shaft was a small bottle—maybe a perfume bottle—made of iridescent blue glass. It looked very old. As my eyes became more accustomed to the feeble flashlight beam, I made out a similar bottle farther down. Bits of broken glass, nails, and chunks of rotting wood lined the tight passage.

The refuse had clearly been embedded during heavy rain, but I wondered whether the material had washed all the way from the cabin or whether the cabin residents had used the little cave as a convenient Dumpster. The practice was—and is—depressingly common. Most cavers at one time or another have approached a landowner to politely suggest that things tossed down "that ol' hole in the ground" don't just disappear. The selling point is seldom the damage litter does to mineral formations or cave life, or even the general illegality of the practice. But farmers take notice when you tell them that trash thrown into a cave often washes directly into their own water supply.

The farmer was long gone, and this wasn't trash. The sparkling, fragile bottles seemed elemental to the cave. I was glad to have found them. I stretched my arm into the tube to retrieve the closest for examination.

I could just touch the smooth glass, but dried mud held it fast to the wall. I opened my Swiss Army knife. The flashlight again in my mouth, I shoved my head and right arm down into the shaft. I began to working the knife blade along the edge of the glass. Blood ran to my head. I felt a little guilty, as though I were prying out a stalactite or gypsum flower.

Cavers, as a general rule, are among the most fervent conservation advocates alive. The need for conservation is hammered into them with every underground visit. No human can walk down a virgin tunnel without leaving some sign of passage. A careless or clumsy spelunker can destroy ten thousand years of geologic sculpture in a second. One of the major expenses of any caving organization is building entrance gates to protect particularly delicate or little-traveled caves. Earlier that year, I had helped repair a vandalized gate at nearby Odyssey Cave.

But even cavers become tolerant of man's intrusion when desecration reaches sufficient age, whenever human evidence is suddenly "discovered." The caver who spends two weekends a month hauling beer cans and batteries out of abused suburban grottoes is the one most likely to let the air out of your tires and call the sheriff if he catches you disturbing the junk left by Civil War–era miners in one of the many saltpeter caves dotting the South. God help the teenager caught spraying his name and the date on a cave wall—or smudging a charcoal deer left by some teenaged tribesman of a thousand years ago.

Old things belong. I had seen on the cover of the *National Speleological Society News* a photograph of a Coke bottle that had been carelessly set, sometime in the 1920s, beneath a dripping stalactite. By the time the photo was taken, the green glass had accumulated a quarter-inch layer of calcite. The name and location of the cave was kept secret by the photographer, for fear someone might try to steal the bottle.

I remembered that photo as I hung upside down, working my find loose. It might have been the distraction of the memory, or the guilt of it, that caused me to drop my knife when the blue bottle suddenly broke free of the wall and slid a yard deeper into the tube. I stopped myself from cursing, or I would have lost the flashlight too. I could reach no farther without becoming stuck upside down. The bottle was beyond my grasp, and my knife had rolled almost out of sight.

I considered my situation. I was damned uncomfortable at the moment. To proceed further without another caver and perhaps a belay rope would be stupid if not insane. I wormed my way out of the squeeze, stood to catch my breath, and then climbed into daylight. A piece of glass similar to the bottle I'd lost lay in the burnt earth of the foundation. I raked around a bit with the toe of my boot and uncovered a cast-iron stove lid. I juggled the small disk from hand to hand, admiring its weight. I brushed enough dirt from the waffled top to reveal the legend: ARMSTRONG BROS. F'DRY. Further excavation was tempting—the rest of that stove had to be down there somewhere—but our group was due to rendezvous in an hour, and I still had a mile of woods to walk. I tossed the lid back where I'd found it.

I considered telling my friends about the little cave, talking someone into a search-and-rescue mission to save my stranded knife, but thought better of it. I would report the entrance as merely another blind lead. Those old bottles, like the Buick and my grandfather's plow, belonged where they were, had paid the debt of time necessary to become indigenous.

I let them lie. And they, with my open Swiss Army knife, are surely there now.

There's something that I like about that.

9

TIGHT SPOT

Whenever I find myself talking about caving with a group of strangers, a question that always comes up is "Don't you ever get claustrophobia?" I generally answer that the human body can fit into some fairly small places, and in caves small places often lead to big ones. Wriggling through a squeeze is part of the total experience, I say. Successful cavers think of the goal beyond. They've learned to calmly ignore the panic that might otherwise set in when one is compressed between tons of rock. No, I tell people, I don't feel the least bit claustrophobic underground.

Of course, I'm lying. Squeezes scare the hell out of me. (*Squeeze*: any crawlway whose passage requires the removal of gear, clothing, or skin.) Some of the less pleasant squeezes I recall include the Agony, the Back Scratcher, the Claustrophobia Crawl, the Gun Barrel, the Eighteen-Hour Girdle, the Crisco Crack, and, of course, the Grim Crawl of Death. All involved a few anxious moments. But the only time I've ever known—and been forced to overcome—true subterranean panic was at a small, allegedly easy place called the Devil's Pinch, deep beneath the limestone hills of West Virginia.

The Devil's Pinch connects two very different caves named Bone and Norman. Norman's damp ceiling bristles with calcite formations in a dozen hues of ocher and umber. The mazelike tunnels of Bone are colored a uniform pale gray. Beads of water glisten on Norman's walls, and dripping stalactites dig tiny craters in the mud-slick floor. Bone stays dry as a you-know-what. A river runs through Norman, filling blue pools and chirping happily over small rapids. Its course has determined the twists and turns of the arched corridor that forms Norman's central trunk. Bone's floors are covered with a loose powder similar in color and consistency to the stuff Apollo astronauts once kicked up on the moon.

The only thing these two cave have in common is a chance connection at the Devil's Pinch, an undulating tube about three body lengths long, a yard wide, and seven to ten inches high. It's the height that gets you. That and the sloping floor, and a ceiling lined with knifelike ridges that can dig at your chest like an excited cardiologist. Hence its name.

After Bone and Norman became a single cave, Bone-Norman, by virtue of the connection, it became popular among West Virginia cavers to take recreational through-trips, entering at one and exiting through the other. An experienced team that knows the route can pretty well see both caves in four hours. When my longtime caving partner Lee Pearson and I found ourselves in West Virginia with an afternoon to kill, we decided to try the through-trip ourselves.

Our guide was Miles Drake, a wiry and powerful Washington, D.C., window washer whose underground prowess is something of a legend in caving circles. I had met him two years before while exploring vertical pits in the Cockpit Country of western Jamaica, and found him to be—like so many of the best American cavers—a competent climber, obsessive about his gear, and more than a little eccentric. Along with the three of us were three novices, new members of the D.C. caving club to which Miles belonged.

It had been a few years since Miles had been through the Devil's Pinch. He couldn't quite remember which of Bone Cave's myriad stoopways and belly crawls led to the connection. He knew we had to crawl "about fifty feet" to a steeply sloping chamber, at the bottom of which would be the Devil's Pinch.

Normally, you expect to spend some time finding the proper route in a rambling cave like Bone. You expect whoever's leading to occasionally say things like "Okay, that rock is familiar.

We turn left at that hole underneath and it should open into a stoopway." You expect the hole to lead nowhere, and the guide to say things like "Well, it's a rock just like that one, only now that I think about it, it should be on the right. Yeah, that's it. Check the *right* wall." Getting a little bit lost is part of the total experience.

While Lee and I weren't exactly happy after crawling 500 feet down five different "this is the one" holes, we weren't exactly discouraged either. We were underground, among friends, and seeing cave that we had never seen before. The novices, however, were not so generous. Two in particular, women I'll call Fran and Hannah, were not entirely comfortable spending an hour on their hands and knees, lost, squirming through dust that filled their boots, powdered their hair, and sifted its way through their underwear.

They were making increasingly loud noises about heading back for the entrance—if Miles could find it—when suddenly we emerged into a steeply sloping chamber above a rocky crawl that had to be the Devil's Pinch. Miles went through first. "Oh, this is it all right," he said. "You don't forget a nasty place like this." Miles was, by far, the smallest member of the group.

He made it through, then turned to coach the novices. Lee and I took up the rear. All I could see of the passage ahead was the soles of Lee's size 12 boots. I could hear Miles shouting that if Fran slid one arm forward and dragged her packs behind, she should be able to wriggle through the tightest spot without any problem. Her muttered curses made me a little nervous, but I reasoned: Hey, she's a beginner. If she makes it through, I can make it through.

In twenty minutes, both novices were standing in Norman Cave.

I'm six feet tall and weigh about 195. Lee was a few pounds lighter, but three inches taller, and big-boned. When I saw his boots push ahead, and heard him grunt and power his way to the other side, I breathed easy. He was *nearly* as big as me. "Coming through," I said.

The floor sloped downward and to the left, with a trench a few inches deep running along the left wall. Floor and ceiling were solid limestone. They hugged my chest and back, but I could push with my toes. I tossed my cumbersome helmet ahead of me in such a way that the lamp was pointing back, lighting my way.

I had forgotten to remove a backup flashlight from my shirt pocket. It dug painfully into my chest as I inched forward—but the ceiling dug into my back, and the floor sloped downward, helping me slide along. I exhaled to remove the friction from my rib cage, and slid through.

With a short hands-and-knees scramble, I was standing in Norman with my companions, in a comfortable tunnel the size of an airplane hangar. "Thank God I don't have to try that bastard uphill," I said. That was when I realized something was wrong. Fran breathed so heavily she had nearly hyperventilated. Hannah was in tears. Miles, Lee, and the other novice, a man who had barely spoken all day, stood looking discouraged. We had been underground perhaps three hours. Clearly, the extensive crawling and the uncomfortable pinch were more than Hannah and Fran had bargained for. They were ready to go home.

Miles admitted that he forgotten just how much crawling was involved in Bone. He apologized for leading inexperienced novices through such an unpleasant place. "But look at the bright side," he said. "It's all walking passage from here. We'll be out in an hour or two."

"Do you know the way?" asked Hannah, her tears subsiding.

"I'm sure I can find it."

Poor choice of words. Hannah and Fran started arguing that we should go back the way we knew. Lee and I argued for pressing ahead. Miles just looked embarrassed. The other novice resolved the argument by saying, "I've had enough," and scrambling back into the Devil's Pinch—uphill.

We had no choice but to follow. Again Lee and I took up the rear. This time, the others took a good hour to pass through. Their echoed groans and curses were far more pronounced. Lee and I slipped out of the crawlway and walked around in Norman, briefly enjoying the river and formations. Every few minutes, we'd hike back to see how they were doing. At last they all had made it through. I remembered to slip my flashlight into my pack, and fell in behind Lee, who quickly gained distance up the crawl.

By dragging one arm and reaching forward with the other, I narrowed my shoulders, but lost one hand for pulling. While pushing with my toes had worked coming in, I made little progress against the slope. I would move forward and feel the ceiling press me into the blades beneath my chest. A knifelike fin of rock that ran from below my left foot to somewhere well beyond my left shoulder seemed far more pronounced than it had coming in. And the trench that had helped me earlier was now in my way.

I pushed with my toes, slid forward another inch, and felt the ceiling press me that much more into the knife. I could see Lee reclining comfortably in the passage ten feet ahead, waiting for me. Another yard and I'd be through the worst. But I couldn't move.

I felt panic rising and paused to breathe deeply—but I was in too far. As I inhaled, my ribs swelled against the constriction and stopped. I could take only half breaths, could move forward only when I exhaled. What if I exhaled too much? What if I reached a point where I couldn't inhale at all?

I closed my eyes, lay my face on the cool rock, and fought the idea. Even if I passed out, Lee could pull me through from the other side. But what if my coveralls snagged, trapping me where I couldn't breathe?

I decided to take off my coveralls. I used my right hand— the one I could see—to slowly push myself back down the inches I had gained. Exhale, move, pause, inhale. Exhale, move, pause, inhale. At last I stood and stripped off my coveralls, wadded the coveralls into a ball, shoved them ahead of me with my helmet, and lay down on the bedrock in my boots and Fruit of the Looms.

The limestone blade—a mere irritant before—now tore at

my bare chest, not deeply, but enough to open the skin. But with a few more millimeters of room, I moved uphill a bit more easily. Soon I was to the point where I had turned back. I called Lee toward me, and tossed him my coveralls and helmet. After he moved them out of the way, I asked Lee to slide in close enough to grab my arm.

"Pull when I tell you to," I said. I took four slow half breaths, then tried to relax fully as I exhaled, "Pulllll." I moved forward six inches, tried to inhale, and could not.

My heart beat in my ears. I made no sound, hoarding the scant oxygen left in my lungs. I had a sudden vision of black lake water closing over my head—the time at age eight I jumped off the old wooden high dive at my uncle's lake in Illinois. The water had stretched on forever as I kicked my way toward distant summer light. There in the Devil's Pinch I remembered the panic, the kicking, and suddenly gulping heavy air. By the time I swam back to the dock, I had pushed the moment of fear to the back of my mind, and dove again, and again. By the end of the day, I had forgotten the black water that had tried to hold me down. Until now.

My arm felt as if Lee were yanking it out of its the socket. I desperately dug both toes into the rock and pushed. The knife scraped my chest once more, I slid forward an inch, and I could breathe again. My ribs were free of the Devil's Pinch. I gasped at Lee to let go of my arm. I closed my eyes and lay again on the bare rock, waiting for my breathing to return to normal. I worked the pinch from belly to hips to thighs, and I was out.

"Well, that wasn't much fun," I said to Lee. "But it was better than law school."

10

TIME ON MY HANDS

In the fall of 1980, I entered law school for the dubious reason that I had been exposed to a number of lawyers. My junior and senior years, I had held a part-time job as doorkeeper in the Florida House of Representatives. I was one of four college students in navy blazers who ceremoniously shut the big brass doors whenever the Speaker sealed the chamber for an important debate or vote. I had landed the job because my mother was a paralegal for a large Florida law firm; one partner was a senior state representative.

It was interesting work. At close range I scrutinized the legislative styles of dedicated idealists and dangerous Machiavellis. I shook hands with governors, U.S. senators, and sundry minor celebrities honored on the House floor. I met the lobbyists who hovered outside the chamber like flies at a screen door. Eventually, I persuaded one of these, a bearded lawyer employed by the Sierra Club, to help my cave club draft and—after months of my own Machiavellian conniving—see passed into law the Florida Cave Protection Act. The law still prohibits the sale of cave formations, wanton destruction of cave life, breaking into a gated cave, and various other subterranean evils.

From watching the Sierra Club lobbyist, my mother's acquaintance, and a few other legislators, I perceived as the good guys, I developed just enough romantic ignorance of the law to sign up for the LSAT. Perhaps I took the test because I was completing my bachelor's in English a year early, and I didn't want to leave Tallahassee: I applied to no school but Florida State. The College of Law stood a pleasant two-block walk from the comfortable old house where I lived with several other cavers. Whatever my motives, I did well on the test and signed up for student loans.

A couple of partners in my mother's firm professed an interest in my future, and my father, a vocational counselor who had just retired from a state agency, was delighted at the prospect of a son in law school. Kathy, my girlfriend of two years, seemed reasonably happy at the idea of an attorney in her future. (We had nervously steered conversation away from the M-word, but I think we both sensed it hovering in our future; we were married on May 5, 1983.) My caving friends looked at me a little askance when I mentioned my plans, but so long as I remained willing to slither through mud, they would tolerate the presence of a potential lawyer. Actual lawyers advised me to stick out the first year no matter how awful it got, so I did.

It did get awful: memorizing ancient cases, dodging the Socratic harpoons tossed by glib professors, suffering the presence of smug and impeccably dressed future corporate raiders. Still, I survived the first year in the top third of my class, at the sacrifice of a number of caving trips. Toward the end of the spring term, and then when I enrolled in two summer courses afterward, I felt confident enough to carve out long caving weekends for myself, despite disapproving clucks from the members of my study group.

As my second year progressed, two unrelated events occurred that at last wrested me out of school and toward my present life. The first was a trip report I heard at a weekly cave club meeting in the spring of 1981; the second, a death following January.

Our club president, a powerful caver and accomplished pilot named Karen Witte, had returned from Guatemala in March. After driving through Mexico for a week, pausing occasionally to rappel pits that ranged up to 1,200 feet deep, she and a Texan named Ernest Garza had rafted down a Guatemalan river through a jungle region called El Petén. They explored and mapped previously unknown caves at several places along the river, their carbide lamps illuminating Mayan pottery, calcite-encrusted skulls, and painted hieroglyphics. At a cave called Naj Tunich they bumped into a team from *National Geographic*.

George Stuart, the magazine's staff archeologist, was writing an article on the recently discovered Mayan site; the photographer was Wilbur E. Garrett, the magazine's editor-in-chief. Stuart asked whether he might hire Witte and Garza to produce an accurate map of the cave. Although Stuart was an accomplished archeologist, the two cavers quickly realized that his team knew virtually nothing about proper caving technique. They lacked helmets and cap lamps, their shoes were wrong, and their hemp ropes weak and dangerous. Witte and Garza lent extra equipment and taught the team how to use it. They agreed to map the portions of Naj Tunich relative to the article.

As she described the experience at our club meeting, Karen passed around Garrett's photos of complex glyphs, ceramic pots, and statues. She said that during mapping she and Garza continually smelled the copal incense used by Mayan priests, which littered the floor in ancient ashes. With a straight face, she described the strange chanting that they often heard coming from a distant passageway—but of course there was no one there. In a day and a half, she and Garza surveyed the major chambers. As they prepared to break camp, Stuart asked how soon the two could draft their raw data into a finished map.

"Well, we have to plot everything on a computer," she told him. "That produces a simple line drawing of the plan and profile of the cave. We flesh that out using the cross sections and sketches from the survey book. It'll take us a few more days to raft down to where we leave the river, then a week to drive back to the States. I guess if we get busy as soon as we get home, we can send you a map four or five weeks from now."

Stuart frowned. "That won't work at all. This story's already overdue."

The two cavers shrugged, no skin off their backs. Stuart asked what sort of computer and software they needed. They listed the requirements.

"How's this?" he said. "A helicopter will meet me at the closest farm tomorrow. You could leave with me, fly to Washington, and finish the map on Geographic computers. I'll put you up in a hotel, pay all your expenses, and when the map is done I'll fly you back to the jungle. You can pick up your trip where you left off."

They grinned and agreed. After describing the helicopter flight, Karen pulled out a snapshot of herself and Garza standing glassy-eyed in the marble lobby of *National Geographic* headquarters. They carried bulging backpacks and wore stained jungle fatigues. She mentioned the culture shock induced by the jungle–D.C.–jungle experience, and told us to look for the drawing based on their map in the August issue.

I hung on every word. Old blue bottles in a tiny grotto paled in comparison to vast chambers full of Mayan skulls and statuary. Karen had caved among the coolest junk imaginable; I couldn't help but envy her. Toward the end of the meeting, she shared a tidbit Stuart had dropped before putting them on the plane back to Guatemala: "I'll be going to El Petén again next winter," he had said. "It seems like a good idea to hire a few cavers to come with me. Would you two be interested in assembling a small team?" So, Karen concluded, anyone who wanted to take the trip of a lifetime and be *paid* for it should talk to her.

I did, to the extent that I soon made a pest of myself. I had done a lot of grunt work for the club, I reminded her, had led novice trips, dug open mud-filled crawlways, built and installed gates, stapled copies of the newsletter, mapped some of the tightest, grungiest leads in Climax. I could rig pits and read survey instruments. I ran four miles a day and was in the best shape of my life. I was more than ready to take a winter semester off from law school. After several weeks of lobbying,

Karen relented. When Stuart called her to set up the trip, which she expected him to schedule for January 1982, she would mention my name as a likely team member.

I neglected Constitutional Law for the intricacies of Mayan lore. The Maya, I learned, were a people endlessly fascinated by time and its passage. They worshipped the fourth dimension from the unchanging setting of the cave, which they saw as offering physical connection to the spirit world.

I too was interested in time. Once, while leading novices through a small cave called Waterfall in southern Georgia, I had found an amazing thing: two shells, a sea urchin, some crinoids lay spiny upon a bit of Eocene sea bottom, a scene preserved in miniature from just after the time of dinosaurs. Each detail was crisp, beautiful, terrifying. I reached to touch a stem and stopped. There was too great a power in a thing so old. I did not know—and do not know now—the name of my grandfather's grandfather, whether he drank or preached, farmed or kept shop. Less of him remained than those bits of shell, which had gathered no dust in his lifetime, or mine, or humanity's.

One night in the middle of that fall of 1981, a government-sponsored death squad beheaded several peasants in the village closest to Naj Tunich. George Stuart called Karen to let her know that it was simply not safe to travel to El Petén for at least the coming year. She passed the bad news to me. I moped through classes and skipped my final exams.

One night in January 1982, as I was mustering courage to crawl to the dean of the law school and beg forgiveness, my grandfather, a lifelong smoker of unfiltered Camels, died of lung cancer. I slipped out of town without a word to anyone. After the funeral, I stayed on at the farm where my mother was raised, ostensibly to help two uncles who were looking after my grandmother. For several weeks, we sat around telling stories, playing poker for matchsticks, taking turns cooking dinner.

When at last I caught a bus back to Florida, I announced to

friends and family that I was taking the next semester off. I decided to take whatever job I could find and in my spare time bang out a best-selling adventure novel. I would simply fictionalize the expedition not taken and set a caver very like myself in the midst of Mayan treasure and a civil war. Piece of cake.

At my grandfather's funeral one of my many cousins—who also had an interest in writing—had offered me space in which to finish a book if I ever "got serious." I surprised him by taking him up on it. Dennis Ulrich was a young doctor, with a new practice in the eastern Kentucky coal country. He possessed a primitive personal computer, a big farmhouse with several empty bedrooms, and no particular desire for rent.

I had a title, *Murder in a Silent Cave*, and a ten-page prologue, which I rewrote endlessly. I couldn't seem to get much further. Every weekend, I'd drive to Cookeville, Tennessee, to visit Lee Pearson. He and I would explore caves with names like Run to the Mill, Camp's Gulf, Xanadu, Valhalla, Pharris Pit, Stamp's Pit, and Grassy Cove Saltpeter Cave.

One day while browsing a London, Kentucky, newsstand, I discovered *Writer's Digest* magazine. The copy I picked up contained an article co-written by two widely published English professors, who, according to a blurb at the bottom of the page, taught at Eastern Kentucky University, located an hour north. That afternoon, I drove up and tracked down one of the teachers, clutching the latest version of my prologue. The teacher, Hal Blythe, didn't have to be anywhere and was nice enough to take a look at it while I waited. He convinced me to enroll in the class he co-taught with Charley Sweet.

Over the next few weeks, I wrote the several short stories they assigned, read a dozen of the books they recommended, and began to realize that I had set myself up for a task at least as hard as making it through law school. I joined a writers' group based at the college, and went to readings of several published novelists who visited campus.

One day near the end of the term Hal called me into his office to ask what my next step would be. I told him I didn't have a clue. He suggested that, if I really wanted to finish the novel, I should look into graduate creative writing programs. Several, he said, provided financial assistance to qualified students.

"Where do you think I should apply?" I asked.

"Well, of course there's Iowa. It's the oldest MFA program. Columbia is very good, if you don't mind New York, but I think one of the best outfits going is the professional writing program at USC."

I wrote all of this down, and promised I'd look into it. New York struck me as too exotic and far too expensive, but the other two sounded interesting. What Hal didn't know was that I was both southern and naive enough to believe "USC" stood for the University of South Carolina. I had no idea what the letters MFA might abbreviate.

I went to the college library to search for information on the two schools and three letters. While there I picked up a novel that caught my eye, and saw it was about a lawyer who becomes disillusioned with his profession and takes off to explore Mexican ruins. Hmmmm. The book was good, and I stayed up late reading it. Perhaps it was lack of sleep, or my positive experience in Hal and Charley's class, or the pure and undeniable fact of coincidence. Whatever the reason, I did something the next morning that I had never done before: I wrote the author.

8 March 83

Vance Bourjaily
Iowa City, Iowa

Dear Mr. Bourjaily,

My God, sir, how could I not write you? After all, what is life itself, if not an extraordinary accumulation of coincidence? A man's car breaks down in Hoboken, a dog farts in Phoenix, and as a result 32 companies fold and James Watt is sodomized. Trivial occurrences, meaningless in themselves, may combine synergistically to determine births, battles and this letter, which I hope you will take the time to read.

Here is a true story:

A young man, 23 years old, the son of two southern Illinois natives, studies law at Florida State University. On weekends, he seeks refuge from the rigors of legal initiation in the wet dark of limestone caves. . . .

In seven or eight paragraphs, I outlined the failed expedition to Guatemala, my plans to write, my move to Kentucky, and the helpful advice I'd received from Hal Blythe. Then:

While at the library finding addresses for some of the top writing programs, our boy decides to pick up some pleasure reading. He cruises the fiction shelves and stops at an attractive brown binding. Opens the book and sees a line of Nahuatl. Hey! Turns a page: a small town lawyer goes to Mexico. No shit? Flips to the beginning: southern Illinois. Well I'll be a monkey's ass! Looks at the title: *Brill Among the Ruins*, by Vance Bourjaily. Hmmm, heard of him, never read him.

That night, our young writer sits engrossed, laughing, crying, and marveling at the prose shining before him. By daybreak, he has finished the book. He goes to town to mail his inquiries to the various graduate departments, and decides to stop by the library to find out more about the man who has kept him up all night. He finds the appropriate volume of *Contemporary Authors*. No! Can it be? "Home: Iowa City"? "Office: Iowa Writer's Workshop"? Somewhere, way off in the distance, he can hear the sound of monkeys typing *Hamlet* and housewives winning the Publisher's Clearing House Sweepstakes.

That was this morning, the young writer is me, and now you know, as Paul Harvey would say, the rest of the story. . . .

As it turned out, my letter was forwarded from Iowa City to Arizona, where Bourjaily had taken another job. He wrote back in April, thanking me for the nice things I had said and offering some general advice on finishing novels. This was followed by a warning:

Now for the wretched, stodgy, geezer advice. I've been around writing programs for 25 years now, seen people go through as good as Tim Williams (National Book Award, 1972), Gail Godwin, and a really long list of others. There's only one I can think of, among former students who've published a lot, who has made enough money to live on, invest (and maybe keep living on the proceeds, and maybe not), and that's John Irving. He pulled the lever when the slot machine was loaded and ready; but he isn't—and would not claim to be himself—that much better than John Yount or John Casey (Harvard Law, now at Univ. of Virginia), for a couple of really fine examples, both publishing, both still teaching, too.

For a student, a writing program (I'm at the Arizona one now, may stay, may not) is okay for a couple of years. The other students make it okay, if they're good and you like each other. And if they're good, they publish books. And if they want to raise and feed families, they teach writing.

If law's any fun for you, go ahead and get the degree, and practice it somewhere. Like Louis Auchincloss. Like François Villon (no, don't do it like Villon). Like Goethe. They lived interesting lives. Writing teachers don't, unless they've put some interesting years behind them (I guess I'll claim I did) before they turned to teaching.

Yours,

Vance Bourjaily
University of Arizona

That might have been enough to send me crawling back to law school, but by the time the letter arrived, I had been offered an assistantship and graduate fellowship to attend the University of South Carolina (Iowa turned me down). I accepted, and after Kathy and I were married in May, the two of us moved to Columbia, South Carolina, to start graduate school. (She qualified for a fellowship in the business school.) I wrote Bourjaily to tell him of my decision, resolving, at least, never to teach writing until I had "put some interesting years behind me."

He answered that the fact I couldn't be talked out of it was a good sign, and that I should say hello to William Price Fox for him. He and Fox had taught together at Iowa for several years. They had once ridden the back of a circus elephant through the streets of Iowa City.

One of things Bill Fox taught me was that you can't write a novel about a place you've never been. I laid *Murder in a Silent Cave* to rest, and went on to other things. I did wind up teaching, as Bourjaily had predicted, but the years before I taught were nothing if not interesting.

HELLHOLE

11

It is a few minutes past noon, Tuesday, September 2, 1986. I have been up for two hours. I slept most of the previous twenty-four, having been awake for most of the seventy before that. What kept me up was the thirty-seventh annual Old-Timers' Reunion, near Dailey, West Virginia, and the ten-hour drive between it and New Jersey. OTR is the world's oldest regular gathering of cavers. Over the Labor Day weekend, 1,600 of the muddy beasts, male and female alike, set up a Technicolor tent city on the banks of the swift, sweet Tygart River.

The event's sponsors recently purchased a permanent site, so in addition to tents, RVs, and trash-bag biveys, this year a few dozen cavers erected more substantial structures for group use: A roomy pavilion, in which four rock bands performed, fifty-eight kegs of beer were consumed, and seventy-three antique carbide lamps auctioned. A junk-food cafe. A first-aid center and security office. Three large-capacity, wood-heated showers, labeled "his," "hers," and "theirs." An unusually large hot tub, a nude beach, and "dry" and "wet" saunas, all of which can be reached by hiking a short wooded path marked by a sign reading "To Ruinous Activities." An obstacle course designed to simulate the cave environment during the annual Speleolympics. A platform wired for ten pay phones. A row of twenty-five chemical outhouses. And more. Much more.

The former pasture that held this event nestled between twin mountain ridges, from whose blue-green slopes deer and locals would sneak at dawn to gawk briefly at the spectacle before skedaddling light-footed back up rocky trails. Despite perfect weather, the OTR paths and roadways were quickly churned to mud by booted and knobby-tired traffic in the heavy evening dew. The smell of twenty-five chemical outhouses mixed with the smoky haze that hung over camp—a haze fed by cookfires, fireworks, and occasional controlled substances—which lurked in fecal pockets that seemed to writhe and pulse with the music and rebel yells pumping from the pavilion. In short, the place resembled the final hours of Woodstock. Fortunately, only three or four farmhouses lie within five miles of the OTR site, and the residents of these were apparently satisfied by the hand-lettered cardboard sign some wag had hung on the gate: *Reunion—Family Members Only*.

The experiences of the group with whom I traveled were more or less typical. Jim Van Fleet, Tom Stockert—both of the Northern New Jersey Grotto—and I met at ten-thirty Thursday night at Jim's house in Union, New Jersey. Having moved from South Carolina only two months earlier, I had met my traveling companions for the first time at the July Grotto meeting. Three weeks ago, I accompanied them on a trip to Knox Cave in upstate New York; Jim invited me to ride with him and Tom to OTR. We crammed ropes, cave gear, coolers, clothing, tents, and ourselves into Jim's Tercel and headed southwest, stopping every few hours to change drivers and eat doughnuts. At dawn we entered West Virginia on State Road 50. Our first glimpse of the sun came while driving through a pass at 3,500 feet. We rounded a bend and there it was, rising over a lake of pink fog far below us, a frozen storm sea broken by a few green islands of mountaintop.

We followed a hand-drawn map to the OTR site, arriving at approximately 7:45 A.M. Friday. We located the New Jersey encampment, already occupied by twenty or so cavers who had come down the day before. We pitched my big dome tent, tossed our gear inside, found a place to park the car where it wouldn't be blocked in by new arrivals (not an easy task), and finally arranged to join a caving trip scheduled for that afternoon. At 9:30 A.M. we fell into our bags and napped for an hour. Unable to sleep, we agreed to wander about OTR until it was time to go caving.

I found Vendor's Row, a strip of mud and straw occupied by a half dozen purveyors of rope, helmets, carbide lamps, cave maps and books, obscene climbing posters, rappel racks, $100 fancy fluorescent coveralls made of tough ballistic nylon, available in a variety of hot colors, $10 Army-surplus coveralls made of itchy green stuff, carabiners, "Bats Need Friends" bumper stickers, etc., ad infinitum, nauseam, et expensium. All credit cards accepted. I stocked up on a few things, then met the cave crew at noon at Ray Sira's GMC pickup—which was of sufficient ground clearance and wheel radius to serve as a landmark throughout the weekend—and set off for Hellhole.

Located down a gravel road about twenty miles from Seneca Rocks, in a rocky sheep pasture just beyond a limestone quarry, Hellhole is a classic American vertical cave, explored by the country's first organized caving club in 1939. Its three entrance shafts beckon from the bottom of a steep sinkhole. The middle entrance is the smallest of the three, a yard or so in diameter, but it is preferred as it gives a free rappel (no ledges to bump against) all the way to the bottom. The bottom is 165 feet below the place where you step over the lip. It takes a while to get into the cave from the middle entrance. You have plenty of time on the way to think about the stitching of your seat harness, which has been moldering in a closet for nearly two years, perhaps rotting or unraveling.

Or you can think about the U.S. marine home on leave several years ago, well before a local grotto strung a high chain-link fence around the sinkhole, who hung a flashlight over his neck, dropped a manila rope down the left-hand entrance, and tried to hand-over-hand it to the floor. He made it eighty feet down to a seven-inch ledge—about where you are now—before his grip or nerve failed and he died. But what you try to think about is the beauty of this vast chamber, spinning slowly as rope buzzes through your rappel rack, an assembly hall of the underworld clearly lit by three parallel rays streaming from the entrances, now distant tree-limned holes that you can block from sight with one hand held overhead.

Your eyes adjust and you continue dropping. You make out the tiny winking lights of cavers already standing on the rock-strewn hillside that is the floor. You concentrate on putting proper pressure on the brake bars of your rappel rack, so that you will land in a way that is not so fast as to knock you down but not so slow as to make you appear overly cautious and lead to embarrassment. But your rack is a good one and you know it well and you touch down with the grace of a heron lighting in the reeds of the swamp you once hunted as a boy. You begin to despise yourself now for thinking and acting and writing like Hemingway, but, goddamnit, caving does this to you.

So we dropped into Hellhole and spent five hours exploring the cave out beyond the Shipp Room, poking through small holes and big, climbing down and up and over, admiring formations, losing the preferred route entirely, saying "No, it can't be up that thing," but checking and "I'll be damned, there's a bootprint up here. Yes, it goes. Let me take off my pack and pass it through. Holy shit, would you look at that black hole ahead." As we were coming back into the main chamber, we met a group returning from a ten-hour surveying trip. We had known from the trucks parked on the surface and two ropes rigged at the pit that there were other OTR folk in the cave, but we hadn't seen them until now. One of the surveyors explained that the West Virginia floods so much in the news last November had opened a previously plugged crawlway at the bottom of Little Hellhole, a 40-foot drop in a seldom-visited area of the cave. Just three weeks ago, a curious caver pushed this crawl into a large canyon passage. The virgin underground canyon continued for four miles—so far—and the tired survey group, composed mostly of students from Virginia Polytechnic Institute, informed us that it was still going.

Some of our group (especially Tom, Jim, and I) were eager to check out this new discovery; others were ready to climb out and return to camp. We compromised by heading back into the cave as far as the beginning of the crawlway, so that any of us who returned in the future would know the way to the new stuff. The climb to the surface, like all rope climbs, made me regret beer and graduate school and the big meals of married life. I eventually made it out on Gibbs ascenders, which, when properly attached to the rope, make climbing out of Hellhole about as dangerous as walking up fifteen flights of stairs. Unhurt and only slightly huffing, I stood a while in the gravel road, inhaling fresh mountain air and enjoying sunlight. Eventually, we changed out of our muddy grungies and headed back to camp to eat and party, making it in about sunset.

I had planned on meeting that night with Mike DiTonto, a twenty-four-year-old Maryland caver. He had been designated leader of the ongoing Cockpits Expedition in Jamaica; DiTonto and I had corresponded back in January when I tried to convince *National Geographic* to send me there on assignment. The Cockpit Country is a region of densely forested limestone hills in the heart of the western Jamaica highlands, a green, rocky place seen by very few whites. Charles Cobb briefly mentioned the Cockpits in a 1985 *Geographic* article on Jamaica, saying the region "is pitted with deep limestone sinkholes, and underground streams course everywhere. Bush-covered hummocks jut up, giving the land an eerie malevolent look." But it is more than jungle that makes the land malevolent: The Cockpits are ruled by the fiercely independent Maroons, rumored to be among the chief growers of Jamaican ganja, known to be general badasses. So while cavers have theorized for decades that vast caverns must exist beneath the Cockpits—the region receives over 150 inches of rainfall per year, yet has virtually no surface water—little exploration has taken place. It was simply not safe for outsiders to travel there. Until now.

Four years ago, DiTonto flew to Kingston, determined to see the Cockpits firsthand. He was able to penetrate no farther than the region's outer fringes, but did manage to befriend a Maroon guide, a bush doctor named Minocal Stephenson. DiTonto returned with other cavers during the next dry season. Armed with gifts and patience, they managed to set up a trip into the interior of the region the following year. Finally, in February 1985, DiTonto and eleven others were led into the heart of Cockpit Country for a ten-day stay. What they saw there amazed them.

Each bowl-shaped valley held several vertical shafts, ranging in depth from 100 to 400 feet. At the bottom of most shafts were horizontal caverns. DiTonto's group surveyed sixteen virgin pits and five caves. They descended one pit, since named Minocal's Glory Hole, to a depth of 213 feet, followed the passage at the bottom to a second shaft, 50 feet deep, then descended that to a yet another pit, which they were unable to descend because their remaining 100-foot rope was too short to reach the bottom. By the end of the brief 1985 expedition, his team had located dozens of other pits and cave entrances that there was simply no time to check. The locations recorded, the group reluctantly began the long hike back to the nearest road, already planning the next year's trip.

As it turned out, the 1986 trip was a bust—several key team members couldn't raise the cash for airfare. Their holes in the jungle will wait for 1987. Next February, DiTonto will return to the Cockpit Country for three weeks of what promises to be significant finds. I want to be there with him.

Understandably, DiTonto and his team have been shy about press coverage, fearful of upsetting their present good relationship with the local Maroon population. But they consented to my proposing an article on the expedition, provided I wrote it for *National Geographic*. (Joe Judge, a senior editor, expressed some interest, but the expeditions committee ultimately turned the idea down because of "similarities to the 1985 piece on Jamaica.") Now, I had heard, DiTonto was willing to let me take the story anywhere I could sell it. If the group attracted some publicity, they could hit up PMI Industries for a rope donation. Nick Nichols had given me the phone number of the Jamaican tourism bureau; he said if I had a magazine assignment, they would donate to the expedition round-trip tickets on Air Jamaica, and perhaps lodging in a seaside resort.

DiTonto and I had planned on meeting Friday night at OTR to discuss the expedition and the state of the magazine industry. My problem was that despite dozens of letters and phone calls over the past year, I didn't know what he looked like or where in the temporary city he might be camped. So I wandered over the grounds, walking up to campfires and asking if anyone knew DiTonto and where I might find him. I met some interesting people this way. Those who claimed to know DiTonto described him variously as tall and of medium height, skinny and potbellied, bearded and clean-shaven, camped with VPI and PSC (groups at opposite ends of the campground). Many people said "He was just here a few minutes ago. Here, have a beer, I'm sure he'll be back."

My quest for DiTonto began taking on the proportions of what I have heard described in literature classes as a Night Sea Journey. At some point I was led by an energetic caver who wore glow-in-the-dark earrings made of miniature Cylume sticks—oh, foul bearer of temptation!—to believe that DiTonto was engaged in Ruinous Activities. So I followed her down that wrong, crooked path to the river's edge, resolved to diligently but with restraint examine every den of Ruin for the missing DiTonto. Wooden racks of clothing hung at the path's end. A sign instructed all visitors that similar articles were to be left upon these before proceeding further.

Having no interest in Ruin, I ignored the sign. I had set only one foot beyond it when I was accosted by a young woman, clearly a rule keeper of some sort, who asked if I had come merely to gawk, and if so why don't I just gawk at this, or these, or maybe you'd like to see this, and if not, then I had better obey the sign, which I promptly did so as to avoid seeing any more of those things I had definitely not come down this path to see. I can accurately report that DiTonto was not in the wet or dry saunas, on the beach, or in the enormous hot tub. Two cavers among the thirty or so that lounged in its

steaming green water believed that DiTonto might be listen-
ing to the bluegrass being played at the edge of camp by a few
musical cavers from the Buzz City Grotto, a spurious Virginia
cave club. With some difficulty I located and reassembled my
flannel and denim accouterments, then set off for Buzz City,
pausing to visit my New Jersey brethren and their fine bour-
bon and ice water.

As I refilled my football cup, I heard Barclay Foord, a Jersey
caver who spends his summers out West, describing a conversation he had just had with one of the directors of the Bighorn
Caves Project in Wyoming. This April, I'm joining a scouting
team in Great Expectations, also in the Bighorns, but south of
the caves being mapped by the Bighorn Project. The director,
whose name I was in no condition to catch, was telling Barclay
that he was one of five cavers who went ridge-walking on Van-
couver Island in August. He said they found and descended a
pit of more than 800 feet, deeper than any single drop in the
United States, and discovered a huge but dangerously unstable cave at the bottom. Plans were being made for a full-scale
assault.

I made a mental note to find this person later, but my mental notebook being what it was at that point, I never got
around to it. Besides, I was on a quest. Sometime past midnight I arrived at Buzz City's big blue party tent, led there by
the clear notes—unmistakable to any James Dickey fan—of
"Dueling Banjos." I quickly forgot about Mike DiTonto. These
were not your average Sunday-afternoon pickers.

The skinny mandolin player, whose name I believe was Ed,
was about forty years old and had those wrinkles on his neck
and forehead that come only with decades of work in the sun.
He had those wrinkles at the corners of his mouth that come
only with hundreds of smiles and winks aimed at sweet things
in the audience. Despite regular slugs of Yukon Jack between
numbers, his fingering was quick and sure, his lyrics crisp and
true. He wandered through the crowd as he sang, clogging
with various admirers without missing a word or a fret.

Ed and the banjo player, whose name may have been Irving,

led the rest of the band (two guitars, a harmonica, a dulcimer, and the only washtub bass I've ever heard played to sound like an actual bass) in "Uncle Pen Played Fiddle," "Cripple Creek," "Salty Dog," "Maggie Don't Weep," and so many others I forget. The happy bunch that stood around them sang all choruses and begged for favorites in the silences brought on by slugs of Yukon and trips to the designated bush.

Ten minutes or so into every instrumental, an amazing thing would happen. Irving would catch Ed's eye, or Ed Irving's, and they would grin and then close in on each other, their faces growing suddenly grave, circling, each watching the other's right hand as in a knife fight. When each knew the other was ready, one of the two would holler "Let her run!" and they did, pushing the tempo to double time, then triple time and faster, sending out new leads and following them, laying foundations and building towers and parapets of bluegrass with such skill and speed that I began to whoop or cry or both, that I was certain I couldn't take any more, that I expected the surrounding mountains and caves and hollows that spawned this music, which held it ringing now in this dark, palmlike valley, to close in and grab it whole, to yank it under as gods aroused, leaving only another rocky pasture beneath the starry sky.

They were that good.

I fell into my sleeping bag at four and rose at eight to go caving again. Saturday we saw several of the well-traveled horizontal caves (no rope pitches) at the end of Dry Fork Road, a twelve-mile cow path possessing very few stretches where we could drive faster than ten miles per hour. This road was no good for wheel alignment or hangovers. But at the end of it we found a fine river for swimming. The river flowed into the upper entrance of Sinks of Gandy Cave and out of the lower entrance not quite a mile away.

In addition to cave entrances, many of the nearby sinks held the skeletal remains of clumsy cows and sheep. We picked up a few souvenir skulls. We entered a cave called Stillhouse by crawling through a generation's leavings of tin cans, broken glass, and table scraps. Inside, far beyond the garbage dump, I found a high fissure that led to a chimney up through a previously unknown, unmapped entrance. I climbed the chimney, cleared away rotten wood and other debris from the fifteen-inch hole, and popped out in a pasture, face-to-face with a surprised cow, which is the best way to surprise a cow if you stop to think about it.

So the weekend went. I didn't find Mike DiTonto until noon Sunday, just before Tom, Jim, and I set out for our last cave. By this point, DiTonto and I had left frustrated messages for each other all over OTR. He was nothing like the descriptions I had received Friday night. Tall and muscular, with reddish brown hair and beard, DiTonto was soft-spoken to the point of my having to strain for every word he said. Or maybe, like me, he was just hungover. Here is our entire conversation:

"Hello at last. I'm Mike Taylor."

"Oh yeah. Hi. Mike DiTonto."

"How are things shaping up for February?"

"Pretty good. We have some Jamaican cavers lining up more stuff for us to check out. I think it'll cost everyone about eight hundred dollars apiece. I have eight definites so far. You still want to go?"

"Sure."

"Sounds good." There was a long pause.

I said, "Well, I'm supposed go to caving five minutes ago."

"Where you headed?"

"Sharps."

"That's a fun cave. You'll like it. I mapped the west trunk. It has a very cool waterfall."

Another silence. "Say," I said, "do you know anything about a second entrance to Stillhouse?" I described the chimney I'd found the day before.

"No. That's definitely not on the map." A long pause.

"Well, nice meeting you."

"Yeah. Nice meeting you too."

And then we did Sharps. Jim, Tom, and I broke camp about 10:30 P.M. Sunday, packed the car and found a Pizza Hut, and set out for New Jersey a bit before midnight. I made it home at 10:30 A.M. on Labor Day, slept until five, got up for five hours, and then slept until the mailman woke me this morning, dropping the usual junk mail and rejection slips into my noisy-hinged box. I'm beat, I have a freelance piece on frozen yogurt franchises that is due today at a business magazine, and I am going to Jamaica in four months.

12

A TRIP TO THE LIBRARY

"Hellhole" began as a letter to Ken Autrey, a friend of mine from graduate school. I mailed it that September morning along with a postscript thanking Ken for a book he had recently mailed me, *Continental Drift* by Russell Banks. The novel told the story of a furnace repairman from New Hampshire and a political refugee from Haiti, and the strange coincidences that brought them together in Florida. I had liked it very much.

Ken wrote back to suggest that I contact a friend of his, Mimi Schwartz, who taught freshman composition at Princeton. She was starting a small writers' group, and he thought I might like to join. I considered it. All of my new friends in New Jersey were cavers. I missed the company of other writers, even struggling ones. Especially struggling ones.

But instead of immediately seeking out Mimi Schwartz, I busied myself preparing for Jamaica. I read *Catch a Fire*, Timothy White's biography of Bob Marley, which gave a cogent, moving history of the Rastafari movement. I read a funny and informative NSS background paper called "Caving in Jamaica," written by Ron Canter, who was to be a member of our Cockpits team. I thumbed through several Jamaican tourism books, fiddled with my climbing gear, and bought 300 feet of new PMI caving rope. I took several weekend cave trips with the Northern New Jersey Grotto, stretching my crawling and climbing muscles into shape. Once I had lined up a firm article assignment with *America*, I called the Jamaican tourism bureau and talked them into three round-trip airfares to Monetego Bay. I called Nick Nichols and tried, unsuccessfully, to persuade him to shoot the expedition—*America* just couldn't afford him.

Eventually, though, I did get in touch with Ken's friend. At her invitation I drove to Princeton to read bits of fiction and prose with her monthly discussion group. Mimi proved to be a serious but congenial writer, and the group reflected these attributes. They provided an intellectual counterpoint to the earthy, intensely physical cavers with whom I was spending more and more of my time. By this I don't mean to say that the cavers were ignorant. Many held master's degrees; most had read and traveled widely. But there was little restraint among them, little philosophy that was not tied to corresponding, intense action. For them, degrees, books, science, ideas, careers, and family seemed to become very small things next to the physical immediacy of the cave. Caving was not a hobby, or an intellectual excursion into Platonic or Freudian metaphor, but a *reality*, one more involving, more *real*, than anything the surface world could offer.

Mimi and her friends reminded me of another sort of reality: the reality of stories. To them, stories could be eternal as limestone, forceful as an underground river. Books could be discovered and explored as thoroughly as any blowing crevice in a mountain ridge. I am sure I oversimplify—the cavers and writers I knew were ordinary people, after all, private individuals with ambitions and fears that I could know nothing about. I don't mean to imply that one was a group of childish miscreants and the other of intellectual prudes. But I saw a quiet intensity about the writers at work which was different from the quiet intensity of cavers pushing a crawlway or divers gearing up for a sump.

And I liked the town, with its ample Victorian homes and paneled coffee shops. A sense of importance seemed to hang in the air. Einstein had lived here, I knew, and several writers whose books I admired—John McPhee, Toni Morrison, Joyce Carol Oates, and Russell Banks—lived here now. I toyed with notion of trying to sit in on one of their classes, but I couldn't afford the audit fees. I lacked the bravado to sit in without paying.

I think it was this notion that impelled me, while on a research trip to the Westwood library in early January, to look up some other work by Russell Banks. I had read only *Continental Drift*. I found that our small library owned just one other novel by the author. As I stood in the stacks, I skimmed a few pages of *Hamilton Stark*, enough to see that it was a postmodern puzzle in which an author from New Hampshire describes the novel he *wants* to write about a friend named Hamilton Stark. The premise intrigued me, dealing as it did with the elusive boundary between truth and fiction. I opened the back cover and scanned the brief biography of Banks printed on the dust jacket. The last line read: "Currently, he is working on a book of nonfiction to deal with life in Jamaica, the West Indies."

Excited, I flipped to the front of the book. *Hamilton Stark* had been published in 1978. I went to the circulation desk and asked the librarian to check for other works by Banks held in the Bergen County system. She found *The Book of Jamaica*, published in 1980, listed at nearby Ridgewood. I drove over and checked it out. The dust jacket called it a novel, not nonfiction; for whatever reason, Banks had changed his genre. But I assumed there was at least some reporting here that might be useful to the forthcoming expedition.

I read the book that night and the next day. Its four parts told the story of an English professor on sabbatical who goes native in the Cockpits, meets a Maroon obeah man, and is transformed after a dramatic encounter in Peace Cave, an ancient Maroon hideout. Eventually, the protagonist travels to the remote John Crow Mountains and engages in an act of cathartic violence. After I finished the book, I sat down at my computer to write, for the second time in my life, a letter to a novelist whom I had never met.

11 January 87

Mr. Russell Banks
Princeton, New Jersey

Dear Mr. Banks,

I am a 27-year-old freelance writer recently graduated from the master's program in creative writing at the University of South Carolina, where I studied under James Dickey as a John Welsh Fellow; I am also a devotee of your work. But these facts have nothing to do with my reasons for writing you. I am writing you because of an odd string of coincidences, and because the Cockpits are full of caves. Explaining these reasons requires that I give you a brief personal history; please bear with me, and feel free to skip down a bit if I begin to blather.

While an undergraduate at Florida State in 1979, I joined a local group of cave explorers. Amid the hundreds of miles of limestone passage crisscrossing the hills of North Florida and South Georgia, I began a continuing affair with the subterra. . . . During my second year at law school, I had a chance to accompany a National Geographic expedition. . . .

While at USC, learning what all creative-writing program participants learn—that is, how to write for PMLA and become a professor of English—I met Bill Emerson, a journalism prof who had turned to teaching after the two magazines he ran failed in the sixties. The magazines were the *Saturday Evening Post* and *Look*, and Emerson spoke of the craft of writing with an exuberance I had seldom seen in the English department. I took his course in 1985 and sold three class assignments to national markets.

My wife, meanwhile, was earning a "usable" master's degree in Personnel and Employee Relations. Kathy and I finished our respective programs this past May—her best job offer came from the Sony Corporation in Bergen County, which was ideal for me because it would put us close to New York, but not too close. (Patience, Mr. Banks—the point is coming!) So we moved up here, and I began writing for the

first time without the distractions of grad school. Naturally, I
tried to maintain correspondence with school friends and caving buddies, and one week in early August this correspondence introduced me to your work. An English Dept. chum
mailed me a copy of *Continental Drift*, along with orders to
drop whatever I was doing, and read it. When I finally read it I
was amazed. About the same time the book arrived, I received
a letter from Mike DiTonto, a caver I knew in Virginia who
had made several trips to Accompong. . . . Would I, DiTonto
asked, like to interest some magazine in this expedition so
that I could go along at their expense?

While researching Maroons in the local library, I decided
to pick up some of the earlier works by this guy Banks, to see if
they were as thought-provoking and densely packed as *Continental Drift*. This led me to—you guessed it—*The Book of
Jamaica*. And the other day I found something surprising in
the four-month-old copy of *Esquire* on my nightstand. There
in the back of the magazine was Russell Banks again, this time
stating a beautifully simple goal which made the work of many
authors I admired seem suddenly insignificant: "To make my
readers know that the inexpressible is the same for inarticu-
late *and* articulate people." Then I read *The Book of Jamaica*,
and saw the mojo rising.

Yesterday, after exchanging a great many proposals, bud-
gets and the like, and after a long search for a qualified
caver/photographer, I received the assignment to do a story on
the Cockpits expedition for *America*, Nissan's college-oriented
travel/adventure magazine. I'll be going into Accompong February 14, and will be camping near there until March 1, rappelling into virgin pits and caves, surveying the larger systems.
Relations with the locals are likely to be tense, as a few months
ago the Accompong airstrip was bombed in a U.S.-financed
anti-drug operation. Several Maroons were killed or seriously
injured, courtesy of de land of de free.

My question, Mr. Banks: May I drive down and meet with
you sometime before I fly to Montego Bay? I would appreciate
any advice you could give me on safe travel through Accom-

pong, any insights on the people that might contribute to their portrayal in my article. I was also wondering whether any of the characters in your novel were drawn from actual residents of Accompong who might know and remember you. Perhaps I could bring a gift and your regards to someone who could assist our group in entering "de duppy sinkholes."

Thank you for working your way through this roundabout account. Please call or write if there is any chance of our getting together. I look forward to hearing from you.

Michael Ray Taylor
Westwood, New Jersey

Banks called a few days later. My letter had been forwarded to him at the University of Alabama, where he was teaching on sabbatical, so he couldn't meet me in Princeton. But he offered to mail some inscribed copies of *The Book of Jamaica* to use as letters of introduction.

He said that three of the novel's main characters were in fact drawn from life, and that one of his subjects, Mann O. Rowe, the "Secretary of State of the Maroon Nation," had written to say that he had never received a copy of the novel when it was published. Banks had wanted to get copies to these friends for some time. He promised that, as I had hoped, his name and the books he sent me should help us receive safe passage through Accompong.

Two days after his package arrived, I boarded an Air Jamaica flight for Montego Bay.

13

IN THE COCKPIT

Forty thousand inhuman voices screamed around me.

A hot, foul-smelling wind from eighty thousand leathery wings hit me full in the face. Daylight and the steaming Jamaican jungle were far behind. Guided by a small cone of yellow light, I stepped gingerly from a limestone chamber the length of a football field into a four-foot stoopway. As point man on the first exploration of Welsch Ratbat Cave, I was expected to press ahead, to find where the passages went. I tried to imagine what Harrison Ford would do in a situation like this.

"Bats," he would say rakishly. "Why does it have to be bats?"

Assuming what felt like a suave expression, I turned to Mike DiTonto, leader of the 1987 Jamaican Cockpits Expedition. "BATS!" I shrieked. It came out as rakish as Opus the penguin. "UGH! PTOOEY!" I added, sliding down a six-foot slope of ripe guano. I ducked just in time to avoid the low ceiling.

At this point I should mention that I've always liked bats. Most North American species are cute little fuzzballs, more like the gerbil you kept in the third grade than something that wants your blood. They eat mosquitoes and pollinate peaches. Without bats, we would have no tequila, bananas, or kapok. Contrary to public perception, they are almost never rabid. In only the rarest of circumstances do they entangle themselves in long blond hair.

But I wasn't so sure about the Caribbean giants flapping past my head. These animals looked like they belonged on motorcycles, wearing tattoos. I pried myself from the muck and edged through the fluttering cloud toward the boulder I had picked as survey station, the next point in the connect-the-dots game that maps a cave. Fred Grady, a Smithsonian Institution paleontologist, took compass and inclination readings on the black smear I burned into the boulder with the steady flame of my lamp. We stretched plastic survey tape to the station to measure distance from the last shot. Several bats found this activity curious, and buzzed us for closer looks. The measurements taken, I sat in the mud as DiTonto sketched the tunnel's features into a survey book. The smell from my guano-slick coveralls was making me woozy.

I heard the ghostly voice of Chip Clark, staff photographer for the U.S. Museum of Natural History, echoing through the warehouse-sized chamber behind me. "Would you look at those," he said. "They're like walnuts."

"Amazing," said another team member. "Let's get a shot."

Assuming the photo crew had discovered some unusual mineral formation, I clambered back over the guano mound and through the gloom for a look. I found them admiring the bathood of a large male that hung immodestly from the ceiling.

"Kiwifruit," said the second team member.

"No, cantaloupes," offered a third. "Big dried cantaloupes."

"Okay, forty-two-point-seven feet," said Grady, coiling the tape in the low tunnel. "Come on back. Let's set the next station." I glanced at the bat before I returned. Kiwifruit.

The passage beyond the boulder was the diameter of the average driveway culvert. We slugged through on hands and knees. The bats moved with us, squeaking and pinwheeling. Seven shots later, we were belly-crawling through black ooze, the ceiling only two feet above the uneven floor.

I kept thinking of those "Come Back to Jamaica" commercials: reggae rhythms, bikinis, rum punches. I should have been lying on a sandy beach, soaking up rays. Instead, I was lying in old guano, no doubt soaking up deadly microorganisms. The Jamaica of my dreams was never like this.

The journey had begun three weeks earlier at another sort of cave, Mike DiTonto's basement apartment. DiTonto shared a house in suburban Hyattsville, Maryland, with four to six other cavers (the number varied with expeditions, jobs, and romances). Seniority entitled him to the lowest room, which he liked "because it's cool and dark. I can work and sleep when I want to. When I was little, I liked to sleep in the basement at my parents' house."

DiTonto's furniture consisted of a mattress and a finely appointed drafting table. The walls were covered with intricate maps of some of the pits and caves he had explored in five years of work in Jamaica. I had come to see the maps and study expedition objectives.

The Cockpit Country is essentially an ancient, jungle-covered limestone plateau, so dimpled and contorted with sinks that there are no flat surfaces, no paved roads, no easily navigable paths anywhere within its 400 square miles. The area receives over 150 inches of rainfall annually, yet it contains no surface water. All water drains underground, no one knows where or how deep. Cockpit residents commonly walk miles to community cisterns to obtain water for drinking and washing. For years, cavers had theorized that vast river caverns must exist beneath the Cockpits, perhaps at record depths, 1,000 feet or more below the surface. Until Mike DiTonto came along, the land and the people had made the place too forbidding to explore.

In 1982, DiTonto, then twenty-four, first traveled Jamaica with Adam Fincham, a Kingston caver and the son of a prominent Jamaican geologist. With help from Fincham's father and a Smithsonian biologist, DiTonto was able to meet Minocal Stephenson, a guide, herb doctor, and bush naturalist from the Cockpit town of Quick Step. Mr. Stephenson was on good terms with the often inhospitable inhabitants of the bush. Every winter since that first meeting, DiTonto had led caving expeditions to the Cockpits, finding many more pits and caves than he had time to enter, each year closing in on the megasystem he believed hid beneath the surface.

Both the 1984 and 1985 expeditions—which DiTonto staffed with volunteers from the National Speleological Society— had turned up many new caves, but most of these were "dead-bottom pits"—that is, vertical shafts with little or no horizontal passage at their bases. By analyzing his maps of the pits, comparing their features with the surface topology above, DiTonto could better judge where to direct group energies in future expeditions. The 1986 findings suggested that the best potential for large virgin caves was in the most dangerous part of the Cockpits: the Maroon lands. He spread a coffee-stained topographic map over his basement floor, dirty clothes giving the paper landscape relief, and began to talk.

"One important thing to remember about traveling in the Cockpits," DiTonto began, "is that nothing ever happens according to schedule. But if you take it easy things do happen." Despite his large frame and heavy features (I had heard one caver refer to him as "the Neanderthal"), the red-bearded surveyor spoke gently; I had to lean toward him to make out what he said. "Jamaica is a poor country. It's hard to worry about somebody's deadline when you're worried about where your next meal is coming from. You can go crazy down there if you try to hurry things."

This was fine by me. I am, after all, from the South. DiTonto's next warning was more troublesome: "You also have to remember that the Maroons have some really bad feelings against Americans right now. If anyone does anything foolish in Accompong"—he pointed to a tiny cluster of black dots, representing houses, in the center of the map—"does anything that can be interpreted as hostile, someone might get killed. I just wanted you to know that. No risk me neck to defend de bomboclot who act uncool."

I had not yet discovered *The Book of Jamaica* and knew nothing at all about the Maroons; I paid close attention, not wanting to act uncool. Throughout the conversation, DiTonto lapsed occasionally into a Bob Marley patois. At first I thought this mere affectation, but soon I recognized it for what it was: true bilingualism. DiTonto had spent enough time in the bush to amass a wide collection of patois words and phrases, many of which he had typed into a glossary that he mailed to team members.

"If you want help from anyone, anywhere," he said once, "you should make at least an honest effort to speak their language." While it might have been laughable at best—and racist at worst—for a white man to speak, write, or otherwise appropriate the language of rural blacks in, say, the American South, in the Cockpit the attempt would be accepted as a sign of respect.

The Maroons, DiTonto explained, are descendants of escaped seventeenth-century slaves of the Spanish. After waging decades of guerrilla war with the British, they were granted official independence from Jamaican law in 1739. They have enjoyed an uneasy truce ever since. For centuries, the Maroons had grown ganja, the potent pot of the Caribbean, but in the 1970s it became their major cash crop. The Cockpit Country is especially suited to illegal agriculture. The caves underlying many sinkholes have become naturally plugged, or have been dammed by farmers, causing fertile silt to accumulate in lush, tick-infested glades called bottoms. These small, rich plots are difficult to approach on foot, all but invisible from the air.

Spurred by U.S. drug policies, in 1986 the Jamaican government, led by conservative prime minister Edward Seaga, had instituted something called the Ganja Eradication Program. GEP was not making Americans popular in the bush. Just before Christmas, the tiny airstrip in the Maroon town of Accompong—our planned base—had been bombed by helicopter. According to DiTonto's contacts, some locals believed the choppers were from the Jamaican Defense Force, while others claimed they carried U.S. Army markings. Two goats had been killed, a house burned. Whoever actually dropped the bombs, the local population was certain the operation had been directed by the CIA. Consequently, any young American males found wandering in the bush would likely be regarded as spies.

What's more, DiTonto said, the Jamaican government had stepped up its Cockpits patrols. JDF soldiers had skirmished with growers during the past month. If a patrol found us hacking through the bush, toting ropes and strange gear, dressed in Army surplus, *they* would think we were drug dealers, in for a buy. Our exploration permits from the Jamaican forestry service might not help us. "What else could such a ragtag bunch be?" DiTonto said. "Book 'em, mon-o. Toss de key."

"Our main goal," DiTonto concluded, "is to get underground where it's safe. With everything happening in Accompong right now, I want to start out in Quick Step, where the people know cavers and won't give us any trouble. If we feel the right vibes, we'll check out Accompong after a week or so." Although actually farther into the Cockpits than Accompong, Quick Step, in the District of Look Behind, is not officially a Maroon town. Our guide, Minocal Stephenson, claimed some Maroon blood, but he could not guarantee our safety near Accompong as he could in the bush around Quick Step.

The pits explored during the previous two years had ended in plugged crawlways within 300 feet of the surface. DiTonto had decided to try a new tack for the '87 effort. On this trip, small teams would check only a few of the most promising pits, while a larger crew would travel the southern edge of the Cockpit Country, looking for horizontal caves that contained emerging streams. We would try to reach the ever elusive borehole, the monster passage DiTonto felt was there, from below. There was another, eminently practical reason for this tactic: It would keep the body of the expedition out of the ganja fields and thus, we hoped, out of the line of fire.

America magazine had hired Chip Clark, who, in addition to his nature photography for the Smithsonian, was a longtime caver, to take pictures of the expedition. His wife, Jenny, a Smithsonian illustrator, would assist with the lighting. An hour after I stepped from a plane into a blast of heat that rose from the baked tarmac of the Montego Bay airport, I checked into a comp room, arranged by the tourism bureau at a comfortable resort hotel, and met the two of them for dinner. If we had been working on a typical travel article, the editor would have forbidden such gifts as a conflict of interest. Since our subject matter lay deep in the bush, he had encouraged us to enjoy whatever the government offered. We sat at a poolside table, sipping rum, trying to adjust to the reality that we were being paid to cave in Jamaica. Our plan was to travel into the Cockpits by rail to meet the rest of the expedition, who had arrived a week earlier.

The next morning, we hung around the dirty, slightly menacing MoBay train station waiting for the "8 A.M." diesel to Kingston. I watched the ubiquitous wooden pushcarts, expertly maneuvered over the broken pavement by teenage boys who seemed not to notice their heavy loads. The air smelled of the ocean, exhaust fumes, and rotten fruit. At noon the train finally chugged into the station. We rode airy, old-fashioned passenger cars, snacking on mangoes, soursops, fried chicken, and other fare offered by vendors who strolled the aisles. At one point a very dark-skinned man in a heavy wool suit walked through the train preaching in lilting rhythms. As he passed me, he shouted, "All evil desires and wicked deeds come from the art of man!" Or it may have been "the 'eart of man." His voice receded into the next car, echoing in syncopation with the clattering wheels.

After three hours of tropical scenery, we reached our station at the edge of the Appleton rum distillery, where the green ridges of the Cockpits could be seen rising like a dragon's back in the distance. DiTonto met us in a rented Toyota Starlet to ferry gear and people into the hills. The main highway proved little more than a wide, rocky path. We had gone no more than a few miles when we encountered our first roadblock. Two government Land Rovers had parked so as to leave open only a very narrow gap in the center of the highway; in this gap stood three men with assault rifles.

They waved us out of the car and asked our business. We were all smiles and sincerity. DiTonto pulled out our government permits, while I produced a letter of assignment from *America*. Two of the men kept their guns trained on us while the third, who gave the orders, looked through several of

Chip's watertight aluminum cases, apparently to verify that he was a photographer.

I had been ready for such an encounter, I thought. But the idea of someone pointing a loaded automatic at me and the reality of it were very different things. I looked at the man closest to me; his gun safety was indeed in the off position. The thought occurred to me that even a sudden sneeze could be fatal. Immediately, I felt an uncontrollable urge to sneeze.

At last the leader smiled and sent us on our way. "No problem," he said. "Enjoy your visit to Jamaica."

Caving is a unique activity in that the safety of an entire group depends upon the safety of each individual. One caver's macho heroics while climbing an exposed face can injure others beside himself, or necessitate a difficult and dangerous rescue operation. Few expeditions have room for hot dogs. Even for cavers with several years' experience, the first time underground with a new group is always an audition. When you join a team, they'll want to see a certain determination and self-reliance in your thinking, to be sure that you won't turn weird in a tight spot or carelessly rack in backward on the rope and "crater." Thus, on the day after my arrival in Quick Step, I found myself trying to act cool as I bounced down the rock-strewn mountain road en route to the expedition's first cave.

It wasn't easy.

Our rented hatchback held a half dozen cavers, two Jamaicans, and forty pounds of gear. Outside it was about 85° F. Inside was a good ten degrees hotter. Six inches away from the car window was an unbroken limestone wall; six inches from the window on the other side was a 100-foot drop into jungle. Somewhere behind us was the rented VW that held the rest of the team. I was wedged in the front seat, beside and occasionally beneath fifty-year-old Minocal Stephenson, who had to move off the gearshift whenever DiTonto shifted. Our guide had struck me as a very wise and gentle man, but like anyone who lives in a region where there is no surface water, he had not bathed in some time.

Other team members in the car were DiTonto's house-mates Ron Canter and Miles Drake, both Cockpits veterans. Drake, a world-class caver who had participated in big discoveries from Mammoth to Mexico, had once financed his caving habit by selling lung biopsies, spinal fluid, and gallons of plasma. More recently, he boasted of procuring "a real job," as partner in a Washington, D.C., window-washing firm. He did well with heights. But, of course, caving came first.

Not everyone was so hard-core as Drake. The only requirements for inclusion in the expedition had been basic vertical and survey experience, a positive attitude, and the ability to pay one's own way. DiTonto's Jamaican exploits had been so well publicized in caving circles that each year he had little trouble assembling a seven- to ten-member team. He had grown to prefer a mix of hard- and soft-core cavers. He felt that too many experts on an expedition invariably led to personality conflicts; too few resulted in less than significant discoveries. Crammed atop the bundle of gear behind the back seat were Mark Thompson, a medical researcher from Maryland, and Russ Rhoads, an IRS analyst from Washington, D.C., both occasional cavers back home.

Sweating in the vinyl seat, I wondered how many cavers of any sort DiTonto would have signed if he had warned us about the transportation. On downgrades, we made up to twenty-five miles per hour. Upgrades were a slow walk. At one point we were passed by a goat. The jagged rock wall, white in the glaring sun, rushed past scant inches from my face. I had no idea what we would do if we met a car coming the other way.

I found out when a blue minibus appeared at the top of the next hill. ("Minibus": a Jamaican term meaning "beat-up '68 Chevy van lined with wooden benches and crowded with 25 or more passengers.") Since Jamaica is a former British colony, driving is on the left, which I forgot during the instant that DiTonto jerked the wheel to that side, toward the hundred feet of space. I braced myself for the imminent head-on and following long fall. But the minibus had pulled to the opposite side. Amid much mutual horn honking we passed each other in true Jamaican fashion: The van added a new scrape to the collection on its side, we added a few loose pebbles to the pile at the base of the cliff. Both drivers cursed like New York cabbies. I eased my death grip on the dashboard. No problem.

Slowly we dropped from the Cockpits to the quiet village of Siloah, and from there to the vast cane fields of the Appleton Estate, site of our first cave. We had seen the massive rum distillery the day before as the train reached our station at the town of Maggotty. Now we approached the plant from behind, its metal pipes and turrets gleaming like a castle in the sun, the green walls of the Cockpit plateau at our backs. Over all was the smell of boiling sugarcane.

"We will stop here," said Mr. Stephenson, indicating a dusty cement-block building. "De manager's office. Him a very dear friend of mine."

I leaned against the hood while DiTonto and Mr. Stephenson went inside to talk to the manager. As I waited, a large, unmuffled flatbed truck belched alongside. A dozen shirtless, machete-wielding cane cutters stood in the steel bed; the truck pulled a heavy trailer of cane. I watched two men detach the trailer and push it into an unloading area. They moved with an almost studied slowness, yet with such grace and strength that I could tell they meant business, that I could not imagine the trailer or anything else standing in their way for long.

DiTonto and Mr. Stephenson came out of the office, accompanied by a smiling, pudgy Jamaican who was clearly the manager. One of the cane cutters grinned, hopped from the truck, and ran up to Mr. Stephenson. Although the patois they spoke was too quick for me to make out, I soon gathered that the man was thanking Mr. Stephenson for a stomach remedy and asking for some other medical advice. It was a scene I would see repeated often in the next two weeks. Despite a modern clinic opening in the nearby town of Maggotty, everyone in the Cockpits seemed to prefer Mr. Stephenson's care. *Him give you de greenberry tea, fix you up, mon.* Ron Canter, who leaned on the hood beside me, mentioned that

Mr. Stephenson's knowledge of local herbs had amazed a Smithsonian biology team several years back.

Gradually, we piled back into the car, already moving with a studied slowness ourselves. We set out through the fields toward a green island in the sea of cane, a steep 200-foot inverted cone of the sort you see in Chinese watercolors. This freestanding remnant of the surrounding plateau formed what is geologically termed a karst tower. The cane cutters said it was hollow. We parked fifty yards from an obvious, vine-draped entrance the size of a railroad tunnel, the clichéd black archway cavers call Hollywood Cave. Truly virgin passage near such a big hole might be hard to find.

But I wondered if the cave's more remote, untried passages would lead to anything like the new rooms I had found in Florida and TAG. There, I'd noticed that virgin mud, especially in drier passages, tends to develop a sort of thin, sparkling crust, a brittle skin unlike any other soil, almost a glaze. It's as if the slow burning of the centuries has baked ordinary mud into something more. Squishing it through your fingers imparts the vastness of geologic time. I hadn't seen such virgin dirt in years; now, perhaps, it lay only minutes away.

I didn't voice any of these thoughts. I separated my helmet, lamp, and coveralls from a compressed pile that someone had pried from the trunk. We stripped out of our street clothes and began donning coveralls and gear, oblivious to curious stares from a couple of cutters who had seen us pull up. This part, at least, was no different from home. Cavers undressing in a field always attract attention.

It took me a few minutes to fire my fifty-year-old Justrite lamp. Coal miners abandoned carbides for flameless electric lamps thirty years ago, killing the market and ultimately the manufacturers. Now cavers roam flea markets all over the United States, buying up the sturdy and economical antiques. Unlike coal mines, very few caves contain explosive gases. Carbide (which produces acetylene gas when mixed with water) is thus safe. The fuel is cheap, long burning, and the small yellow flame can also be used to heat food, warm cold hands, and mark survey stations. I eventually unclogged the lamp's gas jet and sparked a flame to life. I slid the lamp into the bracket on my helmet, which was little more than a construction cap with a chin strap, but vital protection against low ceilings and rock falls. (I used a heavier, less comfortable rock-climbing helmet for pits.)

Mr. Stephenson had cut some fresh cane and passed chunks around before we went underground. The rough fibers, customarily chewed like gum, were full of juice and sweeter than any candy bar. I wiped the sticky syrup off my hands with a handful of leaves, then pulled on my leather gloves. Mr. Stephenson found a shady spot to relax; he would guard our car and belongings. One of his many sons, Collin, twenty-one, had developed a taste for caving with the 1985 expedition. Since we expected this cave to remain strictly horizontal—that is, to require no rope work—Collin was going in with us on borrowed gear. We thanked his father for the cane, and entered the dark.

The ten-foot-wide passage was relatively easygoing. The hard-packed mud floor was unusually flat, and the irregular ceiling required only occasional stooping. We quickly walked beyond the reach of daylight. As I had expected from the large entrance, others had been here before us. Names, drawings, and other Jamaican graffiti were smeared on the walls in charcoal. A number of dry calcite formations on the walls and ceilings had been broken or vandalized—too much like home. Any truly virgin passage in such a cave would be down a tight crawlway, up a tricky climb, or in some other place too forbidding for noncavers to check.

I began to be irritated by the heat. Caves maintain a constant temperature, always within a degree or two of the average annual surface temperature above. In the States, that range is from the high 30s to the low 60s. With a temperature in the mid-70s, the tower passage was cooler than the blast furnace outside, but still warmer than I thought any cave had a right to be. My coveralls were made of heavy ballistic nylon. Usually a source of warmth and comfort, they now became a dripping sweat suit.

The passage turned and began to parallel the contour of the hill outside. After five minutes, we rounded a corner and saw a bluish glow. We were approaching an oval, vine-curtained window to the cane fields outside. The main passage branched and continued, following the circumference of the hill until it reached a third entrance. Apparently, we were meandering around the circular base of the cone. To connect with cave larger than the circumference of the tower, we would have to find a passage that dropped below the level of the valley outside and headed for the cliffs a half mile away. The tunnels we'd seen so far made that seem unlikely.

Disappointed, we split into two groups. One would finish exploring and mapping the Appleton Tower Maze, as we had decided to call it. The other would drive back into the hills to see a man named Welsch, who reportedly owned two horizontal caves, one of them containing a large bat colony. We planned to reconvene at sunset. I drove with the second group. Welsch's cave did indeed contain crow-sized bats, plenty of them, as well as several hundred feet of dung-lined passage. I lay prone in the guano-filled crawlway, setting station for the last survey shot at its dead end. As I held my lamp on point for Grady to sight, I began singing a Jamaican folk tune I had come across while researching the island:

> De bat come down de chimney
> Hang out in de fireplace.
> When I come in de kitchen
> De bat fly in me face.
>
> Fly in me face, oh, oh,
> Fly in me face, oh, oh, oh.
> I hope de bat he don' come out
> Fly in me face tonight.
>
> De bat, he rat got wings
> All de lickle children know dat
> What I need to know from de Lawd
> Is how to put wings on de cat.

Grady advised me not to quit my day job.

I joked about the deadly spores no doubt infesting our lungs. But for Chip Clark and Russ Rhoads, it would prove no joke: A week after the expedition, both would be hospitalized with histoplasmosis, a lung infestation by a fungus common to tropical bat guano. Rhoads developed pneumonia while in the hospital; doctors drained quarts of fluid from his ravaged lungs. It would be two weeks before he could return home, two months before he could go back to work. Both Clark and Rhoads would vow never to cave in Jamaica again. Several of the team who surveyed Welsch, myself included, would spend the weeks after the expedition fighting milder, flulike symptoms most likely caused by the guano.

But there in the cave, we all felt fine. We could only speculate as to what sort of passage lay hidden beyond the mounds of dung. In the States, we might have spent several weekends digging through the stuff to find out. In the Cockpits, so many unexplored caves awaited us that digging through warm shit seemed a silly waste of time.

Welsch's second cave, which we named Penthouse because of its position above the first, was refreshingly batless. DiTonto and I pushed a relatively easy crawlway for 80 feet into some large chambers. When I stood up in the new passage, I looked at my hands. The crawl had covered them with black, sparkling dirt, a deposit older than Western civilization. I smiled, wiped my hands on my coveralls, and moved on. The vaulted rooms we had entered—one of them measured 100 feet wide—showed signs of earlier human passage. It wasn't long before we discovered a second entrance, on the opposite side of the hill from the first.

Our virgin crawlway had merely connected two short, previously known caves. For the rest of the afternoon, we mapped the small system, knowing that the long one was still down there, somewhere.

Back at the village of Quick Step, we settled into our "field house," a one-room, tin-roofed shed on stilts behind Mr. Stephenson's cabin. Past expeditionists called it luxury living compared to earlier years when they had camped in the bush. Not many bugs here, they said, just a few flying roaches. To replenish our plastic water barrel, we had only to hike a two-mile footpath to the cistern. Best of all, there was little chance of being shot at. The only real drawbacks to a good night's sleep were the nine-day wake being held for a deceased grandfather up the road—it ran from ten to three every night—and a confused rooster who crowed every hour. By the second night, there was talk among us of fried chicken.

Even in a community the size of Quick Step, which had a thousand inhabitants spread over several hills and sinkholes, there were no telephones, sewers, or plumbing. Other than the tiny wooden and cement-block houses, the only buildings were three churches and four rum bar–general store combinations, the largest of these also serving as post office.

After a day of muddy caving, we would splash a few handfuls of water from the twenty-gallon barrel onto our faces and arms. The mud in our hair, down our backs, and between our toes was left to dry to a crust, cementing layers of sweat and bug repellent. Only every three or four days would we feel sufficiently filthy to drive one and a half hours off the plateau to the Appleton Estate, where we bathed in the Black River, a cool dark stream that meandered through the cane fields. Whenever I asked DiTonto about Accompong, he said, "Maybe in another day or two."

Just as we adjusted to constant dirt, we adapted to the bland, starchy diet of the Cockpits. Breakfast was fried biscuits and "tea," a mixture of sweetened condensed milk and boiled mints and herbs, picked fresh each morning from the hillside. Lunch—usually eaten underground—was a can of sardines or a wedge of cheese purchased from a Quick Step rum bar the night before, perhaps followed by a melted candy bar carried from the States. Dinner was invariably rice and yams, desert a Red Stripe beer or Ting grapefruit soda.

A typical field house journal entry: 6:36 P.M., 2/26/87. *Eating yam and rice topped with a small dollop of goat grease. Dirty tin plate, dirty plastic fork. J—— and M—— have been dis-*

cussing pit potential in Venezuela, but now F—— and J——
are comparing experiences with hashish in Turkey and tourista
in Peru. Their separate recollections prove remarkably similar.
Five days ago, I was really starting to notice the effect of so many
unwashed bodies in such close quarters. Now we are certainly
dirtier, but I can't say that I notice it. I guess I'm adapting.

Out in the street twenty children play a sort of baseball
involving an old handball and a woman's slipper used as a bat.
The 10-year-old girl pitching has a mean underhanded curve,
but Mr. Stephenson's 12-year-old son Wayne has still managed
to reach second. Some local men lean against our rental, having
an animated discussion about—who knows? The patois is too
fast and furious to make anything out. Every few minutes a
whiff of ganja seeps up through the broken slats of the cabin
floor, or down through the splayed leaves of bananas and
bromeliads. It's always just a whiff, its source indeterminate.
Even this far into the bush, people are fearful of the Ganja
Eradication Program.

Most nights several of us would drive the thirty minutes of
nasty road to the village of Aberdeen, where we downed a few
Red Stripes at Doc's Place. Doc's brother, Caswell Reid, was
temporarily running things, Doc having been sliced open in a
knife fight three weeks earlier. Caswell, a broad-shouldered
twenty-nine-year-old normally employed as a tire mechanic in
the distant city of Mandeville, gave me a blow-by-blow of the
fight during my third Red Stripe of a cool Thursday evening.

Doc had shut the place down about midnight, Caswell
said, and was sleeping in the little storeroom behind the
counter. About 3 A.M., the would-be thief—a stranger from
MoBay, it was later learned—used a car jack to lift a wide
floorboard in the freezer room. Caswell opened a section of
counter, motioning for me to follow. The freezer room was
where Caswell kept his powerful home-built stereo; he turned
down an ancient Marley tape so I could hear the rest of the
tale, ignoring the complaints of some lanky teens who had
been dancing in the street outside.

"Me brother 'ear a noise and walk t'rough a door, and dis t'ief stick 'im 'ere"—he pointed to his midsection—"with a ratchet." A ratchet is a tricky folding knife popular among rude boys, the Jamaican equivalent of a switchblade. "Me brother fall back into de bar, and reach over and grab 'im machet'. 'Im cut the t'ief on 'im neck. T'ief stab 'im in de 'and. Me brother stagger back, swinging the machet', *whoosh*, like so. 'E open up de t'ief belly for 'im. Doc go for 'elp, and dem find the t'ief like so." Caswell slumped on the floor against the freezer, arms at his side, tongue lolling, eyes crossed and bulging.

Slowly he smiled and stood. "'Im a deader, as the rastaman say. We clean most the blood, but you can see a few speckle of it on dis wall." He paused to examine a wall calendar hung beneath a garish photo of a bikini-clad woman drinking Dragon Stout. He found a date circled in red. "It happen t'ree week ago last night. I come over from Mandeville to run a shop until me brother feel him usual self."

Caswell reached over and cranked up "Rastaman Vibration."

A cheer rose from the street. I resolved never to break-and-enter a Jamaican rum bar. Irie.

14

WHOLLY COINCIDENTAL

The familiar approach to Nyamkopong, if one wishes to avoid risking damage to his car, is from the town of Maggotty across the broad Appleton sugar fields, then swiftly into the highlands, the humpbacked hills of the southwestern Cockpit region, from paved road to unpaved to a rutted trail that loops and climbs steadily away from the bright green flats around Maggotty, through the fistful of cabins called Whitehall, then into the Cockpit itself, dense green planes of land tipped at wild angles to the trail, lips of limestone pouting overhead and lopped off below, with careful terraces wedged into the steep slopes where a lone farmer in knee-high rubber boots shoves his spade into the red earth and prepares the ground for yams, Bermuda onions, corn, and Irish potatoes, the trail rising steadily, switchbacking away from Whitehall now, with a scattering of one-room, tin- or thatched-roof cottages alongside the trail or off a way in the bush, approachable only by meandering and nearly vertical footpaths where a broad-hipped barefoot woman with a five-gallon tin of water from the spring below balanced perfectly on her head ascends as if climbing the stone steps of a temple.

—RUSSELL BANKS, *The Book of Jamaica*

The first thing I noticed about Accompong was that it was ringed by a new chain-link fence. I couldn't decide whether driving through the open gate felt more like entering another country—which the Maroons liked to insist Accompong was— or a prison compound. As we approached the collection of cement-block houses and daub-and-wattle shacks that marked the center of town, young boys ran alongside the Toyota shouting, "CIA!" and "Whitey!"

For variety's sake, that morning I had offered to drive. In the car with me were DiTonto, Mr. Stephenson, another local guide, and Chip Clark. The other members of the expedition were caving in two teams near Quick Step.

"Watch out for those kids," DiTonto said. "You know, when a car hits a pedestrian in Jamaica, the crowd exacts vengeance on the driver before they check the pedestrian's injuries."

I slowed down and looked around. I felt I already knew the dusty town from Banks's book. True, he had changed a number facts for the sake of the story. In the novel, Accompong was Nyamkopong, from the patois word n'yam, to eat. There were only two cars in the fictional town, and I had already counted six. I could only guess at how closely the various residents had been depicted, or whether Jah and the ganja trade were as central to Accompong's spirit and economy as Banks had indicated. And even if the book had been a work of nonfiction, I reasoned, Banks had done most of his research in 1976. A lot could have changed in over ten years. Yet I couldn't shake the feeling that I was driving into a novel.

Following directions from Mr. Stephenson, I parked in front of a bright pink bungalow that belonged to Colonel Harris Cawley, elected leader of the Maroon people. In the novel, there is some bad blood between the fictional colonel, Martin Luther Phelps, and Wendell O. Mann, the Maroon secretary of state. The protagonist is befriended by Mr. Mann, an aging obeah man with ebony skin and blue eyes—"pale blue, like agates, except that the blue outer ring of the pupil held a brown center ring around the iris, like a pair of concentric blue and brown rings around a planet." The enigmatic Mr. Mann becomes a spiritual guide to the narrator, gives the book its mystical heartbeat. Banks had told me that the character was based on Mann O. Rowe. I didn't know whether the novel's colonel was also drawn from life, or even whether the present colonel had been around when Banks was in Accompong. (I discovered later that Harris Cawley, Accompong's schoolmaster, had served for only two years as colonel.) While I was curious to meet Rowe and present him with his inscribed book, I didn't want to insult the headman by seeming anxious to talk to someone else.

But Colonel Cawley wasn't home. A heavyset, laughing old woman, wearing a loose-fitting pastel dress and sandals, introduced herself as Auntie Bea, the colonel's mother, and hugged each of us in turn as though we were her grandchildren. She smelled of cinnamon and sweat. "Him teach at the school, but you may kindly wait," she said.

We followed her into the living room and signed the guest ledger she presented. I was surprised to see recent entries from Kansas City and the Bronx. Auntie Bea explained that Cockpit Tours Limited, an outfit in MoBay, was busing small groups of tourists into Accompong for a few hours every other weekend. On the appointed days, local young men would trade their T-shirts and running shoes for traditional warrior garb, and would shut off the reggae in order to greet the bus with drums and blasts from the *abeng*, the ancient Maroon trumpet. Auntie Bea seemed a bit put out that we had shown up without warning, giving the town no chance to arrange an "authentic" Maroon welcome.

DiTonto had brought a gift for the colonel, a box of used but fairly recent American textbooks and teaching materials for the Accompong school. Because of the Maroons' "independence," DiTonto had learned, the school—built as gift by the Canadian government—received very little in the way of supplies and support from Kingston. He brought the box in from the Toyota to show it to Auntie Bea. He explained that we had come not for tourism, but to cave, and that we hoped to be able cave near Accompong as friends.

"Oh yah," she said, smiling and nodding. "You can go a

c'yahv in Maroon town. Dese people will no harm you. Dey may take all you money, and all you ropes and t'ings, but me say dey no harm you." This was hardly encouraging.

At last the colonel arrived. A well-educated, sharp-eyed man, he wore a white oxford shirt buttoned to the neck, black trousers, and black patent-leather loafers. He gravely shook hands with each of us, handing each in turn a business card that read: "Harris N. Cawley, Colonel, Accompong State, Beth Salem P.A., St. Elizabeth." A blank dotted line on the card was preceded by the optimistic abbreviation "Tel." The colonel mentioned that he had received a letter from DiTonto regarding our planned expedition. He invited us to discuss what was on our minds, and we asked if we could go caving.

He nodded, collecting his thoughts before answering. The town was perfectly safe, he began, but nerves in the bush were indeed raw. If we chose to sleep in the bush, to make camp, there would be no guarantee of safety.

DiTonto tried to imply—without making an outright statement, which would have been tantamount to an accusation—that we would remain blind to the existence of any ganja fields we happened to stumble across. DiTonto also tried to ascertain, in the roundabout fashion essential to Jamaican negotiation, whether Cawley was fishing for a "safe-conduct" fee, which, if paid, would make potential problems in the bush go away. But everything about the man indicated that he was sincere, that he was not after our money, and that, no matter how much we ignored the ganja fields, he felt we would place ourselves in danger should we cave among them. DiTonto clearly believed him.

The colonel thanked us for the school supplies, and we stood to leave. After a few photos in front of his mother's flower garden, Cawley directed us toward a rum bar where we would find Rubber, one of Banks's old friends. He also pointed out a small hill where we would find the home of Mann O. Rowe. Rubber stepped into the dirt street and introduced himself as we approached the bar. A tall, muscular rasta with red eyes and a knowing smile, he seemed genuinely thrilled to receive his signed paperback. He flipped through the pages and located scenes in which the fictional Rubber appeared, reading passages aloud to a small crowd that gathered around us.

One of the men who approached was introduced as Stammer. I remembered a line from the cover letter Banks had sent me with the books: "If you deal with a man named H—— (or Sylvester, or Syl, or Stammer), give him my love, and be careful of him. He's very smart and has always got a secret agenda. His role in the local political scene is extremely complex, especially among the younger men. (And it's a male world you're entering.)" Stammer addressed Mr. Stephenson in what was to me an impenetrable patois, but DiTonto asked them a question which made me realize they had been discussing a particular cave. They seemed to be arguing about the best directions for approaching this cave on foot.

I recalled another of Banks's warnings: "Just keep in mind that the thing people up there are protecting is their livelihood, and they're doing it in a world where basic survival is at stake. What can be confusing is that they're also willing to sell each other out." I could barely make out the text of the conversation, and yet I couldn't escape the feeling that there was a much more important subtext. After a few minutes, without any apparent decision as to whether we would actually visit the cave, or any caves near Accompong, we began walking toward the home of Mann O. Rowe.

In the book, when the narrator first meets Mr. Mann, the old man comes out of his house and stops a dog from barking by patting the air above the dog's head. He then shakes hands with the narrator, "firmly, twice," and says, "Mann. Wendell O. Mann," adding, "like an English gentleman, 'Delighted,' with a pleasant nod of his head." As we walked up to the door, several skinny dogs—all of that vague, tan-colored, short-haired breed ubiquitous to the Third World—began to yap. A man who looked to be in his seventies walked out, dressed in a checked oxford shirt, loose trousers held up by braces, and a battered straw work hat. He quieted the dogs by patting the air above one's head. He shook my hand, twice, firmly, and said, "Rowe. Mann O. Rowe. Delighted." He followed this with a pleasant nod of the head. A wooden sign over his door said Trelawny Town, 1738–39, just as in the book. This was the place name and date—new calendar and old—for the signing of the Maroon treaty of independence.

I introduced myself, clutching the paperback I was to give him, and felt the powerful eyes of the old man lock onto mine. Their unmistakable force seemed to emanate from the concentric brown and blue circles around his pupils. His strange eye coloring, not the least bit fictional, was magnified by thick horn-rimmed glasses. "Pardon me for staring, sir," I said, "but you have very remarkable eyes."

The old man grinned. "Ah yes, the blue. This is a sign of my Scottish ancestry, those who were with Sir Francis Drake when he landed at Ocho Rios."

I said that I had brought a gift from Russell Banks, the novelist, and Mr. Rowe nodded as if he had been expecting this.

"Ah yes, Russell Banks is my dear friend," he said. I remembered that the novel's English professor presents Mann O. Rowe with a copy of a history book, *The Fighting Maroons of Jamaica*, inscribing it: "To my dear friend, Wendell O. Mann."

The sense of déjà vu was unlike any I had ever experienced. I felt giddy. I had traveled through the looking glass, crossed the boundary between truth and fiction, seen words made flesh. I handed Mr. Rowe the book, and offered Banks's apologies that the copy he had mailed just after publication never made it to Accompong.

Mr. Rowe said, "Yes, I have waited for it for many years. But the mail office in Kingston is no good."

Over the next half hour Mann O. Rowe spoke line after line of Wendell O. Mann's dialogue. Later, when he had taken me to his small, cluttered bedroom in order to remove, from a dark wooden box beneath his bed, the decaying parchment treaty of Maroon independence that he guarded as secretary, I saw on a small wooden bookshelf a hardcover edition of *The Book of Jamaica*. Tiny scraps of paper marked many of the book's pages.

The last photo of Sheck Exley, taken moments before he entered
a submerged, 600-foot-long horizontal cave leading into Zacatón.
(Kevin Downey)

Support cavers at the surface lower dive tanks into the enormous sinkhole at Zacatón, in advance of a world scuba depth record attempt by Jim Bowden and Sheck Exley. The water at the point where the rope is rigged has been plumbed to a depth of 1,085 feet.
(Kevin Downey)

Jim Bowden checks one of many decompression tanks staged at regular intervals in the deep pit. Each of the tanks mounted on his dive harness carries a precise mixture of gasses that will let him breathe at specified depths.
(Kevin Downey)

Sheri Engler walks
through a stream passage
in Great Expectations
beneath the Bighorn
Mountains of Wyoming.
She wears a full wet suit
beneath her coveralls
to protect her from
the 39° F water.
(Ron Simmons)

Don Coons climbs over
Lower Gonzo Falls, one
of the many waterfalls
that cascade through Great X.
He once accomplished
a solo "crossover" trip,
meeting Pete Shifflet
in the middle of the cave
as the two traveled its
length starting from
opposite entrances.
(Ron Simmons)

With daylight and the Jamaican jungle beckoning overhead, I pause to touch a sheer wall while climbing Minocal's Glory Hole, a 213-foot-deep pit in the Cockpit Country. (Chip Clark)

Steven Cohen, a novelist by day and a caver with New York City's Met Grotto by night, admires calcite soda straws in a side passage of the Old Croton Aqueduct, somewhere beneath the Bronx. In nature, such formations would require a thousand years or more of growth; these are no more than eighty years old. (Kevin Downey)

A caver stands on a field of flowstone amid the totems of Tower Place in New Mexico's Lechuguilla cave. When traversing such pristine formation areas, cavers routinely remove their boots to avoid scuffing the translucent minerals. (Kevin Downey)

Great splays of crystalized gypsum form the stalactites of the Chandelier Ballroom in Lechuguilla. At least one of the heavy gypsum stalactites has fallen since Patricia Kambesis first discovered the room in 1988. (Kevin Downey)

A Lechuguilla caver examines an unusual helictite growing from a cave wall.
(Kevin Downey)

Traces of iron and other elements
infuse these bulbous calcite
formations, tinting them a rosy
pink. (Kevin Downey)

A delicate aragonite bush "grows"
in the Great Beyond passage
of Lechuguilla. (Kevin Downey)

A member of the first American caving expedition to China—sponsored by the Cave Research Foundation in 1988—stands before a fortification built into the entrance of Zhenyan Cave during the Taiping Rebellion in 1850. During times of political upheaval in southern China, whole villages have retreated into the enormous caves that dot the countryside. That's me fiddling with my gear near the base of the steps. (Cal Welbourn)

The 400-foot-tall entrance of the Zhijin River Cave in Guizhou Province lies at the base of a spectacular limestone canyon.

(Kevin Downey)

A woman of the Blue Miao tribe carries water toward
the entrance of Dragon Cave in Guizhou Province.
Although the region receives the highest annual rainfall
in China, surface water is scarce: It all flows into vast caves
beneath the mountains. (Kevin Downey)

I remembered a scene in which the narrator examines Mr. Mann's dog-eared copy of *The Fighting Maroons of Jamaica*. He finds pages of penciled corrections and apocryphal marginalia. The discovery occurs just after he has presented his dear friend with a new, inscribed copy as a parting gift.

We drank a glass of overproof rum mixed with water, and my giddiness evolved into a kind of queasy stupor. The world of the story and the world in which I sat talking to an old Jamaican kept converging like two images on the focusing line of my camera lens. I became unable to extricate Mr. Rowe from Mr. Mann, Accompong from Nyamkopong. It was as if the part of my brain that processes experience and the part that records stories had been hard-wired together. The fiction, which I had experienced first, seemed, if anything, more real than events unfolding around me.

I know that Mr. Mann pulled the treaty from under his bed, because I have a copy of the photograph Chip took of the old man proudly holding it aloft. But the same scene is in the book on page 180. I am reasonably sure that, upon his learning I was a journalist, Mr. Rowe asked me to convey greetings to George Shultz, his fellow secretary of state, just as Mr. Mann asks Banks's narrator to carry a message to Henry Kissinger. I believe Mr. Rowe delivered a convoluted narration of the history of the Maroons—involving Christopher Columbus, Sir Francis Drake, and Queen Elizabeth—but I don't how closely it resembled the one that ends on page 109. And I recall with some certainty that I talked to the old man longer than the rest of my group would have preferred.

Later that night, back in the field house, DiTonto announced that we had sufficient cave leads in the areas we were presently exploring. He would wait for a future expedition, for a time when the Ganja Eradication Program had been forgotten, to set up a base camp in or near Accompong. I scarcely paid attention. I was staring at my open notebook. I found that I couldn't record the day's events without checking them against the novel. I had kept an unsigned copy of *The Book of*

Jamaica and began thumbing through it. For the first time, I noticed that an epigraph preceded the text. In the soft yellow glow of my carbide lamp I read:

> The role that causality plays in our culture has its counterpart in the role played by analogy among the Meso-Americans. Causality is open, successive, and more or less infinite: a cause produces an effect, which in turn engenders another. Analogy or correspondence, by contrast, is closed and cyclical: the phenomena evolve and are repeated as in a play of mirrors. Each image changes, fuses with its contrary, disengages itself, forms another image, and in the end returns to the starting point. Rhythm is the agent of change in this case. The key expressions of change are, as in poetry, metamorphosis and mask.
>
> OCTAVIO PAZ, *Laughter and Penitence*

One page before the epigraph, shining from the paper like some mystical utterance from Wendell O. Mann, was a standard publisher's disclaimer:

> All the people in this novel, including the narrators, are imaginary; any resemblances to persons living or dead are wholly coincidental.

15

River Beneath the Bush

Called "Tawn-tawn" by the locals, the village of Thorton lies well within the Maroon interior of the Cockpits, but outside the fenced "state" of Accompong. Mr. Stephenson had a friend there who knew of some caves. Thorton lay at an elevation that promised good depth potential, so I accompanied DiTonto and Mr. Stephenson to scout the caves before we committed a full survey party to the area. Unfortunately, Mr. Stephenson's friend was ill and couldn't take us to the entrances himself. His brother-in-law offered to lead. We walked up a steep hill behind the village, swatting at vines and the ticks that jumped from them.

Very quickly thirty men with machetes appeared from nowhere, surrounding us. Mr. Stephenson explained that we wanted to go in "dema c'yahv up dere." One replied in angry patois, punctuating his comments with scowls and spitting. The others stood silent. Following Mr. Stephenson's lead, we walked purposely toward the entrance of the first cave. Our escorts stayed with us.

"Don't worry about dem machet'," DiTonto whispered. "They're a common farm tool around here, not a weapon." I looked at the man walking beside me, a shirtless Rastafarian wearing cutoff jeans and split rubber boots. His dreadlocks were stuffed under a thick wool cap, and his eyes were beet red from ganja. He saw me watching him, smiled, and began casually paring his nails with his thirty-inch blade. A farm tool? I wasn't so sure.

If I had to guess, I'd have said these guys had a crop all right, nearby, and it wasn't yams or sugarcane. Trying to seem a friendly foreigner, I asked the man the patois term for his lavender-colored cap.

He touched the flat of his blade to the side of his head. "Das? Me call it a tom." His voice was music in a low register. "Das be the tom of I and I." He glanced at my headgear, a black jungle fedora purchased from an Army-surplus shop in New Jersey.

I asked if he'd like to try it on.

He did so, grinning. "A sportin' cop, mon," he said, pulling the brim low over his red eye. "But too much small about de mane." He handed it back.

We reached the first entrance, a manholelike opening between twin boulders. DiTonto and I dropped into a low circular chamber. Our company followed us in until the room resembled the interior of a minibus. Twenty of us stood hunched in the five-foot-tall cell. Its floor and ceiling sloped together like the insides of a clam. At one end was the top of a chimney, a narrow vertical slot. DiTonto climbed down into it, and two machete-bearing men followed. Others crowded around the lip, accidentally kicking down loose rocks. At least it *looked* accidental. DiTonto and the two "cavers" chimneyed about twenty-five feet to the floor of a horizontal passage.

I heard a rock bounce off a helmet, followed by a curse from DiTonto. "Get those people away from the lip!" he demanded. "These guys don't have helmets down here. Someone's going to wind up with a concussion, and they'll blame us."

Mr. Stephenson was outside the cave, smoking a Craven A with the brother-in-law. I started telling the crowd around me everything I knew about caves and caving, trying to explain why DiTonto and I would travel all the way to Jamaica to crawl into muddy little holes. Soon the angry looks began to be replaced by smiles. I realized that I had convinced them we were harmless idiots, a couple of mental cases. It calmed things down considerably.

DiTonto popped over the lip of the chimney, bleeding from a gash on his cheek. He ignored it. "There's one lead down there," he said, "but it's unstable stuff. Not worth pushing with these guys knocking it down behind us." We left the first cave and headed up toward the second, still escorted, but no longer in danger, if we could trust the apparent change in mood.

I led into the second cave, which proved a carbon copy of the first: a low-ceilinged entrance room followed by a steep twenty-foot climb-down. DiTonto managed to keep everyone else from the lip as I descended a slick wall covered with the milky formation called flowstone. At its base I found a six-by-ten-foot hollow full of noticeably stale air. The only lead out of the sepulchral alcove was a mucky, sewerlike crawlway, not worth pushing under hostile conditions. The chances of big cave seemed less likely than the chances of incurring further wrath. We quit Thorton.

As I relaxed on a pile of firewood at the field house, composing a journal entry on Thorton, the last of sunset glowed violet-red through the macca bushes, and I set my notes aside. I could hear Mrs. Stephenson and two daughters puttering in the "kitchen" down the hill, a flimsy lean-to covering a charcoal hearth. That night, after too many days of rice and yams, we were going to have fresh meat: A goat had been butchered upon our return. Behind the pot that held our simmering supper was an iron cauldron expertly filled by Mr. Stephenson as he gutted and skinned the animal. It was *mannish water*, containing the goat's skull and brain, sections of entrail, peppers, secret plants, and all manner of things designed to promote virility and generally to put hair on your chest.

Several cavers had watched his preparations. Mr. Stephenson's delight at their obvious squeamishness reminded me of the time my grandmother, who lived out her life on small farms in southern Illinois, made squirrel's head stew for two high school friends I had brought up from Florida. She had discussed the gustatory merits of squirrel tongue and brain until both turned green and stumbled into the yard. My grandmother and other rural ancestors had a lot in common with the people of the Cockpits, I realized. All were experts in making do with what was at hand; all could differentiate plants and their uses the way my high school friends distinguished rock guitarists. As a teenager, I tried to fit in with my farm relatives, without much success. I made a horrible mess of butchering chickens, and, although I was a crack shot when it came to skeet or tin cans, I never managed to kill squirrel or quail.

A full moon rose from the silhouetted jungle. My reverie was interrupted by a sudden shout from behind: "Here, Michael!" I jumped as though struck by a machete, scattering loose firewood down the steep hillside. It was Minocal Stephenson, holding a steaming tin cup. "Here, you must try mannish water. It is very good for you."

I politely took a drink, and smiled. It tasted like a spicy beef broth, except for floating pieces of rubbery stuff, which had no discernible taste but which I tried to avoid just the same. When Mr. Stephenson turned to offer Ron Canter a cup, I filtered out the larger gobbets with my teeth, and tossed these to the dog. My chest was hairy enough as it was.

In the following days, we targeted horizontal entrances at the edge of the plateau, searching for springs that could reveal deep river systems. Each black gape in the limestone bluffs seemed the way in, the portal to one of the greatest caves in the hemisphere. It was under us, somewhere. It had to be. Where else could the water go?

But by the middle of the second week, the horizontal caves had all ended abruptly. I asked to join the smaller vertical team. The next day they were to drop a shaft that had been on everyone's mind since 1985, a jungle pit so deep that its first explorers had run out of rope: Minocal's Glory Hole.

Ed Devine and Ray Keeler had first entered the pit in 1985

while ridge-walking—following limestone outcrops—with DiTonto and Mr. Stephenson. They estimated the depth of the entrance shaft at 150 feet, and were surprised when it turned it out to be deeper. Only a foot of slack from their 200-foot rope—which they had hung from a second line stretched across the wide mouth—rested on the bottom. Devine secured the slack to a rock with a length of webbing to prevent the rope from springing out of reach whenever he took his weight off of it.

Offset from the room at the base of the entrance shaft was a second drop. The two had carried only a 24-foot cable ladder and some webbing down with them, but they were able to climb down the first 20 feet of the second pit to the top of a break-down choke, a jumble of boulders wedged in the shaft. After carefully testing the footing, they attached the top of the steel ladder to a solid-looking rock and unrolled it. That put them within eight feet of the floor, which they reached via a hastily tied *étrier*, or webbing ladder. They quickly found a third pit, whose depth they could only guess at. Devine and Keeler had left the cave; no one had been back since. I was to help find where the third drop went.

On Wednesday morning, five of us went through the now familiar routine of piling into the sweltering car. Instead of heading through Quick Step we drove uphill, north on the limestone highway. The single lane degenerated from a graded surface to a jagged, bone-jarring path and then to twin ruts which gave out in a grassy clearing. Beyond us were unbroken miles of bush, the rolling green sea of the Cockpits into which we were about to plunge.

Somehow quieter, more subdued than when en route to other caves, Miles Drake, Chip and Jenny Clark, Russ Rhoads, John Stephenson, and I hiked through the steep terrain. We discovered that a mile in the central Cockpits was like ten anywhere else. Even with the expert work of John's machete, the bush was so thick that each of us could see no farther than the caver immediately in front. Walking became a personal challenge. I was continually struggling uphill or trying to keep from falling down. It was like climbing an endless series of huge, vine-covered ramps. The vegetation carpet hid a ready supply of loose rocks—some the size of bowling balls—that seemed hungry for weak Yankee ankles. Every blow of the machete shook loose dozens of chiggers and ticks, and we were forced to stop every five minutes to brush each other off. This was genuine Saturday-matinee jungle. I wished I were watching it from an air-conditioned seat, munching popcorn and Gummi Bears.

The hike was made all the more frustrating by the way our teenage guide flew through the bush ahead of me. Collin's younger brother moved like a Valley girl in a new mall, stopping only to give me looks that said: Come on, no one can be *that* slow. I shrugged and grinned as if to say: I don't know why *those* guys are so slow either. Luckily, none of the others noticed these exchanges. Exotic pollens slapped my face. My hay fever knew no bounds.

After more than an hour of grunting, stumbling, and sneezing, we approached a clearing perhaps ten yards in diameter. There were no trees because there was no land, just a bottomless black hole.

I was sweating from the hike, but no matter how many pits I descend, the first glimpse of one always gives me chills. One look at that yawning blackness reminds me that this is serious stuff. One bad knot or unlocked carabiner can mean the equivalent of a twenty-story fall.

As we uncoiled our ropes, Drake tossed a rock into the chasm. It fell for what seemed forever before a muffled crash echoed like distant thunder from below. We rigged the pit using a modified Tyrolean highline—hanging our main line from a horizontal piece stretched between two trees at opposite sides of the pit. This kept the rope from being slashed by jagged rocks when our weight pulled it against the lip. Since I was the quickest one into my harness, I won the honor of the first rappel.

A locking carabiner secured my rappel rack—a friction device designed to control the speed of a long rope descent—

to my seat harness. My rack was essentially a two-foot rod of quarter-inch steel, bent into an inverted U, its parallel halves bridged by sliding aluminum nubs. I carefully threaded the eleven-millimeter nylon rope through these, locking each crossbar into place.

I eased back to the lip, inhaled, and stepped backward over the edge. For a brief instant, I felt the familiar but unnerving sensation of falling as my harness and buckles snatched up less than an inch of slack before tightening firmly against the rope. I released tension and began to slide gently downward. The mossy walls seemed to spin as the twisting rope threaded through the rack. I sped up, rope squealing through the bars like tires on sand. Overhead, daylight became a bright, shrinking hole. As in many pits, the entrance was the narrowest spot; the darkening stone walls moved away from me as I descended. Finally, I saw the slack end of the rope resting on the floor below. It looked like a jumble of string thrown across pebbles, but the pebbles grew to boulders as the ground rose to meet me. Soon I was standing where only Devine and Keeler had stood before.

"Off rope!" I shouted, my voice echoing through the shaft to the cavers 200 feet up.

"Okay!" came the standard reply.

As the next caver racked in, I began walking about the rock-strewn chamber, examining it in the blue twilight that filtered from the surface. The room was about 40 by 80 feet. Surprisingly, it was full of life. Small frogs clustered around a puddle. In a wall fissure I saw what I took to be a snake—very rare in Jamaica—but on closer examination it proved to be a ten-inch black millipede. Wiry cave crickets scuttled over every surface. Against one wall lay a shadow darker than the others: the second pit.

It seemed to take hours for the rest of the group to join me; Chip Clark was photographing the pit as he descended, and nothing is so slow as a cave photographer. When we were all together again, we decided that Drake, Rhoads, and I would push downward, while the Clarks took additional pictures.

John Stephenson remained above, making sure that no Cockpit farmer would come home that night shouting "Mama! Looka dis fine long rope me find a-bush."

We had rigged the main drop with a 300-foot line, so that we would have enough slack to deliver us to the bottom of the second drop. I carried a 150-footer with which we would rig the third. The three of us descended the second drop without difficulty. After a few minutes of rigging, I was poised to step into the third, the pit that had halted exploration two years earlier. Again, it appeared that by luck I would be the first one down—but I realized there was more to it than luck. I had made sure that I was ready to go and standing by the rope before the other two. It hadn't happened accidentally.

Unwritten etiquette requires members of a push team to rotate leads, to take turns in the discovery of new passage. In the rare cases where a single caver is shown preferential treatment, it's usually because that caver is the most experienced or has done the most previous work in the particular system. I hadn't spent a fraction of Miles Drake's time underground, and this was my first trip to the Cockpits: I had no business leading into every drop in this cave. But I had read of Minocal's Glory Hole in the NSS News eighteen months earlier, and from that moment it had stirred my imagination. I was willing to push the ethics of the situation, to indulge in a bit of bad form for a once-in-a-lifetime chance. Drake and Rhoads seemed willing to let me.

I rappeled 40 feet to a boulder, bounced off that, and dropped another 20 feet into a sloping room. It was no more than 15 feet across at its widest point. Several dun-colored stalactites hung from the slanted ceiling. I counted three horizontal leads, none of them bigger than the underside of a desk. I called for the other two to come on down.

We each pushed a crawlway, wanting this to be the day, wanting Glory Hole to be the key to a vast underworld. Time for the expedition was running out—we were ready *now*. So we tore the tight, muddy passage from the cave, shined light in all its ugly recesses. But the cave refused to cooperate. I heard Drake rearranging rocks in a parallel passage. He sounded as if he had reached the bitter end.

"What have you got?" I shouted, my voice traveling through the stone maze that separated us.

He grunted and slid what sounded like a small truck out of his way. "It's pretty grim," he said. "There's a little room ahead of me, but there's a lot of loose junk in here. Seems pretty dead. What about you?"

I looked at the crawlway ahead, a muddy tube beneath a ceiling of chalky, unstable boulders. "It goes, at least another ten feet, then it looks like it makes a ninety-degree turn to the left. Hang on a minute." I slid forward, trying not to touch and possibly disturb the loose ceiling. I reached the corner and looked left. "It drops down about three feet into a six-foot-diameter chamber," I shouted.

"Mumphrobble gwarn . . . gaggen?" he replied faintly. The intervening limestone was swallowing and distorting sound.

"What?" I shouted, a bit louder.

In a faint, tinny voice that could have come over a Jamaican long-distance line, Miles answered, "Say! Again! Can! Not! Hear! You! Speak! Slowly!"

I turned to shout in the direction from which it seemed his voice had come—not behind me, but through a five-inch hole ahead and to the right. I took a deep breath. "I! Have! A! Small! Room! Stay! There! I! Will! Check! It!"

A distant "Go! Ahead!" snaked its way through the break-down. I dropped into the muddy pocket. The room held no obvious leads. One side was blocked by a wall of bright red mud. A faint breeze came from a small hole at the top of the wall. I shoved my hand into it, and a chunk of mud the size of a cinder block fell someplace beyond, rolling and thumping.

Bracing my back against a boulder, I began kicking down sections of wall the size and consistency of forty-pound lumps of potter's clay. I leaned through the gap and saw a chimney about a yard wide, twelve feet deep. "I've! Got! A! Chimney!" I hollered, wondering if Drake was still within earshot. "I! Will! Check! It!"

"Fine by me," he calmly replied, suddenly close by. I looked into the crawlway and saw the flame of his lamp.

"How'd you get here?" I asked.

"I just dug my way in a big circle. None of this stuff seems to be going anywhere."

"How's Russ doing?"

"He's sitting at the bottom of the pit, waiting for us. The thing he checked went, oh, maybe five feet. If that."

"I think I've got some airflow here."

"Really?"

"Hang on, I'll find out for sure." I slithered through the broken wall into the slick, muddy throat. Bracing my feet on opposite sides to control my speed, I slid to the bottom. My crash landing was cushioned by the half dozen unsculpted busts I had kicked down moments before. There *was* airflow. I pulled off a mud-caked glove and wet my finger to trace the breeze. It emanated from a rocky crack less than six inches across. More cave was here, but it was too small to follow. Minocal's Glory Hole had become yet another DBP on the topo map, a dead bottom pit. I reported the depressing news to Drake, and heard him crawling back to the room where Rhoads waited.

Covered with two inches of mud, I began the gooey climb out, kicking footholds into the claylike wall with the toe of my boot. I slipped six inches for every foot of height I gained. I wondered if my eagerness to be first had jinxed the trip, had prompted the cave to hide an obvious 500-foot, formation-draped drop into monster borehole. This far below the surface, such superstition seemed as likely a proposition as a muggy jungle sitting overhead. Some Cockpits residents believe duppies live in limestone pits, evil spirits that malicious obeah men summon from the shafts in midnight ceremonies. I could imagine those spirits now, laughing as I struggled up the slick chimney. *Looka dis fool buckra. 'Im t'ink 'im find somet'ing. Find 'eself we supper, 'im not tek c'yare.*

Panting, I reached the broken wall and fell into the chamber. The voices in my head vanished as I crawled back to the bottom of the third pit, saw I was not alone after all. Rhoads had already gone up. Drake was clipping his ascenders onto the rope. By the time all five of us stood at the bottom of the entrance drop, I was exhausted and muttering. I looked at my watch and was surprised to see that somewhere up there it was 7 P.M. I had no idea so much time had passed. Ahead of us we still had the long climb out, then the job of derigging the pit, stowing gear, and hiking through the bush in the dark—I knew it would be well after midnight before our car crept into Quick Step. Any duppies summoned from the cave tonight would reach the village well ahead us. I was hungry, thirsty, and caked with mud, dreading the climb and hike. And yet I felt a strange elation. I had been the first human to touch the bottom of Minocal's Glory Hole. True, it had turned out to be a DBP, no different from a dozen others. But I had reached the lowest point, first and alone.

The Clarks had set up two large flash tripods to illuminate the pit as Rhoads climbed. Chip had also given him a flash-gun made from a five-cell flashlight to fire from the rope. Rhoads was hanging about thirty feet above the floor, screwing in a bulb, when I shouted, "Yo! Hold up a minute."

"What is it?" he asked.

"Ain't it great?" I hollered, raising both arms to gesture at the huge pit that held us. "Ain't this what we came here for?"

He answered with some obscenity I couldn't quite catch. But I thought I could see by his smile that he felt it too—whatever the discomforts, all three of us had been where no one had been before and where no one was likely to go again for a long, long time. This one wasn't the dream cave, but it was ours, and we felt that much closer to the waiting rivers beneath the Cockpit.

When we reached camp at 2 A.M., the "nine-night"—the wake across the street—was just warming up. Over a late supper and Appleton overproof we discovered that the day's other exploration group had enjoyed considerably better luck. Falling Cave, near Aberdeen and Doc's Place, contained a flowing river, the first anyone had seen in the Cockpits. Generally speaking, a lot of moving water means a lot of passage, and this rule held in Falling. On the first trip, DiTonto, Ron Canter, Fred Grady, and Jack Kehoe had mapped a half mile of walking cave with no end in sight. DiTonto said the cave was "going north like gangbusters" toward the interior of the plateau.

The remaining three days of the expedition were spent pushing Falling. In places we were able to walk along the bank of the river that had carved the cave, but often we waded to our necks. In the States such wet passage would have required thick wet suits. In Jamaica, the 72° F water was a delight. We relaxed in sparkling tubs created by yard-high mineral deposits called rimstone dams.

Once again I felt virgin mud between my fingers, as Grady, Mark Thompson, and I surveyed dry side leads above the main passage. In addition to glittery mud and milky calcite formations, a pool in one tunnel revealed a surface crayfish (as opposed to the blind albino species indigenous to caves) well over a foot long. His claws looked like something from the prop room of a Tokyo movie studio. I had to crawl scant inches above him to continue mapping, and did so a bit nervously.

When I mentioned the monster later to one of the Jamaicans on the surface, he said, "Yah, mon, dem is very good eating, dem is. But dat a lickle on' you find. Down in de river bottoms dem grow like so." He held his hands a yard apart. I was glad I had run into only a "lickle" one.

I was still surveying side passage on the last day of the expedition, so I hadn't been able to visit the farthest discoveries made by the Falling push team. As we headed out of the cave, I ran into Miles Drake, who was escorting a group of four boys. The oldest couldn't have been more than twelve years old. All were barefoot and shirtless.

Curiosity had gotten the best of them, and they had miraculously managed to reach a photo team working halfway down the cave. Unhurt, they had traveled by the light of a single beer bottle half full of kerosene, a burning rag for a wick— caving by Molotov cocktail. Now they carried flashlights borrowed from the cavers they had surprised. Drake had been coming out from the back of the cave anyway, and had volunteered to take them to the surface.

As we stood in the water, he described the day's find: a steep canyon passage, only a few yards wide, rising sharply above the water, punctuated by tricky climbs and jagged rocks, unlike the rest of Falling. They had named the canyon the Meat Grinder. Drake suggested that if I hurried, I might reach the push team before they finished mapping their way out of what they had found. The water had made him cold. He was calling it a day once he saw these courageous and fool-hardy young explorers to safety.

I turned around and headed back into Falling Cave alone. As I waded through the blue stream, my lamp cast odd shadows over its surface. Tiny diamonds of reflected light danced on the damp walls. The tunnel stretched before me in an unbroken line. I splashed through a thousand feet of it before I remembered what lay ahead: the Duck, a place about a half mile into the cave where the ceiling dropped to within two inches of the water.

I had passed the spot four times previously while surveying. The water was only a yard deep at the Duck, but to reach it you had to swim across a deep pool—difficult in boots and cave gear. Once across, the best way to pass the low spot was to squat and waddle with your head tilted back, staring at the roof, so that both your nose and your lamp stayed above the water. Or, with an electric lamp and thus no need to wait for a wet flint to dry out, you could simply hold your breath, duck under, and pop through. Wet lamp or dry, it was only a foot to the place where the ceiling rose out of reach and you could walk again. The Duck was not such a hard spot, as cave sumps go.

But then I had never passed it alone. Now, as I recognized the pool in front of it, I was reluctant to leave the comfortable walking passage. All I had to do was swim a few feet, climb up a submerged bank, and zip through—less than two minutes, tops. But I couldn't seem to step into the deep water. A caver should be able to do alone anything he could do in a group, I told myself. Don Coons did a Great X through-trip alone, I recalled. So did Pete Shifflett, and he's a diabetic. I had heard of brazen solo rappels of deep pits in Mexico and TAG. Such actions are derided by some, considered dangerously foolhardy, and perhaps they are. Yet those who accomplish them are often accorded a great deal of private respect. So why was I sitting here, worried about a Mickey Mouse swim?

I stepped off of my comfortable rock, floundered across the pool until my foot hit the opposite bank, and managed to splash out my light as I clambered to a solid purchase. I sat alone in absolute darkness, a mile inside the earth, my helmet pressed against the roof. The thin elastic surface of the water wrapped around my chin. Okay, time for a backup light. I fumbled open my cave pack and groped through soggy Hershey bars, floating carbide bottles, grime. At last I felt the shape of my waterproof flashlight. Taking care not to release any gear to the flowing stream, I pulled it out, closed the pack, and pressed the switch. The Duck swung around, ten degrees left from the spot my mind had placed it in the darkness. I slid over to it, took a breath, and popped through.

"Mickey Mouse," I said to the empty room on the other side, pretending that I was shaking only from the coolness of the water. I began climbing across a low waterfall, when I heard voices ahead of me. The push team was already coming out, I was too late to see the new canyon.

I greeted the cavers as they approached, then turned and went with them back through the Duck—no problem. As we walked, they described a series of difficult climbs and loose, sharp rocks. They said the passage continued beyond the point where they had decided to quit surveying. "Have to leave something to suck people into next year's expedition," DiTonto joked.

I hadn't seen the deepest area of Falling, but I had seen deep waters and passed them, and was satisfied.

It would be up to future teams to learn whether Falling Cave led to a truly big system. But even if it ended before punching through the heart of the Cockpits, at nearly a mile of surveyed passage it was already the region's longest known cave. By the end of the trip, the 1987 Cockpits Expedition had mapped twice the passage of any previous expedition to Jamaica, a fact that later prompted the National Speleological Society to award Mike DiTonto a certificate of merit for outstanding cave exploration.

There was a great flurry of gift giving and hugging between caver and Jamaican on our last morning in the Cockpits, and for the first time on the journey (at least in public) ceremonial spliffs were passed around. Most of Quick Step turned out to see us off. Despite ubiquitous ticks and bland food, each of us was already scheming to come back on DiTonto's next team.

On June 17, 1995, I took a break from compiling my Cockpits account for this book in order to fly from Little Rock to Denver on assignment for *Sports Illustrated*. I was writing a short piece about a guy who planned to rappel off the Royal Gorge Bridge near Canon City, 1,053 feet into the Arkansas River. I had a layover in Dallas–Fort Worth and killed the time in a bookstore. I had barely begun to browse the fiction shelf when the bright yellow cover of *Rule of the Bone*, a new novel by Russell Banks, jumped out at me.

I bought the book and read it on the plane and in my Canon City motel room that night. The novel is narrated by a likable fourteen-year-old dope dealer who calls himself Bone. Bone runs away from home in upstate New York and meets I-Man, an exiled Jamaican. Together the two embark on a journey that, like the trip taken by Huck and Jim, never lacks for adventure and yet never fails to reveal deep truths about the society in which they travel, a soulless world where neither one quite belongs.

I-Man comes from Accompong—called by its real name this time—and the two eventually go there. In the chapter titled "Bone Goes Native," the narrator tends I-Man's ganja in a Cockpit bottom, meets Rubber, and undergoes a magical transformation in the Maroon Peace Cave. Bone spends most of his time in Maroon lands "sattar in the bush," because "having white strangers or any kind of outsider camped in the village was definitely not encouraged or at least that's the feeling I got." But he does see that "they had a chief and everything and even a secretary of state who were these really old guys that I saw a couple of times from a distance but never got to talk to."

When Bone describes his time-traveling, out-of-body experience in the cave, he says, "I'm remembering it now while I'm telling it so I'm like in two places at once, here and now and then and there." I read this aloud in my Colorado motel room.

Time and place really do fall away, leaving only stories behind. On the surface, I needed to get up early the next morning to meet with the rappeller and his support crew, but I was caught up in an enjoyable book and so chose to stay up late and finish it. Below the surface, I was like Bone in his vision—"this was like real and I didn't have any memory of how I got there or any plans for getting out." There is a surface world and there is a world underground. The only real one is the one you are in at the moment. The other one stops existing until you return to it.

Caves and stories and the coincidences of a chaotic life— which is to say, of any life ever lived—are good, useful paths between the two.

16

THE GATHERED
WATERS

On a clear February evening that offered a pleasant hint of spring, I sprinted through midtown Manhattan toting a bulky canvas duffel. Dodging pedestrians and double-parked cabs, I ducked into Grand Central Station at Forty-second Street, barely making the 7:10 Hudson Line, Metro-North. As the train lurched northward, I moved through the cars searching for a seat. The climbing gear in my bag clanked and rattled. I felt suspicious eyes on my ragged jeans and flannel shirt, both of which bore dull brown stains from dozens of muddy caves. I had come from the New York Public Library, where I had attended a lecture on travel writing given by Ian Frazier. I was bound for Ossining, where I planned to meet some cavers for the exploration of an urban ruin.

The year was 1990, and I was thirty years old.

Since becoming involved with the Northern New Jersey Grotto in 1986, I had joined its members in expeditions to China, Mexico, Jamaica, and elsewhere. Between trips in 1989, several of us began puttering about a 150-year-old aqueduct that has been sealed and largely abandoned for most of this century. In that time, it has developed aspects of a natural cave: stalactites, stalagmites, bat colonies, natural springs, streams, and sumps. Through dozens of trips, most of them clandestine, I had traversed over twenty miles of the brick-and-marble structure, slogging beneath the most desolate sections of the Bronx and the ritziest Westchester neighborhoods.

After the lecture, I had tarried at a display describing a restoration project then underway in Bryant Park, behind the main library. A plastic panel held a photograph of the Murray Hill Reservoir, built in 1841, which once covered the present sites of park and building. In the photo, a frocked pedestrian crosses Forty-second Street toward the camera, while a buggy blurs down Fifth Avenue and past the elevated tank, a massive masonry structure modeled after the base of an Egyptian pyramid. The reservoir—parts of which were incorporated into the library's foundation—was designed by John Bloomfield Jervis. He was, I knew, the same pioneering engineer and architect who surveyed the route of the Hudson Line upon which I rode.

The bright electric cars rattled north through Yonkers, Hastings-on-Hudson, and Dobbs Ferry, disgorging commuters at every stop. I envisioned Jervis and his crew working through these wooded river towns in 1849. He was chief engineer and a founding director of the Hudson River Railroad; the latter position made him a target of a citizens' group opposed to any development that might spoil the view. With the Utilitarian enthusiasm of the age, Jervis had argued that "the shores washed by the river would be protected by walls of the railway; and the trees, no longer undermined and thrown down by the river, would grow more beautiful; and the railway thus combining works of art with those of nature would improve the scenery." Whether or not his railroad had added anything to nature, the view from my seat was pleasing. The Palisades stood in dark relief against a winking backdrop of stars and aircraft. Nyack glowed dimly to the north. Breezes swirled patterns across the black water.

Near the Tappan Zee, a lighted mast swayed slightly in the chop. I imagined it as a steamboat's stack. Jervis could not have helped but watch the heavy steam traffic, his chief competition, with each passing day of railroad construction. The Hudson Line must have offered the fifty-four-year-old man an element of nostalgia. He had spent an earlier decade, from 1836 to 1846, toiling just a few hundred feet inland, planning and supervising an entirely different sort of line. This other route—which, like the railroad, still parallels the Hudson exactly as Jervis laid it out—was the Old Croton Aqueduct, a crumbling architectural masterpiece hailed as a marvel of the modern world when it opened on October 14, 1842.

It was where I was headed.

An oval conduit of hand-laid brick and mortised stone, the Old Croton winds thirty-eight miles from upper Westchester to Central Park. It abuts the grounds of vast estates, the parking lots of corporate headquarters, and dozens of suburban backyards. It snakes unnoticed beneath burned-out alleys of the Bronx, crack streets of Spanish Harlem, and forty-five blocks of Amsterdam Avenue. It descends thirteen and one-half inches per mile.

Jervis was offered the position of chief engineer of the city's first aqueduct only after the Board of Water Commissioners fired the original architect, Major David Douglass, for incompetence. The appointment led the self-taught, intensely religious and private man into the public eye, where he became the recognized Father of American Engineering. For decades, tourists crowded the balustrades and walkways above his great achievement, which was celebrated in guidebooks as New York's symbol of industry and innovation—until surpassed by a more visible symbol, the Brooklyn Bridge, in 1883.

In its day, Croton water slaked the thirst of Boss Tweed and Mark Twain, of Cornelius Vanderbilt and Jumbo the elephant, of presidents and kings and the residents of Sing Sing. It filled the boilers of the ironclad *Monitor*, the ill-fated *Central America*. It spun the turbines of the Edison Illumination Company and of countless callous sweatshops. It drove the pistons of the Ninth Avenue Elevated. It extinguished fires. It splashed the sweltering childhood streets of five generations. Without it, the population of such a dry and drought-prone island could never have grown northward, could not have accommodated wave upon wave of immigration.

Between 1842 and 1890, the Old Croton served as Manhattan's principal water source. The $12 million tunnel crossed the Harlem River at High Bridge, bringing up to 72 million gallons daily to a receiving reservoir in Central Park. From there, it was piped into the Murray Hill tank for distribution. The ready supply planted the false notion of free water in the collective mind of the city; it inaugurated an enduring policy of watershed acquisition. At its opening, the Old Croton Aqueduct was the most expensive public works project undertaken by any government since ancient Rome. It was expected to meet all of New York's water needs for centuries. After less than fifty years of operation, it had become obsolete.

In 1890, the Old Croton was supplanted by the longer, wider, deeper New Croton Aqueduct. Three decades later, the Catskill system reduced the original's reserve status to third string. With the gradual opening of the Delaware system in the 1950s, the Old Croton's flow was cut to a trickle. In 1955, the city sealed it south of Yonkers. The headgates were closed in 1965. As part of a 1968 "conservation" effort headed by Winthrop Rockefeller, a hundred-foot section of the aqueduct was destroyed in order to make room for State Highway 117, a bypass routing traffic around the Rockefeller preserve.

The surface above the conduit north of the Bronx became the nation's longest and narrowest state park, immediately popular with suburban hikers and joggers. The tunnel's interior remained more or less intact. Sometime after the close of the present century, work will be completed on New York City Water Tunnel Number 3, proclaimed as "the largest construction project ever undertaken by the City of New York." Even then, much of the Old Croton will be maintained as a backup of last resort. Although "maintained" may be too strong a word.

The city, state, and municipal agencies that claim overlapping control of the tunnel's future remain, by and large, ignorant of its present condition. Short sections at the far northern and southern ends of the line were called back into modified service in 1990, and again deliver water to New Yorkers. Every summer weekend, a restored two-hundred-foot strip in downtown Ossining is opened to tourists. In 1991, a water tower built into the system at High Bridge was restored as a New York historic landmark by the city Parks Department. Despite such activity, as much as half of the thirty-five miles of surviving aqueduct has seen no official visitation in decades.

The dozen or so engineers and administrators nominally in charge would be surprised to learn, for instance, that the Old Croton is home to the largest concentration of the bat *Pipistrellus subflavus* observed to date in the state of New York. They probably don't know that the tunnel's arched and rock-ribbed ceilings bristle with stalactites, helictites, and soda straws superior in length and clarity to any found in the state's natural caves. While some authorities have in fact acknowledged that the Old Croton carries a shallow river of polluted ground seepage, they were certainly unaware, on that agreeable February evening in 1990, that I would be slogging through it in less than an hour.

The train reached the Ossining platform. I wrestled my duffel through the automated doors and walked through a nearly empty commuter parking lot. My instructions were to meet Ian Baren, Tom Stockert, and the Guru in "whatever bar is closest to the Ossining station." On other subterranean missions, I managed to find these three in Guangzhou, Budapest, and San Luis Potosí. I knew them to be competent, quirky, and prone to lateness.

A red neon glow led me across the parking lot to the Waterfront, a Jamaican grill, where a cooler displayed bottles of Red Stripe, Dragon Stout, and Desnoe and Geddes Ginger Beer. A wire rack bulged with assorted patties, Jamaican versions of the British meat pie. Jerk pork and chicken appeared prominently on a chalk menu, along with the curry goat special. From a back room came the familiar whump of reggae played through a blown speaker, and in some unseen place a woman scolded a petulant child in sharp patois. I was momentarily brought back to the Cockpits. It seemed an auspicious beginning to the night's activities.

Presumably off-duty guards from Sing Sing, a short walk away, crowded barstools and most of the Formica booths. I spotted Ian

Baren alone at a corner table, poring over a spiral-bound Westchester street atlas, tracing the route of the aqueduct in felt-tip highlighter. I had first met Ian, a twenty-eight-year-old Westchester native, while caving in South China in 1988, on an expedition sponsored by the Cave Research Foundation, the NSS, and *National Geographic*. After receiving his bachelor's in Chinese language and literature from Hobart College in the mid-1980s, Ian had worked for an import-export company in Hong Kong. (He once described his job there: "I go to little Chinese villages and buy ceramic items. We drill holes in Hong Kong, then ship them to Trenton, New Jersey. I think they get made into lamps.") Ian had proved an optimal choice as translator for the first American caving expedition in China. Besides speaking a flawless Mandarin, he had caved in college with James Wells (son of pioneering cave diver Oliver Wells and great-grandson of author H.G.). Ian was unusually urbane for a caver. He dressed well. Even in old clothes and muddy boots, he looked almost preppy.

I carried two Dragons to the table. Lifting a bottle of the sweet stout, Ian smiled and said in mock Oriental bureaucratese, "Ah, comrade, here is drinking toast to glorious underground explorations in spirit of mutual cooperation for betterment of East-West friendship. May you eat bitter. Before explorations, we must be having brief social chat."

"Yah, mon," I answered.

By chance rather than design, Ian had returned to Katonah to work in a family architectural hardware business just a few months before the tanks rolled into Tiananmen Square. He soon became active in both local cave clubs, the Met Grotto and the NNJG. Having grown up on the shore of the Croton Reservoir, Ian held a long-standing interest in the New York water system. Not long after an initial "breakthrough" trip in August 1989, he had become one of the more prolific tunnelers.

Tom Stockert, a fiber optics engineer at a Rutgers lab, had invited his brother Craig up from central Jersey for the trip, Ian said. He expected them in the next half hour. "God knows when the Guru will show up," he added.

The bar was warm. Ian unbuttoned his flannel shirt to reveal a T-shirt that bore the phrase "Using Fully Automatic Weapon." This was the motto of a Hong Kong gun club with which Ian had fraternized. He once told me that the club made regular runs to a mainland Army base, where, for a very reasonable fee, a certain colonel allowed members to fire Chinese antitank guns and heavy machine guns.

While we waited for the Guru and the Stockert brothers, I tried some of the curry goat. The hot, fatty dish came with rice and "peas," Jamaican red beans. I ordered a second Dragon Stout with the meal, and also water. I made it a point to drink a glass or two of tap water whenever in Ossining.

In 1987, the village contracted with the New York City Bureau of Water Supply to recommission two miles of the Old Croton Aqueduct, between the New Croton Dam and the town waterworks. Ossining had disconnected from the Croton system in 1888, after establishing its own small reservoir. Back then, the town was still called Sing Sing. The name change was brought about in 1901 by several local industries. Product labels proclaiming "Made in Sing Sing" had not been a boon to sales at a time when the entire nation was aware of the big house located "up the river."

By the 1980s, a century of growth—residential, industrial, and penal—forced Ossining to find a second water source. The city planned a small filtration plant atop the original tunnel and, inside, a five-foot-thick concrete plug to prevent any water from flowing downstream of the new outlet. An Ossining engineer walked the upper Old Croton in an afternoon, and declared it sound between dam and waterworks. Anything south of that point was of little concern. The plug and filtration plant were finished in late 1988; headgates that had been shut for decades were opened a year later.

Half of Ossining's water now comes through the Old Croton. Although I had no way of telling which half was the source of the moment, I preferred to believe that the sparkling beverage before me had traveled the bricks of Jervis' masterpiece. I savored a draught of history, then rose to seek the water's source. The Stockerts had arrived at last, with the Guru in tow.

The geology that makes Manhattan water poor keeps it cave poor as well. The island is underlain by some of the nation's oldest, hardest, most impermeable rock. South of a fault line running roughly from Morningside Heights through Yorkville, the principal formation is Manhattan schist. A thick hodge-podge of micaceous stone, it's great stuff for anchoring sky-scrapers, but not so good at holding water. What scant moisture does flow into and through the schist mixes en route with alluvial silt to become a brownish, noisome tea. In the eigh-teenth century, the burly toughs who delivered water from New York's most reliable spring were known as Tea Water Men. Their name derived both from the suspicious cast of their product and from the fact it was unfit for consumption straight. Brewed tea and beer were the drinks of the day because few could stomach the water.

Much of the underlying formation north and east of Cen-tral Park, beyond the schist, is limestone, the rock W. H. Auden rightly associated with "a secret system of caves and conduits," with "springs that spurt out everywhere with a chuckle." The world's largest caves and springs always occur within limestone, for chemical reasons. Rainwater and sulfur-bearing groundwater—both naturally acidic—dissolve ever widening channels in the calcite-rich stone. The surrounding undissolved portions remain structurally sound. Given time and a fairly constant overhead climate, small chambers can expand to the dimensions of Shea Stadium.

Yet no Carlsbad lies beneath 125th Street because the city's limestone is the Inwood, compacted remains of a seabed some two billion years old. This Precambrian layer has been buried deeply and often, most recently by Ice Age glaciers. It is packed harder than some granites. History records a few small wells of more or less potable water in early Harlem, but the tiny chan-nels that fed them were unclean and sluggish.

In order to find caves large enough to stand in, the hundred or so members of the region's two cave clubs must drive two hours west or four hours north. Even then, only three caves within a 200-mile radius of the city reach sufficient length to occupy experienced explorers for a full day. The largest and most complex—McFail's, west of Albany—is off-limits during the winter, when its sensitive bat population is in hibernation.

Another interesting cave, Single X, is frequently closed by the farmer who owns it. He fears a lawsuit, or at least bad press, should some hapless caver expire beneath his property. His fear is fueled by knowledge: To reach the main passage of Single X, one crawls 400 feet against the current of a stream that maintains a hypothermia-inducing 45° F temperature year-round. Airspace above the water ranges from three to ten inches, unless there is a sudden, heavy rain—which reduces airspace to zero.

That leaves Surprise Cave, near Port Jervis, another winter bat hibernaculum. Vandals have caused such severe damage to Surprise's formations that NNJG members have gated the cave at the request of the state agency that owns it. Access to the key is limited to a few summer months. Then the cave can become so crowded with Scouts, explorer clubs, and other organized novices that on Saturday afternoons the main passage resembles a suburban mall.

But local cavers will go to great lengths to get underground. In 1988, for example, a handful of NNJG members caved in Alabama, Arizona, British Columbia, Georgia, Jamaica, Mexicos New and Old, South China, South Dakota, Spain, Tennessee, Virginia, West Virginia, and Wyoming. Urban cavers routinely sacrificed time and money to their unlikely passion, not to mention occasional careers and marriages. The discovery of a little-known, multimile subterranean system less than ten minutes from the George Washington Bridge—not only replete with formations and bats but large enough to allow one to walk upright—had proved more or less irresistible, in spite of the cave's questionable speleogenesis.

Irresistible at least to the Guru and company.

✻   ✻   ✻

By 1990, maps and a year of close investigation had revealed perhaps two dozen portals between the Old Croton and the outside world. Only a few were of human proportion. Entry could be gained through certain manhole covers on Amsterdam Avenue and in the Bronx and Yonkers. With appropriate keys and permissions, one might stroll down a lighted stairway through the Ossining weir house and directly into the "tourist" tube. With further keys and more complex permissions, one could proceed beyond the locked gates at either end of the raised aluminum trail and into unrestored "wild" passages, where petrochemicals leaked into the tunnel from several home fuel-oil tanks and perhaps from the storage tanks of nearby service stations. The gas smell was strongest—and its attendant glistening rainbow of oil-soaked mud formations the thickest—near a sixteen-inch iron pipe that took off for Sing Sing. I once looked down the filthy tube and tried to imagine a prisoner desperate enough to use it as an escape route. If such a convict somehow made it uphill through the thousand feet of sludge and into the tunnel, I would call that punishment enough.

A few miles below Ossining lies a quarter-mile segment blocked by water to the north and a brick wall to the south. This section can be accessed only by climbing, and then rappelling into, a five-foot-wide, thirty-foot-tall stone ventilator shaft. South of the Pit Entrance is the northern terminus of the longest continuous section of the Old Croton, which extends for fourteen uninterrupted miles. Although we talked of organizing a "death march," seeing these fourteen miles in one uninterrupted slog, in practice we tended toward trips of three to four hours and two to four miles.

To reach the Hibernaculum entrance, you must chop your way through thick brush at the base of a wooded bluff below the aqueduct. A thirty-inch-diameter hole in the side of a low wall reveals a winding pipe, made of brick in some places and iron in others. You are to crawl three hundred feet uphill inside this. It was designed to carry waste water from the aqueduct, but more recently it has served as a den for a long series of small animals. Past incumbents lie in state. Entering the Hibernaculum means taking, on hands and knees, a brief paleontological tour of rural Westchester.

I dropped to all fours and fell in behind Tom, for the Hibernaculum was the section we had chosen to enter that February night. Our plan was to walk south for three miles, from the point where the runoff pipe entered the system to a manhole cover that would spill us into an office complex. After leaving the Waterfront, we had stationed Ian's car near the intended exit; the others followed in the Guru's truck. Ian and I piled into the truck, and the five of us drove upstream to the parking spot nearest the crawlway. It was exactly like staging vehicles for a canoe run.

The Guru is Bob Cohen, a Bronx native who works as an audiovisual technician at a small city college. Bob holds the elected title of Guru—an office created especially for him—in both local grottoes. Bearded and dark, he delights in showing off his heavy Bronx accent, his odd sense of humor, and his very large four-wheel-drive truck. He is fond of vegetable stir-fry and carries in his truck a wok and gas stove to facilitate impromptu cookouts. His physical appearance might best be summed up by the image associated with the words "mad bomber."

The pipe angled upward at a grade of about twenty-five degrees. Flakes of iron rust crunched beneath my gloves. I was thankful that I remembered kneepads. Ahead of me, Tom dislodged a bouncing thing that resolved into a rusted can, one dating from a time when tin cans were actually made of tin. The odd acoustics amplified the rattling can into a ricocheting bullet. *Ping, booing, pingyang.* The iron pipe ran straight and true. Where builders had found it necessary to bend the line, they had used brick. Odd-shaped wedges were precisely inserted between rows of regular brick to pivot the tube up, down, left, or right as required. Near the upper end of the passage, a smaller pipe joined the main line in a sweeping brick splice. The symmetry and evident forethought of this joint, the sheer practical math, made me think of flying buttresses, Gothic spires.

After ten minutes of crawling, I stood at last in a small marble chamber. From there, I climbed down a ten-foot canted timber into the Old Croton Aqueduct. Precisely laid bricks stretched in rows before me, somewhat like the cross section of limestone in an illustrated geology textbook. The parallel walls drew together in an overhead arch, its apex eight or nine feet above the submerged floor. The passage was approximately eight feet wide.

We walked south. Periodic ropes and mats of tree roots had grown through the mortar and pried apart brickwork. Some of these roots had rotted away, and through the holes left behind tiny jets of groundwater spurted into the aqueduct. When I plugged two springs with my fingers, another leak shot with increased pressure several feet away. I removed my fingers; all three returned to the same level. Similar spouts appeared every few yards. An army of Dutch boys could not have saved this dam. A few lower holes must have drawn water off, for the depth varied by up to a foot as we moved along.

A shadowy pipistrelle darted about the mist, the shrill clicks of its echolocation seeming to curse our intrusion. Perhaps in response to our presence—but more likely as a result of unusually warm weather—it had ended hibernation a few weeks early. Hundreds of others still slept, anchored to the brick. Pearls of condensation glistened on their inverted backs. The wakened bat flitted past my head and up a shaft in the ceiling twenty yards downstream. We had walked this section a month earlier with Emily Davis Mobley, a caver from upstate New York. In addition to operating Speleobooks, an extensive cave-oriented bookstore housed in a 200-year-old octagonal barn in Schoharie, Emily has led dozens of bat counts and conservation efforts. Under her guidance, we recorded 361 pipistrelles and two big brown bats. Although the pips were in hibernation, the big browns were, interestingly enough, awake and in coitus.

I paused briefly to look up the stone chimney. It was about two feet in diameter, tapering as it rose. The shift in girth made estimating its height difficult, but Craig and I guessed that it stood between 25 and 35 feet tall. Through the small circle at the top, I saw a few stars, and the hazy glow of a nearby streetlamp. There was the distant sound of a truck shifting gears, and for a moment I remembered that Highway 9 was not far away. I moved along.

Thirty minutes later, Ian and Craig stopped behind me to take photographs. I shifted from one foot to the other in the cold shin-deep water. Bob and Tom became a faint splashing, far ahead. A thin cushion of mud oozed between my boots and the hard surface underneath. The flame from my helmet lamp sparkled in tiny yellow reflections on the right-hand wall, thrown back by a curtain of translucent calcite. To my left lay an unexplained cement patch perhaps two feet square. Someone, presumably the patcher, had scratched into it his name and a date: "D. Mulligan, March 3, 1865."

Between 1835 and 1842, some 3,500 Irish masons were recruited to work on the tunnel. After the job was completed, many stayed on to work for established contractors; these formed the nexus of the Irish community that would welcome refugees from the potato famine a few years later. Anti-Irish sentiments ran high among the Knickerbockers. One local resident who leased land for a work camp was Washington Irving. In an 1840 St. Patrick's Day letter to *Knickerbocker* magazine, Irving observed:

> A colony of Patlanders have been encamped about this place all winter, forming a kind of Patsylvania in the midst of a "witherness." Whether the goblins of the Hollow, accustomed only to tolerate the neighborhood of the old Dutch families, have resented this intrusion into their solitudes by strangers of an unknown tongue, certain it is that the poor paddys have been most grievously harried for some time past, by all kind of apparitions. A waggon road cut through the woods and leading from their encampment past the haunted church and so on to certain whisky establishments has been especially beset by foul fiends, and the worthy Patlanders on their way home at night have beheld misshapen monsters whisking about their

paths, sometimes resembling men, sometimes hogs, sometimes horses, but invariably headless; which shows that they must be lineal descendants from the old goblin of the Hollow.

A drunken riot in one work camp was quashed by militia, and the anti-Irish movement gained support. When water from the tunnel first reached the city in the summer of 1842, lawyer G. T. Strong wrote, "There's nothing new in town, except the Croton Water, which is full of tadpoles and animalculae, and which moreover flows through an aqueduct which I hear was used as a necessity by all the Hibernian vagabonds who worked upon it. I shall drink no Croton for some time to come. Jehiel Post has drunk some of it and is in dreadful apprehension of breeding bullfrogs inwardly."

I killed my lamp, saving carbide during the wait. I removed a glove, stretched to touch the cool brick, and leaned against it in darkness. Although I stood fifty feet ahead of the other two, my eyes soon adjusted to the scant light of their cap lamps, reflected from around a slight bend. Subtle textures in the mortar and bulges in the brick cast long shadows over the wall. I tried to ignore the chill of the stream.

In my brief experience of that cold and difficult crawl beneath the Bighorn Mountains, the watery place aptly named the Grim Crawl of Death, I kissed a rock wall for no particular reason. I had stopped to catch my breath at a relatively tall spot where I could keep my entire head—as opposed to just my nose and one eye—above the rushing stream. The white dolomite beside me held curlicues of black chert. The fine details of black on white had been so crisp, so beautiful and unexpected, that I had leaned into the rock and kissed it. Now, recalling that moment in Wyoming, well out of sight of the others, I did the same for the rough letters of D. Mulligan's patch. I caught a whiff of mold as my lips touched the gritty cement.

To wander underground is to court fear. Common spelean features—darkness and bats, abrupt pits, hidden rivers, impossibly tight constrictions that allow some to pass but not others—lend caves a sinister romance. Cave images and anec-

dotes permeate world mythology. Similar descriptions of subterranean connection to some spiritual underworld, to an
ancient place of magic, can be found in Mayan codexes, Buddhist scrolls, Greek manuscripts, and the works of writers
from Dante Alighieri to Berke Breathed.

New York City has spawned suitably urbanized versions of
the stygian mythos. Most children, for instance, have heard
that the sewers teem with alligators. Many more imagine that
they are also home to burly, pizza-loving turtles. The green
scum half filling the Croton beneath Amsterdam Avenue is
remarkably like the river of slime Dan Aykroyd discovered in
Ghostbusters. Adults who should know better, people I consider my friends, have admitted a fascination with the gentle
mutant who sulked beneath the city a decade ago in the television series *Beauty and the Beast*.

Tunneling as I know it began in March 1989 with Bob Cohen.
We were hiking to a West Virginia pit when the Guru casually
remembered "an old brick tunnel" that he had played in as a
child. At a National Speleological Society convention the following July, in a mountain campground adjacent to the University of the South in Sewanee, Tennessee, the Guru mentioned
that he had just mountain-biked through the Bronx, checking
out the tunnel's surface. He had scouted three likely entrances
and poked his head into one.

This conversation took place as a group of us paddled inner
tubes across a small lake, en route from our convention campsite to a sauna and hot tub on the far shore. We had tied several six-packs to the largest tube. For some reason, I was
smoking a cigar and wore only a helmet and caving lamp. The
surrounding New Yorkers—clearly enthralled by the availabil-
ity of cheap fireworks in the South—were using cigars to
launch bottle rockets into the night. It was perhaps 2 A.M.

The flotilla consisted of Bob, myself, Tom Stockert, April
Elsasser (a computer programmer with *The New York Times*),
and Mike Newsome, the thirty-six-year-old vice president of a
Manhattan toy company (Ian Baren had been unable to make

the convention). All of us had caved together earlier in the day. That night, Mike, April, and I had played with BrickInHead, a rock band, before an audience of perhaps 300 convention-eers. I played bass.

"So what you're telling us is this tunnel goes," said Mike, touching his cigar to a fuse. *Sssssft.*

"Don't know for sure," said Bob. "Seems to." *Sssssft.*

"What's it—damn. Wet fuse. When you stuck your head in, how did it look?" *Sssssssft.*

"Dark and scary. Water up to your ass, who knows what's in it. And the entrance is in a neighborhood that I think would be a really good place to go if you wanted to get killed." *Sssssssft . . . ftt.* "Hey, a double."

"So I take it, then, that you propose we should do something about this situation?" *Sssssft.*

"That's why"—*sssssssft*—"I've called you all together," said the Guru.

Although Bob alone is Guru, he most effectively does the Guru bit as one-half of the team of Bob and Mike. They could fairly be called the Abbott and Costello, or at least the Ren and Stimpy, of American caving. Together they are great instigators. They spawn international expeditions and adolescent high jinks with equal fervor. That night they debated proper methods and equipment for tunneling, speculated on possible pits and life-forms. All onlookers were hooked before we reached the sauna.

Mike Newsome invented the Kawasaki Digital Electronic Guitar for Kids and the Mr. Christmas Santa Claus Band, among other things, shortly after he arrived in New York in the mid-1980s. He had spent the previous decade at one of the 1960s' few remaining communes, a 250-year-old restored plantation called the Rocks in the Shenandoah Valley of northern Virginia. He does not own a tie. I've seen him cross fifteen blocks of midtown Manhattan barefoot, in November, without showing a trace of discomfort. When not caving or inventing, Mike often relaxes in his office near Union Square by shooting multicolored lasers at an inflated tennis dome across the street, drinking ale, inhaling nitrous oxide, and dancing to a very loud stereo. Simultaneously.

A week after the convention, before I had returned from Tennessee, Bob led Mike and Tom to a manhole in the center of a tree-ringed clearing in Van Cortlandt Park. The Guru dubbed the place the Corner That Time Forgot. Their trip began at 11 p.m. Having taken great pains to remain ignorant on the legality of what they planned, the three hoped to avoid anyone who might educate them on the point.

After prizing the cover aside with a crowbar, they descended a rusty ladder fifteen feet into the tunnel. The last man paused to slide the lid shut behind him. It rang into place with a deep metallic *om* that echoed around them. But it wouldn't do to have some ill-equipped teenager tempted by a hole in the park.

They looked at the passage they had entered. Thousands upon thousands of bricks stretched north and south, merging in lines of perspective broken by occasional roots and rock formations. In nature, stalactites typically grow by one inch per century. Here, acid rain had freed relatively abundant calcite from the tunnel's mortar at a rapid rate. Delicate speleothems that appeared thousands of years old were no more than fifty. One was clumped at the end like a lion's tail; another, no more than a quarter inch in diameter, hung six feet from the ceiling.

During construction, Jervis had insisted that all bricks be laid using hydraulic cement, to guard against future leakage. On at least one occasion, he forced a subcontractor to destroy a completed section of aqueduct after an inspection tour revealed "ordinary" motar. The expensive hydraulic version was imported from France at first, until a domestic supplier was located in upstate New York. The proper grade of lime came from an underground quarry inside Howe Caverns. Ground-up bits of stalactite that had helped to build the tunnel had become natural stalactites once more.

The explorers traveled south, spotting no previous footprints in the soft silt beneath the clear water. (Two years later, tracks from that night were still plain.) After a half mile, they encountered an iron door straight out of Camelot. The shut-off valve had once slid freely along recessed slots, winched from above by hand-cranked chains. Now it was rusted firmly in place. Only six inches of clearance opened beneath it.

The three turned and walked north for two miles, eventually exiting—after a tricky climb—from another manhole, this one in a grassy area decidedly less private than the first. They emerged at 2 A.M. in the center of a busy off-ramp from Yonkers Avenue. From here, they were able, eventually, to hail a cab.

Thus began what became almost weekly ventures. I joined the second trip, from the Yonkers entrance north to a waste weir, a barnlike masonry building housing iron and wooden valves. Rugged sluice gates, made of hickory or some other pale hardwood, were held together by tightly fitted pegs. Attached to the top of one gate was what could have been the anchor chain of a wrecked galleon. From the edge of another hung a two-foot rope of gray rubber, thick as a man's arm. This dangling remainder of what was once a watertight seal had the heft of soft lead. It felt far more substantial than its modern, more pliable equivalent, tangibly a substance from another time. Its age hung heavy in my hand. I remember gently lowering it back against the wood where it had been.

The following week, aided by three hydraulic jacks, the three original explorers passed under the door that had blocked southern travel. That night, they discovered some of the most profuse calcite decoration in the state, somewhere below the South Bronx. Beneath stone overpasses on older parkways one can occasionally see soda straws several inches long. A soda straw found in the tunnel that night was nearly eight feet long. Two others were woven into a complex chain, interconnected by horizontal strands known as helictites. A prominent cave geologist who later saw a photo of the chain formation claimed to have encountered something like it only once before, in a remote passage of Lechuguilla Cave.

The decorated passage ended at the narrow, steep opening of an inverted siphon where the tunnel enters High Bridge. To explore the mud-lined 24-foot siphon pipe, Mike and Tom later constructed the Slime Sled, a sort of mechanic's creeper on outsized, angled wheels. They attached a rope fitting to the back of the sled, which would allow the explorer to be hauled safely back up the slick crawlway.

On my second tunnel trip, Mike, Ian, and I explored north into Irvington, where NYNEX telephone cables had been laid along two miles of the aqueduct. Every few hundred feet, the cables passed through local switching stations. These poorly constructed blockhouses, perhaps ten feet square, protruded halfway into the tunnel. Throughout the 1970s, original brickwork had been blasted away to accommodate them. Bright yellow ropes and unconnected wires poked from holes in the pasty white walls. Chunks of brick rubble lay scattered on the floor. Jagged borders of torn brick framed each station like a ragged mouth. There were twenty-four in all.

At first glance these additions appeared built of concrete block. But the substance had the feel of wet cardboard, yielding easily to the touch. It seemed unlikely to support its own weight, let alone the bulging barriers into which it had been laid. Mike thrust his head through a wall of it and said, in his best Jack Nicholson, "Here's Johnny." Each block of the chalky stuff bore, in raised lettering, the brand name Pyrobar. In smaller print beneath this a boldface legend announced: APPROVED FOR USE IN NEW YORK CITY.

Open any New York history or guidebook published between 1845 and 1900 and you will find several pages devoted to the great Croton Celebration of October 14, 1842. In *Leslie's History of the Greater New York* (1898), Daniel Van Pelt wrote, "The city famous for processions since the days of the 'Federal Ship Hamilton' in 1788, organized one for this day which put all the former ones to the blush." Or in *History of the City of New York (Illustrated)* (1877), Mrs. Martha J. Lamb noted, "While parading the streets, the rejoicing multitudes were suddenly greeted with the opening of the beautiful fountains, and wildest enthusiasm prevailed."

Stephen Allen, the former mayor whose descendant Sarah married my writing professor William Price Fox, recorded in his diary that "not less than 20,000 persons walked in the ranks. They consisted of nearly all the uniformed companies of the Militia; the firemen; the butchers handsomely mounted; the numerous charitable institutions of this city, Brooklyn and Jersey City." The ever acerbic Philip Hone entered in his journal, "It is astonishing how popular the introduction of water is among all classes of our citizens, and how cheerfully they acquiesce in the enormous expense which will burden them and their posterity with taxes to the latest generation."

"The fourteenth of October arrived, and a more beautiful day never broke upon the earth," according to a souvenir volume published to commemorate the event. "A brilliant sun, a sky veiled but not clouded, and a breezy atmosphere were in harmony with the occasion, and with the joyousness of the multitudinous population crowded into the city from all surrounding regions, to witness and share in the grand jubilee."

One hundred guns were fired at dawn, church bells rang, and the Grand Marshal and ten divisions assembled at 10 A.M. to form a seven-mile-long procession. The parade progressed south down Broadway to City Hall Park, circling a sixty-foot fountain of Croton water before breaking into assigned areas for the ceremony. After a division of artillery came the Second Division, which included the mayors of New York, Brooklyn, Albany, Troy, Jersey City, and Newark, the Board of Water Commissioners, several members of Congress, and Governor William Seward, in whose carriage Jervis rode.

Oratory gushed. Chief water commissioner Samuel Stevens spoke; then John L. Lawrence, president of the Croton Aqueduct Board; then Governor Seward. Before Grand Marshal Gilbert Hopkins ended the occasion with "nine hearty cheers for the City of New York and perpetuity to the Croton water"—cheers "given with a heartiness that made the welkin ring again"; before the invited masses partook of a cold collation in City Hall—washed down with "Croton water and lemonade, but no wine or spiritous liquors"; the New York

Sacred Music Society mounted the platform to sing "The Croton Ode," written at the request of the Corporation of the City of New York by George P. Morris. Printed copies of the ode's seven verses had been distributed to the happy crowd, which plunged into the harmonic torrent, bubbling toward these final stanzas:

> Round the Aqueducts of story,
> As the mists of Lethe throng
> Croton's waves, in all their glory,
> Troop in melody along.
>
> Ever sparkling, bright and single,
> Will this rock-ribbed stream appear,
> When posterity shall mingle
> Like the gathered Waters here.

Water and silt swirled about my feet and headed toward Manhattan. The smooth passage amplified and reverberated the rhythmic slosh of approaching cavers. Ian and Craig had finished their picture taking. They sounded like a freight train at low volume. As the two rounded the gentle curve separating us, their lamp beams bobbed with the jerky motion of locomotive headlights. Clouds of vapor, roiling in the subterranean humidity, became bursts of steam.

A fist-sized brown lump hung from one of the tree roots draped along the side. I stepped closer, and the pendant ball resolved into a sleeping little brown bat, a species slightly larger than the more plentiful pipistrelle. The little brown pulled its hamsterlike face from beneath crossed wings. It regarded me with bright black eyes, which could see—contrary to the old saying—quite well. It wiggled radar-dish ears, sniffed the air, stretched the membranes of its highly evolved hands, and took flight.

We continued south, observing other life-forms: millipedes, spindly cave crickets, a lone four-inch spotted slug, and salamanders that in a thousand generations might become blind and white as their troglodytic cousins. A rotted board sprouted a clump of bushy white fungi vaguely resembling Don King's hair. From another board a forlorn seedling—who knows how it got there—curled vainly in search of light. I spotted two smallish brown worms. There was evidence of absent life as well: the signatures of D. Bannen, dated April 16, 1875; Michel Woods, 1871; John Quinn, 1861; an unsigned 1897.

Near a tunnel section that was shored with corrugated steel thirty or forty years ago, no doubt in order to bolster some heavy overhead construction, lay the unmistakable tracks of a large dog. A bit farther was a peace sign next to a signature: "Arlo, 1971." Considering the date, I wondered whether it might have been left by *the* Arlo. Atop a fairly recent concrete ledge, built to support an intersecting local water pipe, some waggish workman had left three rubber spiders. In the flickering lamplight, these hairy-legged blobs appeared animate. Had their purchaser seen me jump, he might have felt his uncertain investment justified.

The tunnel swung inland as we neared Tarrytown. I noticed that the tube was not perfectly oval in shape, but more a pointed arch with a rounded base:

Where it passed beneath solid rock, the city—in the person of the ever frugal John Jervis—had saved on brick by leaving exposed the blasted (but watertight) ceiling:

   or

We crossed a few squat, oddly rounded sections, lasting no more than a hundred feet:

Every quarter mile we passed a ventilation shaft, installed to help maintain a steady flow of water. Without regular airflow, the stream would have slowed or even reversed, as in a siphon. Most of the air shafts had an inside diameter of just over a foot, and rose from the center of the ceiling:

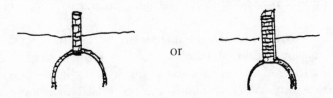

or

The workmanship evident in seams where brick and stone came together, and where smaller runoff tubes intersected the main passage, was exquisite. A few of the larger-diameter air shafts were offset from the tunnel, opening above curved brickwork ledges. These always opened to the right side as we faced south:

Near one of the side-mounted shafts, Ian and I spotted some animal tracks that took a while to decipher. The tracks lay in soft brown silt, six inches below the surface of water that was glass until stirred by our feet. They meandered over an area of perhaps thirty yards, and appeared to have been left by a small bipedal mammal that traveled in short hops:

The tracks were thickest near the stone shaft itself. Its base was piled with moldering leaves. I climbed to the ledge and looked up, and saw overhead the outline of a branch swaying in the moonlight. The animal must have fallen from the tree into the cushion of leaves, then bounced or stumbled into the tunnel proper. But what animal? As we continued beyond the shaft, the hops became shorter and less distinct.

Ian walked beside me, muttering, "Small, two feet, lives in trees."

In six inches of water, I realized, the heavier back legs of a squirrel would rest on the bottom, while its tiny forelegs would paddle to keep its head above the surface. Any land mammal immersed in a 54° F stream would be able to maintain body temperature for a half hour at best. Unless the tracks were very old, whatever left them should be close by and visible.

This thought had no sooner occurred than I saw, suspended in the stream directly before me, floating remains that proved my hypothesis. The squirrel had decayed so thoroughly in the undisturbed water that it seemed a fuzzy projection, a squirrel made of fog, a dream of a squirrel. As I sloshed toward it, it dissolved into mist.

17

THE BRONX, AUGUST 1985

While riding the Harlem Line of the Metro-North this past Saturday, bound for Grand Central Terminal from Scarsdale, I was afforded a sunset view of the dark brown soup that is the Bronx River. The train had stalled somewhere south of Fordham, at a place where the track rises from its ditch to curve through a stand of mimosa, becoming, momentarily, something akin to a zoo monorail. From my air-conditioned vantage, I could see the Bronx as a pleasant stream, churning a light froth where it rushed through short granite rapids. Above the far bank, high cirrocumulus glowed pale pink against a sky that looked airbrushed. The sun's ruddier shades bounced from the bricks of burned-out Bronx tenements—if the buildings had been sandstone bluffs, the scene might have made the cover of *Arizona Highways*. I soaked it all in, this being my last train ride for some time to come.

July had eleven days left in it, but my summer was nearly over. Kathy and I had lived since May on Bleecker Street, in a fourth-floor walk-up procured for us by my professor, William Price Fox. His wife's family had let the West Village apartment below market value, so that we might enjoy the summer of museums, readings, and concerts that so many students have enjoyed in the city before us. Weekdays, Kathy commuted to Sony offices in New Jersey, while I worked on assignments for *McCall's* and *Audubon* in a dark booth of the Pot Belly Cafe. Weekends, we went everywhere we could think to go.

Bill Fox's elderly father-in-law, Charlie Crawford, lived on the first two floors of the painted brownstone, which he owned. Mr. Crawford's sister had passed away the previous spring after living on the top floor for more than fifty years; the family had not yet gone through her belongings. Kathy and I were allowed to recline on her Victorian fainting couch and read her inscribed first editions of Saroyan, Hemingway, and Gibran.

I had perused a shelf, set into an odd hollow in the living-room wall, stocked with musty histories of New York City. These had been collected for their mentions of a Crawford ancestor, Stephen Allen, who served as mayor from 1821 to 1824. Everything in the apartment seemed placed to enrich a first-time New York experience, from the bay window which overlooked a courtyard exactly like James Stewarts' in *Rear Window* to the tiny mouse that, at exactly ten-thirty every night, poked its nose out of the gas fireplace and scurried to the kitchen.

Like most shut-ins, Mr. Crawford enjoyed company. Two or three times during the summer I had gone downstairs to talk with the old man. He spent his days propped in a hospital bed before a portable television, in a room that smelled of vanilla wafers and urine. He and his Jamaican nurse argued so often and so loudly that I surmised they felt a deep mutual affection. On one visit, I began to talk about caving, and Mr. Crawford became excited. He ordered the nurse to fetch a particular cardboard box, and when she brought it he yelled, "No, not that one, you idiot, the one on the *top* shelf," and so on through several boxes of documents. At last he gave up and told me what it was that the nurse couldn't find.

"Stephen Allen, my ancestor, was in charge of the first water tunnel in the city," he said. "It's still down there, the Old Croton. Miles and miles of underground passage. I've got some of the blueprints, if that woman could ever find them. You should go down there and see it. Take you myself, I was any younger. Native stone and brickwork. Amazing."

I said I'd have to do that sometime. Now, as I watched the water flowing under the tracks, I recalled Mr. Crawford's tunnel. I believed that it crossed the Bronx somewhere nearby, but there was no indication on the surface. I opened my brief-case and glanced once more at the August issue of *McCall's*, fresh off the newsstand, and advance galleys of a fall issue of *Audubon*. Each contained an essay I had written, and I felt more sophisticated than I had any right to feel.

Smoke curled from the corner of an empty lot beside the roofless hull of a brick building. I saw no fire, just smoke. In one week, the summer would be over, time to return to South Carolina, early registration, and the start of another academic year. I had gone to Scarsdale to see about my car, stored for two months in the backyard of one of Kathy's friends, another intern. The car was fine, the battery was being charged, and it had been arranged that the friend would drive it down to the Village next Saturday morning and help us pack. Everything was settled. All that remained was for to me go back to the apartment and "make the most of the last few days." I was in no hurry, certainly not enough of one to be put out by the present delay.

I had seen what was necessary of the familiar New York, the essential places that every college student knows from books and movies and dormitory art prints, and was satisfied if not overwhelmed. The summer memories that I had already begun to cherish were personal and unimportant ones, mem-ories that could have been of Toledo or Dallas or any other city: the muffled shouts of Mr. Crawford and his nurse min-gling with the exotic squawking that came from the parrot shop on the corner; the surprising coolness of a few June nights; the gentle and somehow mysterious smile of the Korean girl who sold me "coffee regular" every morning. And now the unexpected beauty of a Bronx sunset.

Lushness and decrepitude were spread before me. I imag-ined myself seated on the upper deck of a side-wheeler, star-ing over the wild boomtown where we were to dock for the night. Thirty yards or so below the rapids, the stream slowed and turned out of sight at a wide oxbow—perhaps twenty feet across, it was certainly wide for the Bronx River. I could make

out water bugs darting over the smoother water there, dancing on the membrane of surface tension that separated them
from unthinkable toxic waste. I could also see the long
shadow of a mimosa, black against the tan surface, limned by
slanted rays. It was while watching this shadow that I decided
the river was soup: I spotted a thin wisp of vapor twisting from
the heart of the projected tree like steam from a Cajun broth.
The tiny plume continued to rise for the next several minutes,
even after the sun had finally and conclusively disappeared
behind a high-rise, low-rent housing project.

I was still watching the strange mist when, like a barge
drawn free of its bank by a sudden current, the train slipped
forward. It slid downstream past the oxbow before the gears
caught, before electric acceleration replaced the feel of floating, and the man sitting in front of me, who had been reading
a newspaper, looked up and said, "Jesus, it's about time."

18

THE CRYSTAL
CAVERN

Deep below an ancient coral reef in southern New Mexico lies a cave passage called the Great Western Borehole. A mile long and 100 feet high, the hall's every surface sparkles with crystallized gypsum. Between its discovery in 1988 and this expedition in the spring of 1991, perhaps fifty people have walked through the white palace in which I stand. Impressive as it is, the chamber is just a small branch of the tree that is Lechuguilla Cave. Still, the corridor is sufficiently vast that I almost miss the torn piece of notebook paper someone has placed in the path before me.

"EMILY BROKE HER LEG," it reads, the letters hurriedly scrawled in black Magic Marker. "THIS WAY." An arrow points toward a twenty-foot patch of blackness to the right, one of many side passages arched into the borehole.

My two companions, the veteran cavers Garry Petrie and Pat Seiser, exchange worried looks. We know that "EMILY" must be Emily Davis Mobley, whose survey team entered Lechuguilla just behind ours early the previous afternoon. Somewhere overhead, it is 10:30 A.M. We've been caving for twenty-one hours.

In five years of nonstop discovery since the 1986 breakthrough into the cave's vast interior, Lechuguilla has revealed itself as America's greatest underground wilderness. The three of us realize that it will soon be the site of America's greatest underground-wilderness rescue. We stand nearly two miles from the desert entrance, and 900 feet below it. Dozens of rope climbs and tight crawlways block the complex path ahead. As we work our way toward Emily, following paper arrows at every intersection, I wonder whether we—or the cave—will be up to the coming effort.

The entrance to Lechuguilla is situated about five miles from Carlsbad Caverns. All passages explored to date lie within the borders of Carlsbad Caverns National Park. With over 86 miles mapped, Lechuguilla is four times as long as its famous neighbor. It presently ranks third longest in the country, behind Mammoth and Jewel caves. The cave is also the deepest in the United States—at 1,560 feet, deeper than any building in the world is tall. But rather than size or depth, it is Lechuguilla's bizarre geology and extreme fragility that make it unique in the world.

Many of the cave's delicate gypsum and calcite formations grow nowhere else. Some see a profit in such rare beauty, but not National Park Service cave specialist Ronal C. Kerbo, who has argued that Lechuguilla should never be opened to the public. In 1990 and 1991, Kerbo's drive against commercialization was successful—despite the threatening late-night phone calls he received—yet Lechuguilla's future is by no means clear. As geologists attempt to puzzle out the genesis of the cave's decorated halls, the only consensus seems to be that much of the rock was carved by hydrogen-sulfide-rich waters indicative of petroleum reserves. Oil companies hoping for a chance to prove the scientists right have sought to drill just outside the park boundary. Yet the most immediate threat to this virgin subterranean realm remains the act of exploration itself. With each human footfall, Lechuguilla is changed forever.

What do you look for when you want to discover a cave? It's always good to start in an area where caves are already known. Limestone is important, especially when it assumes the type of rough surface topography characteristic of karst. You look for closed valleys, places that suck rainwater under as soon as it falls. And if you have a few holes to choose from, the most promising—no matter how small and miserable it may appear on the surface—will be the one that noticeably sucks or blows air. A stiff breeze in a crawlway indicates that a vast space *somewhere* is trying to maintain equilibrium with constantly shifting air pressure above.

When Colorado cavers Dave Allured and John Patterson set out to look for caves near Carlsbad in 1984, they found all of the classic signs at Lechuguilla, a "small" cave known since the turn of the century. First recorded as Walnut Mine in 1914 by John Ogle, a guano miner, the cave historically consisted of a 70-foot natural shaft into 300 feet of dead-end passage. In the mid-1950s, it was known as Misery Pit. The Park Service eventually settled on Lechuguilla, after the spiky member of the amaryllis plant family that proliferates nearby, poking everyone who hikes to the small entrance.

Several times since the mid-1970s, members of the Cave Research Foundation—a nonprofit group dedicated to cave study—had examined Lechuguilla because of its proximity to Carlsbad. Occasional trips confirmed that strong airflow emanated from loose rubble piles in the cave. But each CRF team concluded that digging through the unstable rock would require considerable effort, as well as the risk of collapse. Patterson accompanied the last team to reach this conclusion in 1979. In an area as cave-rich as the Guadalupe region of New Mexico, there were always safer leads to pursue, ones that required no engineering.

Then came Dave Allured. Unlike other western cave explorers, Allured had begun his underground pursuits in an area where virtually every new find was the result of extensive digging: upstate New York. Northeastern caves tend to be wet, slimy holes, choked with glacial debris. New York cavers gladly spend months on projects that yield only fifty feet of sewerlike passage. Allured had carried this molelike approach with him to Colorado, where he conducted several successful digs. A chance discussion with Patterson interested him in Lechuguilla.

An initial trip in the spring of 1984 excited Allured even

more than Patterson's descriptions. He spent the next several months obtaining permission from park authorities for a full-scale dig. This was easier than it might have been because of the efforts of the Park Service's senior cave specialist, Ronal Kerbo. A major voice in American caving over the past twenty years, Kerbo considers himself an explorer first and bureaucrat second, often coming to the rescue of cavers who encounter paper barriers. (He's also an environmental writer and poet, greatly influenced by the late Edward Abbey. When James Watt visited Carlsbad during the Reagan years, two Secret Service agents spoke to Kerbo in advance, to make sure he would do nothing to "embarrass" the secretary of the interior underground. The white-haired caver answered in his characteristic Oklahoma drawl, "I'm sure the secretary can do that just fine without my help.")

Thanksgiving weekend 1984, Allured, Patterson, and Kerbo joined several other cavers with folding shovels, crowbars, and five-gallon plastic buckets. Following the strongest of several air channels along one wall, the diggers began removing fill, a bucketful at a time. An ever strengthening wind rewarded their efforts, throwing dust in their eyes and extinguishing their carbide lamps.

The results were encouraging enough to enable the two leaders to recruit more diggers for weekend trips the following Memorial Day and Thanksgiving. On the last day of the Thanksgiving 1985 dig, four cavers broke beyond the rubble for the first time, into a crawlway bordered top and bottom with bedrock. Although this passage also required digging, the fact that they had passed the loose breakdown made a breakthrough seem imminent.

Among the novice diggers Allured recruited for Memorial Day 1986 were Colorado natives Richard Bridges and Neil Backstrom—whose names would become forever connected with Lechuguilla. On May 25, the three waited for others who had planned to join them in a surface survey above the dig. When the others failed to show, Allured decided to rappel down the entrance shaft and pass a couple of hours digging.

Before long, the three observed the small passage responding to a change in weather above. Whereas it usually blew sand outward, sometimes as fast as thirty miles an hour, it now drew air with such force that dirt disturbed by the cavers vanished into the void. In an hour, they had expanded the slanting passage by two feet. Bridges, taking a turn at the bottom of the dig, shouted for a rope. A ten-foot rappel and a short crawl later, the three stood beneath dripping formations, staring at a caver's dream come true.

Lechuguilla contains unprecedented masses of gypsum. It holds the world's largest-known and most spectacular concentrations of selenite crystals, aragonite, and hydromagnesite balloons. It holds the world's first observed subaqueous helictites. All of these formations are beautiful, all crumble to the touch, and all are everywhere one turns in the cave. The phreatic tunnels branch in all directions, offering explorers more interesting sights in a single trip—and more of the unknown to discover—than many cavers see in a lifetime.

Lechuguilla demands excellence. It has altered the face of caving in the way that the first ascents of Everest and K2 forever changed climbing; perhaps even more so. Lech, as most cavers know it, has precipitated new caving techniques and technology. Cavers wear tan-soled shoes to avoid scuffing pristine floors. On the finest surfaces, even these come off as cavers cross barefoot. Climbing systems, clothing, lights, and sleeping bags have all been designed to handle grueling Lech trips, which typically last from twenty-four to thirty-six hours.

Perhaps the greatest change Lech has brought to sport caving has been philosophical. Because it is a public cave on national park land (and, in part, because of antielitist efforts led by Ronal Kerbo) exploration has been open to more cavers, with more diverse backgrounds, than virtually any major find in history. Because what they have found is so spectacular, caving has been thrust into the public eye as never before.

Normally secretive cavers have been interviewed on the major television networks, in dozens of magazines and hundreds of newspapers. Others testified before the U.S. Congress when it considered declaring Lechuguilla the nation's first Underground Wilderness. The fantastic gypsum sprays of the Chandelier Ballroom, discovered during the first 1988 expedition, have been so photographed that they grace calendars, posters, and the cover of the National Speleological Society member's manual for 1989. Almost any of the active U.S. cavers would recognize the room on sight, yet fewer than two hundred people have ever been there.

Even two hundred may be too many. When Pat Kambesis first stepped into the ballroom in 1988, its floor was already littered with chandeliers that had fallen naturally. One cave photographer who has seen recent ballroom images claims that at least two small chandeliers that were visible in earlier photos can no longer be seen. Perhaps they too fell naturally. But the slightest nudge by a careless visitor would have been enough to send them crashing.

Prospective Lechuguilla explorers must prove complete mastery of caving skills—not only for safety but in order to ensure that cavers pay more attention to the cave than to the perils of moving through it. Occasionally, passages are so profusely decorated that explorers agree to go no farther, to seek out less damageable routes. Not all cave damage is as obvious as a broken chandelier. White gypsum "rock flour" crumples underfoot to a yellowish dust, which can hold footprints as long as the moon will hold Neil Armstrong's. Gypsum bridges lose a bit of themselves with every crossing. Hot cavers leave minute amounts of mud and sweat in deep blue pools—some of which have tested purer than the testing laboratory's "pure" reference water.

Yet even the most ardently conservative caver bristles at the idea of suspending exploration completely. It is an easy matter to find cavers willing to say, "Let me see where this passage goes, and then you can close it forever." Much rarer is the caver who will say, "I believe this passage goes somewhere. I think you should close it forever."

＊　　　＊　　　＊

In essence, Ronal Kerbo said just that regarding his own desire to explore Lechuguilla. Within weeks after the initial break-through, Kerbo realized that to remain impartial in his role as cave administrator he would have to remove himself from the vested interests of the explorer. Despite his recognized caving expertise, Kerbo began to say "no" to the inviting blackness of Lechuguilla. His prowess had made network news broadcasts. With Jim Goodbar, a Bureau of Land Management cave spe-cialist, Kerbo had led a much publicized 1985 climb into Carlsbad Caverns' Spirit World. I had seen the two friends tackle tough cave passages as members the 1988 China/USA Caves Project. More recently, Kerbo had watched Goodbar become one of the more active Lechuguilla cavers.

"It was one of the hardest decisions I've ever made," Kerbo told me over breakfast in a Carlsbad diner in March 1991. "And *some cavers*"—he said this as though spitting out a bug—"see it as a moral or physical failure on my part. They think if I'm not man enough to do a three-day push trip to the Far East, I'm not man enough to have any say in Lechuguilla's future. But how could I tell cavers around the world we'll only allow thirty people in the cave at one time, or three expedi-tions a year, if I know I can go in there and scoop passage any-time I want?"

Kerbo made it clear that *some cavers* include Richard A. Bridges, then president of the nonprofit Lechuguilla Cave Project, which in 1991 oversaw expeditions. All three cavers present at the breakthrough—Allured, Backstrom, and Bridges—later became embroiled in assorted power struggles within the LCP. Of those three, only Bridges still caved in Lechuguilla.

Bridges had become Lechuguilla's spokesman to the world as well as one of its senior administrators. Perhaps as a result of his business background, he seemed more comfortable with park officials and the press than were most project cavers. Because of his press role, Bridges had been reported—mistakenly—as the cave's sole discoverer and the project's sole leader, an error that sometimes rankled other Lech explorers. But the project's toughest, most prodigious hard-core cavers seemed happy with their relative anonymity.

A stocky former salesman with the oil industry, Bridges quit his job in 1989 to explore and map Lechuguilla full-time. He supplemented oil-well income by selling cave gear and by appearing as a "cave expert" on such television shows as *To Tell the Truth* and *Live! The World's Greatest Stunts*. He applied, unsuccessfully, for Kerbo's job as cave specialist at Carlsbad, after Kerbo was promoted to the Park Service's regional office in Sante Fe.

As Kerbo had predicted at breakfast, Bridges was quick to denigrate him: "The thing you have to realize about Ron Kerbo is that he doesn't really know anything about Lechuguilla. He's only been to Boulder Falls, which isn't even into the cave as far as any Lechuguilla caver's concerned. He just likes to stir up controversy. That so-called fight over commercializing Lechuguilla, he created that. He antagonized the people of Carlsbad without any reason."

In truth, some of the people of Carlsbad hadn't much cared for Kerbo from the start. Some years ago, he told a local reporter that he felt mountain lions had at least as much right to eat sheep as ranchers had to graze them on public land, adding, "No one would be upset about it if the lions had pockets. Then they could carry wallets to pay for the sheep they ate." Kerbo was no stranger to threatening phone calls.

The fight over Lechuguilla began when the mayor, Bob Forrest, who owned a local tire store, called a citizens' committee to bring about the tourism development of Lechuguilla Cave. The fight ended when the committee's engineering consultant determined that it would be less expensive to build a perfect replica of the Chandelier Ballroom than to install the elevator, path, and lights that would enable an average visitor to go there.

Emily Davis Mobley operates Speleobooks out of a historic barn in Schoharie, New York, that she has filled with one of the world's greatest collections of cave literature. As writers interested in caves, Kerbo and I were both delighted to see Emily arrive the day before the spring 1991 expedition. Like Kerbo, I had spent hours browsing among the rare works in her collection, many of which travel with her several times a year. Emily's aging white van, with its OLD BAT vanity plates, could generally be found parked on Vendor's Row at every major caving convention. Each year, she and her husband, Bill, who collects chocolate ephemera, invited Kathy and me up for their annual chocolate party, where we would ingest a year's supply of cholesterol and sugar. Only a few weeks earlier, I had been up to McFail's Cave and stopped by Emily's barn to purchase a signed copy of Kerbo's book of cave poems, *Bat Wings and Spider Eyes*.

Kerbo took Mobley to dinner the night before caving began; she promised to spend time catching up with me underground later in the week. I dined that evening with the husband-and-wife mapping team of Petrie and Seiser. We discussed leads the two wished to pursue near a place called the Chandelier Graveyard, off the Western Borehole. It was to be my second expedition, and my fourth trip into the cave.

I had first seen the Chandelier Ballroom in China, not long after it was discovered, when Kerbo presented slides of American caves to Chinese geologists at the Guilin Institute for Karst Studies. The following summer, I had joined a mapping crew led by Carol Vesely that had netted 2,000 feet of virgin passage in a single trip, all of it lined with more gypsum formations than I had seen in all my years of caving. Although the heat of the cave and the length of the trip had bothered me, I couldn't wait to return.

After a long orientation meeting, in which Bridges discussed expedition rules and procedures, we set off for Lechuguilla. The two-mile hike from the parking area led us around the coral heads of the old reef, now home to scorpions and rattlers. We made our way past several of the flowering desert plants that give Lechuguilla its name. By chance, our three-caver team arrived at the entrance rope just moments ahead of the five-caver team that Mobley had joined. The 70-

foot entrance pit was unremarkable, as was the gated steel culvert placed in the passage crawlway below it to stabilize loose dirt, control cave access, and restrict airflow to its natural level.

The wind howled like death as I climbed through the pipe, but the same can be said of many large caves. We passed a few nuisance crawls and climbs just beyond the entrance crawl, including a descent over a sparkling slope of flowstone. But Lechuguilla's unique personality wasn't revealed until Boulder Falls, a 150-foot pit well into the cave. The name refers to loose rocks that rain down whenever you rappel off the crumbling cliff at the end of the entrance passage.

Once beyond the lip, Lechuguilla ceased to be ordinary. I landed in a chamber much larger than the weak beam of my carbide lamp could define. I waited under a protective ledge while the others descended, then we all removed and stowed extra food and gear atop a rock called Pack's Peak. Finally, Garry led us through twin columns called the Pearly Gates into Glacier Bay, a vast hollow fjord lined with gypsum blocks of megalithic size.

The tilted white surface looked for all the world like the fissured top of a flowing glacier. Freestanding gypsum bergs had broken from the mass. They seemed to float toward the distant darkness. The white mineral used to make plaster of Paris is found in many caves, but in minute amounts. Lee Pearson and I once traveled for hours through a Tennessee cavern to see a single gypsum flower three inches in diameter. The *smallest* of the blocks now before me was the size of an upended school bus.

We worked our way down and through the immense slabs, following the well-marked path of the first explorers. Gypsum is a soft, easily crumbled material. My boots sank several inches in the yellowish path. But a few inches to either side, the floor appeared solid and white, exactly as it has looked for centuries. Again and again through the cave, I would see the conservation practiced by Lech explorers in the careful marking of every trail, and in the absence of footprints elsewhere.

Each caver is responsible for removing his or her own human waste from the cave. Cavers double-wrap solids in plastic bags, then store the resultant "burritos" in their packs. Although liquid was deposited in specified in-cave drops in earlier exploration, the resultant smell and increased soil acidity brought an end to the practice. Now cavers carried special canteens for liquid waste; more than one told of becoming fatigued on a long trip and accidentally taking a swig from the wrong bottle. (Exceptions to the no-liquid-waste rule are made for those on multiday trips to remote areas such as the Far East, when explorers must drink—and eliminate—several gallons of cave water before exiting.)

Even cave air is measurably changed by exploration, from simple breathing and sweating. If an artificial entrance were to be blasted into Lechuguilla, the increased airflow would almost certainly dry out dangling gypsum formations in the lower passages and send them crashing down. The Chandelier Ballroom would become a pile of gypsum rubble. Lechuguilla is home to a number of unusual, sulfur-based microbes, which live in outer rock layers and feed on nutrients carried by the wind. No one knows how the passage of cavers affects this tiny, poorly understood ecosystem.

Two hundred and fifty million years ago an inland sea covered most of the American Southwest. Along its eastern shore grew a coral reef of proportions rivaling the Great Barrier of modern Australia. As the reef slowly expanded, earlier layers were cemented into limestone. Eventually, the continent uplifted and the Permian sea drained. Impounded saline lakes dried up, leaving behind vast beds of gypsum. The exposed reef, called El Capitan, rose with the land to form the eastern escarpment of the Guadalupe Mountains, a cave-rich crescent stretching across West Texas and southern New Mexico.

Most of the world's limestone caves are etched out by the downward flow of rainwater, made slightly acidic from carbon dioxide picked up in the air. But the Guadalupe caves seem to have grown from the bottom up. According to the geologist

Art Palmer, who has done extensive fieldwork in Lechuguilla, heated hydrogen sulfide rose from deep petroleum deposits through cracks to mix with water flowing below the surface. Chemical reactions with oxygen in the water produced sulfuric acid, which began to scoop out vaults and tunnels in the limestone. Hot mineral springs bubbled out on the surface, pouring from the labyrinths they had carved. When the water table later fell, the acidic fountains receded. They left behind voids whose encrusted walls glittered with dissolved minerals to rival Coleridge's caves of ice.

It is this unique geological and chemical genesis that gives Lechuguilla its character. Although theories of sulfuric acid cave formation were put forth a decade ago to explain Carlsbad and other caves, Lechuguilla alone has proved them. The sulfur-laden water that rises from Zacatón in central Mexico may be duplicating the process even now. As Lechuguilla's explored limits expand, someday Carlsbad itself may be regarded as no more than a side passage of the long-dead sulfuric river.

The surrounding Delaware basin has long been one of New Mexico's richest oil producers. In 1989, proof of Lechuguilla's petroleum connection interested local oil companies in exploration on land adjoining the national park. The U.S. Bureau of Land Management owns most of this land, which is already dotted with capped oil wells, abandoned decades ago.

Jim Goodbar headed the committee considering oil exploration requests. Predicting where Lechuguilla's passages might go can be as risky as predicting weather. Although no known Lechuguilla passage extends beyond Park Service land, Goodbar had good indication that the cave might reach into the proposed drill area. The indicator was Big Manhole, a cave several miles up the reef from Lechuguilla, right in the middle of BLM wilderness.

Big Manhole is a "small" cave whose description mirrors Lechuguilla's just before the breakthrough. A 90-foot rappel leads to a rubble-strewn chamber; a fierce wind issues from the jumble of rocks. Federal Wilderness rules have curtailed recent digging in Big Manhole by cavers. No one knows where its passages lead. The only certain thing is that they are there. In 1991, members of Goodbar's committee released a special high-grade helium at various key Lechuguilla intersections. Sensitive receptors in Big Manhole sniffed a few molecules of the test gas—just enough to prove that a physical connection between the two exists. In 1993, the Lechuguilla Cave Protection Act became federal law. A "buffer zone" now protects areas surrounding the cave—including Big Manhole—from future petroleum exploration. Under a plan developed by Goodbar, cavers may resume limited digging in Big Manhole in 1996.

Our team had entered together with Emily's, but tortuous passages near the entrance quickly separated us. As we worked our way through 1,000 vertical feet of limestone toward the mouth of the Great Western Borehole, Pat Seiser stopped unexpectedly at a field of boulders. My watch said it was six in the evening. "I think something's wrong," she said. "We should go find Emily's group. I just had a feeling that something bad happened, and I think it involves Emily."

Her feeling passed, and we moved on. In fact, Emily's "bad thing" wouldn't happen for another twelve hours. It would ultimately keep Seiser in the cave for the next four days.

Soaked with sweat, we reached our goal—a rope climb and two rappels beyond the Western Borehole—later that night. Sore, exhausted, I pushed into virgin leads Petrie pointed out to me, setting survey stations as I went. At one point I entered a series of chambers about the size of a three-bedroom suburban home. They dead-ended, an "insignificant" side passage. Tiny shards of gypsum crackled underfoot like fine china. My single crossing of that small side passage will take centuries to fade. In time, cave deposits will cover my tracks. But not in time that has any human meaning.

At last we slept in the Western Borehole, at a camping area near gypsum totems called the Three Amigos. The camp reeked of an overflowing five-gallon slop bucket. Those who had placed it had reasoned that urine would evaporate between expeditions. They had been wrong. But I was much too tired to care about the smell. In the morning, we rose to canned breakfast and the hike out—a hike interrupted by a piece of notebook paper.

We follow the "EMILY" signs to the Reason Room, an irregular chamber 100 feet wide. I hear Emily joking with other cavers as we enter the room. At least she's conscious and in good spirits. We are the second team to see the note and arrive. The fast caver who led her mapping crew has already left to call out a rescue. A makeshift Ensolite splint wraps Mobley's leg. She lies in a sleeping bag on the one of the few flat rocks in the rubble-filled room. When she sees me, she says, "Mike, we've got to stop meeting like this. My husband is getting suspicious."

I realize that whatever the rescue entails, she will be up to it. For the second of what will become hundreds of times, she tells what happened.

Emily's trouble began sixteen hours after the forty-year-old caver entered Lechuguilla. She had sponsored three cavers from West Virginia, all of whom were new to Lech. Together with their crew leader, Mike Mansur, the party toured the Chandelier Ballroom and other scenic spots before starting survey work near the Western Borehole. The Reason Room lay in a side passage called FUBAR, a quarter mile from the lead Petrie had taken me to. A pit in the floor, lined with boulders ranging in size from bowling ball to pickup truck, looked as if it might go somewhere. Mobley gingerly climbed through the rocky jumble, testing handholds. At 35 feet it came to a dead end.

She measured the pit and began her ascent. An eighty-pound hunk of limestone, which had supported her on the way in, popped loose without warning. Mobley fell five feet; the rock hit her left leg. She shouted to her companions, "I'm hurt, but don't worry—nothing's broken." Then, as she tried to stand: "Whoops, I could be wrong about that."

She was. She had sustained a serious fracture just below the knee. By luck, one of the team members was a doctor. Steve Mossberg performed first aid while another caver made paper signs to draw others in the cave to the scene. Within an hour, Mansur left for a bivey area at Lake Louise, where he knew he would find other cavers. He told them the news and dispatched a fast runner to the entrance.

No stranger to cave rescues, Emily has supervised several near her rural home in Schoharie, New York. As recently as the previous December, she helped free five college students trapped in flooding Onesquethaw Cave. Perhaps more than anyone else in the room, she knows the slow and grueling process that awaits her. Seiser, who considers herself a fair masseuse, volunteers to stay with Mobley to rub away the soreness sure to come with immobility.

One of Mobley's New York team members, Bob Addis, joins me and Petrie in exiting the cave. Addis and I are both dehydrated—a danger faced by all big guys in Lech—and need a recharge on the surface before we can be of value to a rescue operation. Just before leaving, I offer Pat Seiser the small inflatable pillow I've carried in my cave pack since Great Expectations, as well as some extra food and polypropylene clothing. She and Emily will use them all in the coming days.

Addis, Petrie, and I at last stood in the cool air of a desert evening. The next morning, I was drafted to help fend off an invading army of the press. I wasn't to see Emily Davis Mobley again until a visit to her home a week after the expedition. Requiring the concerted efforts of over 170 expert volunteers, Emily's retrieval from Lechuguilla became one of the more difficult underground rescues ever accomplished.

From the outset, her comments on how to most efficiently extricate her—and yet not harm the cave—were respected. "Listen," she told Don Coons, "if you have a choice between trashing formations and making me uncomfortable, make me uncomfortable." Throughout the ordeal, Mobley's priority remained protection of pristine passages. As one team would guide her past a given obstacle, a second would follow, removing ropes, communication lines, and any other signs of human passage.

Past disagreements thrown aside, cavers focused on the business at hand. Far overhead, Bridges and Kerbo worked together assigning tasks to Goodbar and Coons, who ran the in-cave effort. Various Park Service officials coordinated surface support, and entertained the growing press contingent. (Duane Alaire, a Park Service media liaison flown in for the occasion, began scheduling twice-daily press conferences, complete with "Operation Desert Rescue" graphics and rope-climbing demonstrations. I was standing next to him when he confidently told an ABC correspondent, "I'm in charge here," à la Al Haig.)

While Kerbo was interviewed on the *Today* show, Bridges answered questions on *Good Morning America*. During these remote interviews, a nervous Art Palmer sat in the New York studio with Bryant, wondering what theories of hydrogen-sulfide speleogenesis had to do with cave rescue. A few blocks away, Kevin Downey chatted on-camera with Joan. Millions of Americans who had never heard of caving suddenly found the Chandelier Ballroom in their living rooms. Publications from *The New York Times* to *People* to *The Globe*, a supermarket tabloid, dispatched reporters who stood frustrated in the Carlsbad parking lot, asking me why they couldn't be allowed into the cave for an interview, just a short trip "in and out."

During the *Today* interview with Palmer, the camera cut to stock footage taken during a 1988 *Today* segment I had helped Craig White and Tom Zannes shoot. For the second time, I saw myself on national television rappelling into the Lech entrance shaft and walking down the LaBarge Borehole. The visuals for the *Good Morning America* segment were slides Kevin and a Swiss photographer had taken for a photo book called *Lechuguilla: Jewel of the Underground*, which was about to be published in Switzerland. Coincidentally, I had edited the text for the English version. Also coincidentally, Emily had signed a contract making Speleobooks the volume's sole American distributor. If I were a suspicious stranger, I might have thought we cooked up the whole accident for publicity. But I knew that we didn't and couldn't do such a thing, that Emily would have given anything to avoid the trouble she was causing, let alone the pain.

Her spirits remained high throughout four days of tedious progress. Her only requests were for pizza, a canned margarita, and (upon hearing of the huge press contingent awaiting her exit) a hairbrush. Those of us working in various capacities on the surface appreciated these requests. Several companies sent dozens of pizzas to the park, one company shipped fifty cans of margaritas, and a manufacturer had a gross of hairbrushes delivered.

When Emily began to get nervous about the way her litter spun and dangled as she was hauled up Boulder Falls, she sang "Joy to the World"—the song about Jeremiah the bullfrog, not the Christmas carol—in order to calm down. This went out in a press release, and Hoyt Axton, who wrote the song, called to wish her a quick recovery and to say, "Me and my mama are praying for you." Before leaving Lechuguilla, Emily named the short virgin climb that broke her leg. That previously blank spot on the complex cave map would forever read: "We Shouldn't Have Mapped This Pit."

Shortly after 1 A.M. on April 4, 1991, tired cavers at last hauled Emily Davis Mobley to the New Mexican night sky and an awaiting ambulance. The National Park Service declared the rescue a stunning success, expressing sincere thanks to the LCP and pledging support for future expeditions. After extensive leg and knee surgery, Emily began the long process of physical therapy, and was back in Lech the following year.

During the media blitz, one television interviewer asked Northern New Jersey Grotto caver Andrew Foord (the only experienced caver he'd been able to lay hands on), "Why do you go through all of this? If you wait five years, won't you be able to take an elevator to see this stuff? Don't they always put in lights and paths?" Flabbergasted, Foord managed at last to explain the ethics of caving and the concomitant drive to explore the unknown.

The drive to explore the unknown—that's what has given humanity knowledge of Lechuguilla, and what, in dozens of small but sure ways, threatens the very things that make it unique. Donald Davis, a bearded, thoughtful caver whom many consider the philosopher of Lechuguilla, says of the cave's future, "Carlsbad Cavern, like Pikes Peak, has been made accessible to anyone wishing to see it. Lechuguilla Cave, like Mount Everest, may forever be experienced by only the relatively few explorers and scientists with the unusual abilities required to traverse the cave on its own terms."

Despite the damage sure to come to the most heavily traveled throughways of Lechuguilla, Davis rests secure in the knowledge that "many areas in the cave may be visited only once, and will remain almost untouched if survey parties take care. And other chambers are there which may never be discovered. These will wait in silent darkness, in the dim and gentle contemplation that is the life of undisturbed caves, until the mountains themselves wear away."

In 1992, the park administration replaced Richard Bridges' LCP with a more democratic volunteer group, the Lechuguilla Exploration and Resource Network (LEARN), which now controls the cave's exploration. After several expeditions in 1994 and 1995 revealed further miles of pristine passage, LEARN decided to suspend exploration for at least a year in order to "give the cave a rest," according to Jason Richards, assistant cave specialist for Carlsbad Caverns National Park. But it is certain that more passage is there and that, someday, more will be discovered.

To traverse the virgin rooms of Lechuguilla in the company of master cavers such as Donald Davis—or Goodbar, Stine, Kambesis, Coons, or a hundred other Lech explorers—is an experience akin to walking Yosemite with John Muir or hunting in Florida with Audubon. Even knowing what eventually became of those pristine places, what lover of wilderness would turn down such an invitation to explore?

Not I.

19

SEARCHING FOR THE SYSTEM

On a cold December morning, I paused at a precarious ledge near the base of a canyon in southern China. I considered my position. My right hand rested against a limestone face 1,000 feet tall. Inches to my left, the ledge dropped 100 feet to a churning white-water river. Sleety mist had leaked since dawn from a slate sky. The dry, sandy path on which I stood, no more than a foot wide, was protected from the damp by an overhanging rock.

Thirty yards down the trail, an enormous cave swallowed river and canyon alike. Its black entrance stood 600 feet tall by 100 feet wide. The hollow space amplified the rhythmic chugging of the rapids below, like a great engine echoing in the moist air. I had just crossed a green patch where water trickled from a crack in the cliff, making the rock mossy and slick. A few feet ahead, I could see another slippery spot, this one below a boulder that bulged inconveniently into the path.

I would have to grab the rock and swing my left leg around it, jamming the toe of my right boot into the crack at its base for balance. The crack would also keep me from slipping on the moss. The trick, I knew, was not to look down.

As I looked down thinking about this, three of our team of eight American and two Chinese cave explorers caught up from behind. I knew that Chris Stine, Pat Kambesis, and Don Coons must have already traversed the exposed ledge, for they had started down the canyon twenty minutes ahead of me, and there was nowhere else for them to go. The time for hesitation had passed. I was blocking traffic.

"Watch out for that wet spot," I advised the caver behind me. "It's slick." Perhaps he would think that was the reason I had stopped, concern for his safety. But only if I moved forward now. I took a step toward the bulging rock, staring at the slot where I would wedge my toe.

Just then a soiled running shoe danced around from the other side, finding and filling the slot. Attached to the shoe was an elderly man, dressed in the traditional loose shirt and turban of the Blue Miao tribe. The bundle of freshly cut wood he had slung on his back seemed nearly as large as he was. He swung casually around the boulder, his load hanging impossibly in space, and nodded hello without looking up. The tribesman breezed past as though we'd met on a crowded city street rather than on an eight-inch ledge above a vanishing river.

I carefully grabbed the boulder and saw that beyond it the ledge widened to a comfortable platform that stretched into the cave. Inside the vaulted entrance, I could see that the three team members ahead of me were already pulling on wet suits, preparing to enter the river below and follow it to wherever it went. The 1991 China/USA Caves Project, a joint undertaking of the Cave Research Foundation, the National Speleological Society, and the Smithsonian Institution, had been years in the making. Now our first mapping trip was about to begin. The cool stone beneath my palms felt like a sesame, a magic door to unknown treasures of the underground world. Determined not to be shamed by the old man, I swallowed my fear and stepped around the rock. I didn't look down.

I unpacked my stiff wet suit, shaking loose the layer of dried cave mud it had acquired the last time I'd used it, while hauling scuba tanks through a cave in upstate New York. Our plan was to split into three teams. Two groups of four would begin mapping the Zhijin River Cave, while a two-man photography team documented the entrance area and details of the survey. I would join the survey team led by the expedition's chief cartographer, Patricia Kambesis. Before pulling on the bulky coveralls I wore over my wet suit, I ate a boxed lunch provided by our hosts: two boiled eggs, three tangerines, and a bar of dark chocolate.

Liang Hong, a graduate geology student at our host institution, Guizhou Normal University, sat down beside me. He would be the Chinese member of our mapping party. Although he spoke very little English and I spoke no Chinese, we were able to learn a few things about each other.

We agreed that my fiberglass climbing helmet seemed more substantial—but less stylish—than his miner's hat of woven bamboo. We discovered that we were the same age, thirty-two, and that Liang had never planned to be a geologist. After several years spent in northern China as an electrical engineer, he had become homesick for his native province. Acceptance into the Guizhou geology program had been a means of moving back to his family. We established that this would be the first time Liang had ever mapped a cave.

As we ate, I stared at the ceiling far overhead. Cave swallows darted about the shadows. I made out the rotting remains of a short bamboo ladder, hanging from a small hole at least 400 feet above the river. The rolling meadows on the surface above hid several sinkholes that drained rainwater to the main passage. Some daring hunter had followed one of these channels in order to reach cave-swallow nests—the prime ingredient in the highly prized bird's nest soup. Loose bits of rope hung from cracks and crevices near the ladder, tiny and indistinct as strands of broken spiderweb.

I could see what appeared to be a stone path notched into a ledge in the distant ceiling. The path ended at a white patch, which indicated a relatively recent break from the darker, weathered stone. I pointed this out to Liang. He pointed in turn to the river below. A boxlike boulder, perhaps ten feet on a side, stood in the middle of the stream, its shape corresponding roughly with the white outline overhead. Incredibly, one corner of the boulder's top was traversed by a carefully notched stairway, which now led nowhere.

I wondered whether anyone had been standing on the staircase when it made its 400-foot fall. More likely, it had broken loose in the heavy runoff of some past typhoon, falling unknown in the night. What I tried not to think about, as we stowed dry clothes and extra food on the ledge before setting off, was whether the boulder had been the ceiling's only loose rock.

The first known explorer of Chinese caves was among the first known humans: the cannibalistic headhunter *Homo erectus*, commonly called Peking man, who roamed northern Asia in the Middle Pleistocene. J. G. Andersson identified Peking man from trophy skulls buried in a cave at Chou K'outien, or Dragon Bone Hill, forty miles west of Beijing. Since Andersson's discovery in 1920, Chou K'outien has become one of the most studied paleoanthropological sites in the world. Decades of excavation have proved that the cave was more or less continually occupied for an incredible 230,000 years of human development, all long before the first Neanderthal crept into Lascaux with a paintbrush.

Even more ancient cave sites have been studied in China. Recently, a group of American paleoanthropologists working in Vietnam, Laos, and southwestern China have confirmed that early humans competed for caves with the possibly intelligent great ape Gigantopithicus. In their 1990 book *Other Origins*, Russell Ciochon, John Olsen, and Jamie James theorize that this period of cohabitation and competition became lodged in a "cultural memory" at the root of modern legends of the American Bigfoot, the Himalayan Yeti, and the "Wildman" of rural South China.

One of the oldest recorded cave expeditions is found in *The Records of the Mountains*, an atlas of mystic locations compiled between 770 and 476 B.C. by unknown Chinese geomancers. These shamans sought the geologic source of *chi*, the life force believed to flow through all things. For a thousand years after the compiling of *The Records of the Mountains*, holy men ventured into caves for mediation, often returning with strange mineral formations and the bones of fantastic creatures. These fossils, called "dragon bones," were credited with healing a wide variety of ills, and the calcite cave formations became prized aphrodisiacs. Both are still used in Chinese medicine.

At the beginning of the seventh century A.D. hundreds of ancient texts detailing cave locations, and describing the mining and use of cave resources, were cataloged for the vast imperial library of the Sui Dynasty, located in Changan, or modern Xian. Several Chinese speleological scholars added to this body of knowledge in the ensuing millennium. Notable among them was Xu Xiake (1586–1641), a Taoist monk who devoted much of his life to exploring and mapping caves. The detailed descriptions he compiled over thirty years spent wandering the southern provinces are so precise that most caves he visited can be found today by simply following the directions in his journals. In 1953, surveyors from China's Ministry of Geology and Mineral Resources checked Xu's map of Guilin's Seven Star Cave and found it completely accurate.

Xu is regarded by modern Chinese as an Isaac Newton of geology. His portrait appears on commemorative stamps, his statue stands in geologic institutes and university squares. He has been depicted as a sort of Taoist Indiana Jones in Chinese comic books.

In sight of the stone and bamboo walkways that crossed the entrance to the Zhijin River Cave, the notion that our team would "discover" anything seemed as culturally biased as the idea that Columbus discovered America. Yet, despite the impressive work of Xu, sandal-shod, lantern-bearing monks were poorly equipped to handle such physical impediments as waterfalls, deep pits, and raging rivers. If a cave passage proved more extensive than one could explore in a single day, carrying sufficient food and light became an almost insurmountable task. When an ancient explorer stopped to rest, the cool, moist cave air could bring the onset of hypothermia. While the entrance areas and more accessible chambers of many Chinese caves have been visited, albeit infrequently, for millennia the greatest depths remain virgin.

＊　　　　＊　　　　＊

Pat Kambesis' crew—Liang Hong, Tom Stockert, and I—followed the main passage. We would "leapfrog" sections of the river with another survey team working under the expedition's field leader, Don Coons. His caving style was as smooth and graceful in China as when I first met him, four years earlier at Great Expectations. I could swear that he floated from ledge to boulder to ledge without touching the rock. He led his crew across the rapids to the left-hand side of the cavern. They began measuring passage width and examining possible side passages high on the far wall. It gave him an excuse for rock climbing.

Our team was looking for big caves. That adjective can have several meanings underground: It can mean "deep"—the maximum change in elevation from the entrance to the lowest point in the cave. (The world depth record is just under a mile, held by a cave in the French Alps.) It can mean voluminous—a space the size of a football stadium, or bigger. (With floor dimensions of 2,300 by 1,300 feet, Borneo's Sarawak Chamber is considered the largest underground room. Carlsbad's celebrated Big Room is only a third as large.) Among experienced cavers, "big" most often translates as long.

When one cave passage leads to a dozen, and each of those tunnels lead to a dozen more, all of them long enough to take explorers many miles from the surface world, a cave *system* has been found. "Deep" and "voluminous" can be experienced in a single trip. "Long" may occupy an entire caving career. Cave systems tend to be geologically rich, formed over time by a number of complex events. Ancient rivers, prehistoric earthquakes, the runoff of retreating glaciers, and other forces can link many smaller caves into a supercave, whose very existence changes the shape and nature of the land overhead. Thus is karst created.

Named after the region in the former Yugoslavia where it was first studied, karst is a limestone landform characterized by steeply eroded hills, sharp pinnacles, underground streams, and caves. To see a karst landscape, look at a traditional Oriental watercolor, or the cover of any coffee-table photography book on China. The world's largest caves typically form in the elevated limestone of karst, where the steady penetration of rainwater can carve out great hollows in the fossil seabed.

China contains more karst—and quite possibly more caves—than all other nations combined, yet very little of it has been examined with modern equipment and methods. Speleological expeditions have become increasingly sophisticated and far-reaching over the past two decades. And as caving has evolved into a global pursuit, the world's cavers have begun to salivate over the vast limestone cake that sits atop China.

By far the longest cave system known to exist is Mammoth–Flint Ridge in Kentucky, which is 350 miles long and still growing. The story of its exploration, by hundreds of cavers working over a period of four decades, is told in *The Longest Cave*, a 1976 book by cavers Roger Brucker and Richard Watson. If there is a longer system in the world—and, of course, no one knows whether there is—the group that discovers it is unlikely to be caving or even living when that system's explored length begins to approach Mammoth's.

Our team had only five weeks in China. Since I had worked several years to procure the bulk of the expedition's funding from *Smithsonian* magazine, I had been allowed to set the dates to coincide with Christmas break at the Arkansas university where I teach journalism. But we felt reasonably optimistic that in Guizhou Province we might find a previously unknown cave system large enough to draw future expeditions, if not future generations.

During a scouting trip the previous year, team members Ian Baren and Tom Stockert and I had traveled deep into the rural province. We spotted more large entrances, disappearing streams, and closed valleys than we could begin to catalog in a week. Several other team members had been instrumental in the exploration of the two largest systems discovered in the previous decade—New Mexico's Lechuguilla Cave, which has

proved far longer and deeper than its famous neighbor, Carlsbad Caverns, and Mexico's Che Ve, which (in addition to having great length) may be deeper than the French record
holder. Both of these systems were discovered in the mid-
1980s, and both have yielded additional miles of passage to
every subsequent expedition. The cavers who had served as
midwife to such finds felt the conditions in this corner of
China were the best they had ever seen.

Because of a big cave's complexity, the only way to make any
sense of it—geologic or otherwise—is to map as you go. Imagine exploring the Mississippi and its tributaries in the dark.
With all the twists and turns, how could you describe where
you had been? What was the greatest distance you traveled
from the river's mouth? Which tributary seemed to be the
largest? Place the river in three dimensions, and you will see
why cartography is the essence of cave exploration.

A skyscraper-deep pit, a glistening formation, a pile of prehistoric bones—cavers can and do find such features around
any particular bend. We hoped to find such things before our
expedition was over, perhaps by the end of the day. But often
the greatest finds emerge weeks after a trip, when a finished
map tells us where we have been and suggests where we might
go next. De Soto seldom knew what he had found until he
completed a number of trips, and a number of maps—and he
worked in daylight, over a period of years.

Individual cave trips usually last forty-eight hours or less,
most expeditions a month or so. If we accurately mapped even
ten miles of passage during our entire expedition, we would
have accomplished more than many first forays into a new
cave region. And we hoped for several caves that would extend
beyond our time and manpower to fully map them. Ideally,
one or more of our partial maps would—when studied in the
light of day—suggest that we had found a system to occupy
expeditions for years to come.

Mapping a cave is a matter of connecting survey stations by
means of a plastic measuring tape. Along with distance, the

compass bearing and degree of inclination between stations must be recorded. A careful sketch of the passage, set down on waterproof grid paper, supplements the straight-line data. Pat Kambesis is known throughout the international caving community for the vivid detail of her cave maps. She was one the chief drafters of the 86 miles of passage mapped in Lechuguilla since 1986. Much of that cave was discovered by Pat herself, including the Chandelier Ballroom, one of the most heavily decorated cave chambers ever found. She has drafted intricate maps that cavers hang as pieces of art.

All of this is to say that she is a perfectionist and a slave driver when running a survey team.

Before she allowed me to set the first survey mark, she forbade the team from working more than a single survey station ahead of her. Reading instruments and measuring distances takes less time than sketching, especially sketching the complex features of a cavern as large as the one before us. If her instrument team became too caught up in the thrill of discovery, the quality of her map would suffer.

"When I say stop, I mean stop," she said.

Stockert winked at me. "Yes, Dominatrix Patty," he said, bowing with his arms outstretched. "We await your discipline."

I played along. "O giver of pain, our wish is but to serve your pencil and your protractor."

"Good," she said, keeping a straight face. "I'm glad you know your place."

Liang looked confused. It wouldn't be the first time on the expedition that one of our hosts looked confused. Cavers almost constantly engage in the sort of banter that would be inconceivable within a Chinese group. When enduring formal banquets on the surface, our team had tried to maintain ambassadorial composure. Underground, this was harder to do. When you are routinely coated with mud and grime, when you travel through places most people can't imagine, let alone experience, when your very survival depends on individual competence and confidence, the social norms of the surface world tend to evaporate. I suppose it is something like going to war, but without the unpleasant part. By the end of the expedition, some of our goofiness would rub off on our hosts: Two senior Guizhou geologists would be seen arguing over which of them could wear a rubber cone head in a group photo.

Despite the fun, Tom and I knew the importance of allowing the sketcher to set the pace. Instead of racing into blackness, we moved as deliberately as astronauts on the lunar surface. For the first hour, I taught Liang "lead tape," the task of setting survey points. Liang would carry the end of our thirty-meter tape (all cave surveys outside the United States are metric), while Tom held the unwinding spool. As the tape neared its maximum extension, I would find a distinct finger of rock to serve as a station, or build a cairn of small stones. Liang would hold a flashlight "on point" while Tom wrote down bearing and inclination readings from the previous station. Whenever Pat shouted that she was ready, we would move forward and repeat the process.

For the first few shots, we were able to continue along the ledge, high and dry above the river. Several stations into the cave, Liang asked why I had chosen to build a cairn five meters short of an obvious natural point, when our tape would have reached it. "We want long measure, right?"

"That point's against the wall," I answered. "Tom would have a hard time seeing our next station if he stood there. Next station, we'll be somewhere down there." I pointed to the river. Our ledge had run out; it was time to get wet.

Liang looked surprised, but shrugged to indicate that he was game. After Tom and Pat caught up, Liang and I scrambled down the face.

Even beneath coveralls, a full wet suit, and a thermal polypropylene liner, the shock of frigid water creeping up my legs made me howl. Caves normally maintain a constant temperature within a few degrees of the annual average of the surface overhead. At the elevation and latitude of Zhijin that should have been about 58° F—but this river had just left a subfreezing canyon.

Ice water slammed into me. I chose each step across the

hip-deep stream with care. At first I managed to keep dry above the knees, then the thighs, then the waist. Protected as I was, I still didn't want to slip on a loose rock and become completely immersed. Without the wet suit, I would have become hypothermic in minutes, unconscious in less than an hour. A general lack of wet suits in South China is one reason so many large river caves remain unexplored.

At last I gave in to the inevitable and plunged into a deep hole to avoid climbing over a twelve-foot-high rock. As I became used to the coolness, I realized that I actually felt better in the river. I'd been sweating in the thick wet suit while mapping the ledge above. When we stopped at a midstream boulder to set the next point, I tried to convey this observation to Liang. That was when I noticed he was shivering.

"Isn't your wet suit working?" I asked.

Liang smiled sheepishly. "No wetta suit," he said.

"What was that you put on when we stopped to eat?"

Liang unfastened the Velcro closure of his coveralls to reveal long underwear made of dark, heavy cotton pile—virtually useless when wet. "No wetta suit," he said.

Daylight still reached us from the massive entrance, now a half kilometer behind us. When the others caught up, we convinced Liang to return to the ledge where we had changed, borrow some warm clothing, and wait for our return in a few hours. We watched the bobbing progress of his lamp to make sure he made it safely up the slick face.

Tom and I decided to trade jobs: I hung the compass and clinometer around my neck like medallions and handed him the tape. The three of us waded from one side of the river to the other as we continued mapping. Pat—the team's only formally trained geologist—pointed out fault lines, side leads, and the contact zones between different limestone layers. We set about learning not only where this cave led but the history of the landscape in which it lay. As she sketched, Pat began to draw conclusions on the characteristics of the particular limestone in which we found ourselves and what effect those characteristics might have on its caves.

At length Coons's mapping party caught up with us, having checked all side leads. They leapfrogged a few hundred meters beyond our team. It was late evening somewhere far overhead when both teams were at last stopped by a sump. Nearly two kilometers into the cave, the high ceiling came down to meet the river. The water continued, but without dive gear we could not.

We trekked out to the entrance and then back up the frozen cliffs of the canyon. A full moon occasionally poked through clouds that still spilled mist and sleet. We were grateful to discover that Liang Hong had hiked ahead to arrange a bus for us at the top of the canyon. Throughout the dark ride to our cold guesthouse, we debated which of the many entrances surrounding us we would try the following day.

Since the time of Marco Polo, expeditions to China have begun with a seemingly endless series of meetings and banquets. Ours had been no exception. By our third day in the country, I had begun to wonder whether everyone could survive the etiquette. I had joined the first American expedition to cave in China in the spring of 1988. That group of twelve, sponsored by the Cave Research Foundation and *National Geographic*, had been chosen primarily for scientific expertise and the ability to serve as goodwill ambassadors for expeditions to come. We had explored several big and impressive caves, but every day spent underground cost us two or three spent socializing on the surface.

While scientific expertise was also represented in the present team, the main qualification for selection had been proven skill in exploring caves. This was another reason I was glad I had found our sponsor; I could never have joined such a team otherwise. Among us were some of the strongest cavers in the United States, rugged individuals used to action. Three days of banquets in Guiyang had turned them into staggering zombies.

Don Coons, a professional caver who also ran a large family farm in Illinois, had been much in the news the previous spring for leading the three-day rescue of Emily Davis Mobley from Lechuguilla. His subterranean skill and daring through-out North America had become legend in speleological cir-cles. Underground, he was a fluid marvel. On the surface, he seemed shy to the point of introversion and easily bored.

By the second hour of a meeting in the unheated lobby of a Guizhou Normal University dormitory, Don twitched like a trapped cat. His face was locked in a grimly polite smile, aimed at the various senior geologists and university adminis-trators who held forth on our impending subterranean success and the value of continued East-West exchange. Don wore a black cap, pulled low, and a brilliantly embroidered jacket made for him by Mayan women in an area of Guatemala where he caved regularly. His feet danced incessantly.

What was to be our final meeting before heading to the field had been delayed while we awaited the arrival of the uni-versity president, who was reputed to be a caver himself. Other members listened drowsily as our surface coordinator, Ian Baren, translated repetitious statements of goodwill from the assembled Guizhou geologists. At length the president arrived. A powerfully built, open-faced man with a winning smile, he delivered an example of classic Chinese oratory, punctuated by shouted injunctions to strive onward. He paused, now and then, to sip tea from an old Tang jar. The American breakfast drink, not the dynasty.

In contrast to the nervous Coons, cartographer Kambesis sat very nearly asleep in the corner of the room. Beside her slouched Chris Stine, a New Jersey caver who had appeared on the cover of *National Geographic* a few months earlier, climb-ing up a flowstone slope in Lechuguilla. I had come to regard Chris as the world's consummate caving bum. Despite a Rut-gers master's degree in hydroponic agriculture, he had been liv-ing hand to mouth for several years. When not discovering and exploring great caves, he took construction jobs, played a mean lead guitar, and slept in attics or on couches. Rounding out our bored assembly were Ian—who was at least kept busy trans-lating the stream of mutual compliments—Tom Stockert,

Mike Newsome, and our team photographer, Kevin Downey. Kevin flitted about the room flashing strobes, I think to wake us up as much as to light the place.

Don grinned at something far away, his feet a tapping blur. As the president's speech drew to a close, one of the professors unrolled a military topographic map of our target area. The map was far more detailed than any we had seen to date; showing it to foreigners was almost certainly illegal. Suddenly, the cavers were very much involved in the meeting.

"My God, look at that!" shouted Don. He traced the course of a dry river with his finger. "It goes into the ridge here and doesn't come out until way over here."

"That stuff on top looks like parts of Puerto Rico," said Kevin Downey, setting his camera aside. "Only bigger. Look, see the karst window right there. It's like Río Camuy."

"Yes!" shouted Chris Stine, waking up. He had not yet looked at the map, but didn't want to miss out on anything. "Yes!" Then he saw the map and became really excited.

"If we camp here," Don pointed, "we can send teams here, here, and here. All of this stuff goes, it has to. We won't see a fraction of it."

Pat crowded among the others. "It could take years to see a fraction of it," she said. "Let's go, let's go, let's go."

The next day, as we drove among the karst canyons near our first base at Daji Dong, Don stared openmouthed at the limestone reality of what the maps had promised. Unmapped, unexplored caves were everywhere. Some of them surely led into "the system." At one point our van crossed a canyon lip to begin a frightening series of switchbacks down the dirt highway. The opposite canyon wall was pocked with holes the size of the Hollywood Bowl. Don looked out the window and said, "Everything that's been done in speleology up to now was preparation for China. This is where the real stuff is. The rest of the world was practice."

The dirt highway passed through the center of two dozen villages. If a village was having its weekly market day, traffic

would stop for hours. One such delay gave us our first opportunity to walk among the Miao minority. Most of the Miao we
encountered had never seen a foreigner. We walked about the
market, drawing a crowd of onlookers that soon swelled to
more than three hundred. As each of us moved from stall to
stall, our personal entourage moved with us. I felt like a Mar-
tian, or Michael Jackson. At last the van honked slowly past
the tables of fresh pork and handmade batik, and we were
again on our way.

Along with the van, our hosts had engaged a small truck to
carry caving gear. Our driver responded to the gasps of terror
he would hear each time the narrow highway presented a hair-
pin turn or sheer cliff by gradually slowing down. The truck
driver was under no such constraint. He sped far ahead of the
van, flying past coal trucks on blind curves. It thus came as no
real surprise when, late in the day, we rounded a bend to see
the highway blocked by our truck and a bus, both skewed at
ominous angles.

The truck had taken the turn too fast, the bus had taken it
too wide. Each had unsuccessfully swerved to avoid the other.
No one appeared to have been hurt in the collision. Both
drivers now stood in the highway, cursing like Manhattan cabbies, while onlookers gathered from nearby homes and out of
the stopped traffic.

Although both vehicles appeared to be in running order, we
were told that neither could be moved until the proper
authorities arrived. The highway was effectively closed. The
nearest police station was an hour away. The nearest telephone that could summon the police was perhaps forty-five
minutes in the opposite direction. It would be a long wait.

While the van set off for the telephone, a few sharp villagers set up food stalls for the growing crowd. Kevin and I
took advantage of the delay to explore the surroundings.

The accident had occurred on a bank above a small river.
We walked past a series of rapids just below the wreck, where
wooden paddles converted the water to mechanical energy,
driving four-foot poles that moved with a continual scrubbing

motion, their tips buried underwater. We tried to deduce the purpose of these simple but ingenious devices. All of our guesses were proven wrong when a man and his son arrived to tend them. Through gestures and demonstration, the man showed us how each pole held a short length of sandalwood, which it scrubbed against a grooved stone set underwater. The washed shavings that accumulated at the base of the stone were collected, dried, and compressed to make sandalwood incense.

"And then you sell the incense?" Kevin asked, pantomiming a transaction. The man shook his head no, looking offended. He pointed to a small building at the side of an ancient limestone bridge that crossed the river upstream of the sandalwood mill. His fingers waved like smoke, and I understood. *We burn it in the temple.*

Kevin stayed to photograph the man and his machines. I reached the building at sunset. It was a windowless masonry square, about the size of my college office. The doorway faced a dark entrance in the rockface that stood directly across from the bridge.

I looked first at the cave. The opening was the sort of beautiful curved arch that the general public typically imagines as a cave entrance but which is in fact rare in nature. Hollywood Cave: Inside, the broad-shouldered hero invariably finds a flat floor, a never explained light source which follows him around, gold, mole people, and assorted skeletons. At some point he is generally attacked by slow-moving, hairy loaves of bread with cardboard wings.

The cavern before me, however, proved small and choked with boulders. It offered little more than a pretty entrance, a rock shelter where a traveler might wait out a storm. An ancient footpath snaked down from an overhead mountain to the cave. The path crossed the bridge to the empty temple and took off up a mountain on the opposite side.

I walked across the bridge, twenty feet above the river, wondering who had laid these stones and when. Standing before the single-room temple were what appeared to be very old

Buddhist prayer wheels. Some had fallen over and lay decaying in a pile. A smell of sandalwood rolled from the open door. In the shadowy interior, I could barely make out two white figures standing at the center of an ash-covered shrine.

The two-foot-tall deities appeared to contemplate the cave across the river. I assumed one statue was of Buddha, and wondered about the second, which appeared feminine. As others had done before me, I left a small offering of paper money on the wooden altar. Later, I learned that both images in the shrine depicted local spirits of the underground, much revered.

Like Mayan cave lords or the Oracle at Delphi, these earth goddesses were believed to traverse limestone pathways connecting the physical with the sacred. They moved freely from the temporal world—a surface governed by cycles of day and night, hot and cold, life and death—into the timeless world of the cave. Outside was logic, order, linear thought. Inside was story, inspiration, magic.

In a decade and a half spent exploring and reading about caves, I have learned that the primitive peoples who worship underground tend to have a high regard for coincidence and prophecy. Those who enter a grotto in order to receive a vision usually do. Like pilgrims in the desert, they have left the known behind. For cavers, a working knowledge of geology and possession of decent lighting robs some of the mystery from cave passages. But all we really manage to do is to set the unknown at arm's length, to push it a bit farther down the next crawlway or higher up the next climb.

We still carry the cavemen inside us.

The otherness of the spelean environment teaches them, has taught me, to see nothing illogical, or even very much out of the ordinary, whenever a person or cavern or narrative becomes suddenly magical, becomes, like Billy Pilgrim, unstuck in time.

20

Feng Shui

Anyone who has stood at a cave entrance and felt its cool breeze, smelling of mud and ozone, should not be surprised to learn that caves take on mystic significance to indigenous peoples in virtually all places they are found. This is especially true in South China, where there are so many. The mystic quality of South China caves is intertwined in the Taoist concept of *feng shui*. "Wind water" is a literal translation of this central phrase of Chinese geomancy, but *feng shui* can also refer to the intrinsic "rightness" of a scene, to the effect of landscape on human destiny, or to "the art of adapting the residences of the living and the dead so as to cooperate and harmonize with the local currents of cosmic breath which rise from the ducts of the earth."

No skyscraper is built in Hong Kong or Singapore without a consulting geomancer, who examines *feng shui* through inscribed compasses and ancient bones. In much of Asia, the process determines where exactly to locate any structure from a tomb to a regional plastics factory. This yin and yang of place is found, as often as not, near the mouth of a cave.

On a misty afternoon during one of my three trips to China, two American cavers and I became the first Westerners to experience the *feng shui* of Coffin Cave, which has been tied to the Liu clan of the Blue Miao for over a thousand years. The short cavern was aptly named: It was stacked floor to ceiling with some seven hundred hand-carved coffins. Instead of family plots, there were family piles. Simple pine boxes lay atop crumbling, inscription-covered sarcophagi. Human bones and ancient pottery littered every visible surface.

According to tradition, every three hundred years all of the coffins are burned to make room for more, and the time for burning had nearly come again. However, closer examination showed only a single likely fire pit, thick with ash, bone, and pottery fragments. We could find no evidence of burning elsewhere in the shallow cave, which we mapped in three survey stations. It seemed more likely that the coffins were burned selectively, as particular family branches died out, with no descendant left to guard the deceased.

We were told that whenever an older member of the clan is dying, family members will ask, "Do you want to go to the country or the city?" Those who opt for the country are given a more traditional Chinese tomb, while those who choose the city are placed in the crowded cave.

Many of the older coffins had begun to decay. Shrouds and bones poked through the sides. I studied the carved wood, wondering about the lives these people had led. Some skulls showed clear bullet wounds. Throughout China's history, the Miao have periodically rebelled against imperial rule. These may have been failed heroes of some ancient rebellion. Or perhaps they fought the occupying Japanese. More likely, they fell victim to the Cultural Revolution.

Standing amid the dusty skulls and piled coffins, I felt as though I were in a museum warehouse. The strangeness of the scene made it somehow impersonal. I could not connect these boat-shaped boxes to respected grandparents, nor those short bundled logs to mourned infants. Whatever *feng shui* Coffin Cave held belonged to the Liu clan. I felt awkward, an interloper. This was not my place. I was overcome by a strange disassociation from the scene that threatened to make any later effort to describe it both overly existential and prolix.

Luckily, one caver, who had lagged behind, whistled softly. I'll call him Floyd Collins. He whistled again, and I walked back around a corner.

Floyd stood alone on a ledge, juggling three human skulls. I shook my head. He was pretty good at it. The whiteness of the bones stood out against his electric-blue coveralls and the soot-blackened walls. There was an intrinsic rightness to the scene. "If Mikhail Bakhtin went caving," I said, "I believe he would term this a *carnivalesque* tableau."

"The hell's Mikhail Bakhtin?" Floyd asked. Rightly so.

I watched him a few minutes more. "If you could just add an apple, you might have an act."

In the spring of 1995, I flew to New York City with eight Henderson students for a journalism convention. We were packed with a couple thousand other college journalists and their advisers in the Marriott Marquis at Times Square. Downstairs, Jerry Lewis sang nightly in *Damn Yankees*. Most of the students in my group had never been to New York, so of course they wanted to see the Empire State Building, Statue of Liberty, Metropolitan Museum, Staten Island Ferry, blah blah blah, yadda yadda yadda. Not that I minded playing Circle Line guide. I still loved and missed most of those places myself.

I finagled our group some media-related tours at Rockefeller Center: Chris Hunt detailed the weekly routine at *Sports Illustrated*. Craig White led us on an informative walk through the NBC news division, and let us watch Paul Reiser and the cast of *Saturday Night Live* rehearse a sketch for an upcoming show. But I also persuaded five of the students to accompany me to Chinatown for an enormous meal of unidentifiable items with Floyd and another caver at New Pell's Dinty. These five liked the food, and they were game enough to agree to a tunnel trip the following night.

So after a day of lectures on how to run a better campus newspaper, we drove to Floyd's apartment and geared up for a midnight walk through the Hibernaculum. Floyd brought out a few relics of our shared past, and somehow we both started telling the story of his juggling act. I could have sworn I'd taken a picture of it, I told him, but I've never been able to find the slide.

"Why on earth would you want to juggle skulls?" asked Lara Crane, a good student bound for graduate school. Lara was to deliver the student charge at commencement in a few weeks. In it, she would quote from the *Tao Te Ching*.

Floyd shrugged. "I knew what I was doing was wrong, and I still feel a little guilty," he said. "I'd hate for any of the Chinese geologists who brought us there to ever find out about it." This part he said looking at me. "But I couldn't *not* do it. I was there, the skulls were there. How many times in your life are you gonna get that sort of chance?"

21

INTO THE MOUTH OF THE DRAGON

Fog rose from the entrance. The hazy column led the team through a maze of muddy limestone paths. Once more I followed Chris Stine, Pat Kambesis, and Don Coons up the mountain's flank, stepping where they stepped, zigzagging toward the spiral of mist. A layer of rime on an ancient stair caused my boots to slip from under me, nearly sent me tumbling downhill. Balance regained, I paused for a moment to stare at the rising vapor, now no more than a hundred yards away. I felt like a child of Israel, following the Pillar of Smoke. Yet this was no Egyptian desert underfoot.

We had begun to intimately understand what had been a mere statistic before this expedition: Guizhou Province is the wettest place in China, with over 200 centimeters of rainfall annually. We had chosen the "dry" winter months to avoid flooding caves, not realizing that dry is a relative term. An old Chinese proverb holds that "in Guizhou, you will never see three consecutive days of sunshine, three taels of silver, or three *mou* of flat land." The relentless rain hammers at the elevated limestone, carving great breathing portals that swallow rivers whole and give rise to legend.

The day before, Ian had thoughtfully distributed vials of snake bile, purchased at one of the Miao markets, to ward off the hacking coughs most team members had developed in the cool, damp weather. Kevin was in bed at the guesthouse, looking miserable. The rest of us seemed only slightly better off;

we took what cures we could find. English labels declared the bile "most efficacious against sputum, crudum cough," among other ailments. It tasted sweet and syrupy.

In single file, we wound among triangular boulders that our team's Chinese geologists termed "dragon's tooth karst." The blades of dark rock suggested to me the fins of prehistoric sharks, the extinct giants whose teeth are sometimes found embedded in limestone. The surrounding terraced fields— many of them smaller than a king-sized bed—sparkled with ice. I wondered whether the tender, hand-planted shoots of cabbage and bok choy would survive the frost. Low clouds hugged the overhead peak, washing the rock in the gray bands of a Chinese watercolor. Rain or snow seemed once more imminent.

We reached the steep sinkhole that held the entrance. I could see what had prompted the Miaos to name the place Long Dong, which, despite the obvious jokes it engendered among the cavers, actually translated as Dragon Cave. What creature but a dragon would dwell in a such a hole, constantly spewing damp fog? The Miao evidently harbored no more fear of dragons than I did. As I crossed the rim of the sinkhole, I saw that a group of women and young girls ahead of us were working their way down to the opening below.

They wore traditional blue scarves and dresses. Their black belts were embroidered with bright, complex patterns that recorded Blue Miao lineage and clan status. The women had high cheekbones and skin the color of polished rosewood. They stood slightly taller than the average Chinese, and moved with an almost regal poise. Empty wooden buckets rested in bamboo carriers on their backs. These explained why the group had journeyed so far on such a cold and dreary day. In a region where the rivers flow underground, few villages enjoy the luxury of surface water. Our team had come to Dragon Cave in search of unknown pits and passageways, geologic mystery. The Miao entered it in order to fetch water.

We caught up them with just inside the cave. Both groups paused to look each other over in the hazy half-light. As we unpacked ropes, helmets, and gear, Mike Newsome pulled a harmonica from his pack and began to play the blues. Shades of Muddy Waters echoed from the arched ceiling. The little girls gathered around him, fascinated and giggling. Their shyer mothers stood back, studying our ropes and gear, speculating in local dialect as to the purpose of each strange item. I noticed one of them tapping her foot to the beat. She wore dirty Western-style running shoes.

Mike and Ian were the principal singers of the caving band BrickInHead; Chris was the lead guitarist and I played bass. Our name had been given us by the Guru, Bob Cohen, who had once seen a man holding a bloody towel to his head in a Bronx emergency room at four in the morning, chanting, "I have brick in head, I have brick in head." Mike worked his way through some of the BrickInHead repertoire: "That Old-Time Carbide Glow," "Cave Gear for Nothing," "Psycho Caver." The rest of us donned coveralls and climbing harnesses, and at last the harmonica concert drew to a close. Miao and caver alike moved deeper into the gloom.

Perhaps 200 feet in lay a carved stone pool. For centuries, pure water had trickled into the basin from a crack in the cave wall. Here, the Miao filled their buckets before beginning the long hike back to their village. Even the smallest girl carried a load of water, the wavering flame of a bamboo torch lighting her way to daylight. A hundred feet beyond the pool the cave floor dropped steeply away. At the base of a rocky 20-foot slope lay blackness—an overhung pit, gateway to the virgin passages below. Our goal for the day was to find the source of the warm breeze that flowed past us to mix with winter air outside, the source of the dragon's breath.

Late in the night of the truck accident, we had arrived at the guesthouse of Daji Dong, which translates as Shoot-the-Chicken Cave. This tourist cave is seldom visited by Westerners, not because of its name, but because of the difficulty involved in reaching it. Should the roads eventually be improved, Daji may one day be ranked among the world's premier tour caves. It is approximately the same length and depth as Carlsbad Caverns, and contains rooms and formations strikingly similar to those found in that national park. Daji receives mention in only one tourist guidebook to China, a thorough if fairly obscure 1988 British publication called *Southwest China off the Beaten Path*, designed for serious trekkers and hitchhikers. The single-paragraph entry begins, "By most accounts, Daji Dong Cave near Zhijin Shan Mountain is the largest in the world."

While we found nothing in Daji to substantiate such an extravagant claim, the cave was indeed enormous, as were many of the unexplored caves we mapped in its vicinity. We began the slow process of what Coons called "putting the puzzle together." We hoped the maps of several caves would help us to see how they were interrelated, to learn the hidden geology of the karst. A dry cave that opened halfway up a cliff might have once carried the river now lying in the canyon. A pit atop a plateau might lead to a segment of passage that, when plotted on our map, would prove to be part of the same extinct riverbed. Meanwhile, the present river that flowed into a cliff and appeared to emerge at a spring five miles away might go someplace else entirely.

Many entrances indicated past human activity in the form of crumbling fortified walls. Such was the case of Hei Dong, or Black Cave. Its borehole tunnels were so dark that they seemed to suck the light from our headlamps. We could seldom see from one end of a chamber to the other in the gloom. The rock was not naturally black, but had been darkened by decades—or, more likely, centuries—of smoke from an extensive saltpeter extraction operation which had reshaped much of the cave floor.

Written records of gunpowder manufacture in China go back as far as the ninth century. All of gunpowder's three main ingredients—charcoal, sulfur, and saltpeter—abound in the southern karst regions. In parts of Guizhou, all three can be literally scooped off the ground. Although written records are unclear, some historians theorize that the first gunpowder may have been mixed in one of the southern provinces. What is better established is that hundreds of years before recorded gunpowder, Taoist monks in Guizhou extracted saltpeter from cave soil for use in alchemy.

As we mapped our way across the stone saltpeter vats of Hei Dong, I asked one of our hosts from the university whether he knew the age of the abandoned operation. He thought for a minute, shrugged, and said, "Before Liberation"—that is, before 1949. I pressed for a more specific date, and he said, "About two hundred years." This was a standard reply throughout the trip. I would observe a crumbling monastery, a bit of porcelain, a human shin; I would ask a local person or one of our hosts to guess its age; I would receive two answers: "Before Liberation" followed by "About two hundred years." In that we were unqualified and unprepared for any sort of archeological excavation, we merely noted in the survey book each item, its location, and its "estimated" age for future researchers.

Using small metal wedges called chocks, Don Coons attached one end of an eight-millimeter line to a limestone boulder and tossed the other end into blackness of the pit inside Dragon Cave. He and Mike Newsome rappelled first.

"On rope!" I shouted down to them. I stepped from a boulder and into space, rope singing through my rappel rack. Although the wide chamber in which I landed lay no more than 100 feet below the Miao pool, I could see that from this point on Dragon Cave would offer nothing but virgin passage. Above the shaft, countless feet had worn a smooth, dusty trail in the cave floor. Below, the only marks had been left by the passage of time.

I waited in the rock-and-pebble-strewn room for Liang Hong to rappel down. Although he had trained thoroughly on the surface, this was his first in-cave rappel. Liang had become more enthusiastic about caving with each trip; I recognized in him the signs of a convert. He had wanted to crawl into a couple of miserable-looking side passages, to see where they might go, as we worked our way past the water bearers. As he had heard others do, Liang let out a rebel yell when he stepped free of the ledge. He landed flawlessly, and joined me in an inspection of the circular chamber.

The mud floor bore tiny depressions in each place where water had dripped. Every limestone flake that fell from the wall stood embedded where it had landed. The slow geologic process by which mountains are swept to the sea was arrested in freeze-frame. No living thing had touched the evidence; the pieces of the puzzle fit. *Surface water fell there for a very long time, and this large boulder, loosened from above, changed the course of the stream, and thus that slot was cut into the wall over there.*

We again formed two mapping teams, spacing ourselves 200 meters apart in the main passage. One danger of being the first person to walk through a cave, especially one as dry as Dragon Cave proved to be, is that the rocks you step upon may shift without warning. About a kilometer beyond the pit, I climbed down a slope toward what appeared to be a lower level. The entire slope moved six inches. I scrambled rapidly uphill. A boulder the size of a dishwasher crashed down from where I had been standing. Such shifting rocks kept several team members on their toes as we moved steadily into the bowels of the dragon.

For that was how the main passage ended: in a mud-slick, bowel-like tube which trapped Mike Newsome for nearly an hour. The old watercourse we had followed divided into several slanting tunnels. When Newsome tried to chimney into what seemed the largest, he found that the smooth sides gave no purchase. He slid several yards into the steep, damp funnel. It tightened about him so suddenly that he could barely breathe, let alone move.

He shouted his situation up to Coons, who relayed it to the others, both groups having met in this final chamber. We lowered a loop of rope down the tube. Slowly, hand over hand on the muddy line, we managed to haul our winded harp player to safety. Seeing the mud-covered Newsome emerge, hearing his description of the tube that had held him, the team unanimously concluded that we had more interesting leads to pursue elsewhere. Dragon Cave was declared mapped, one more piece in a puzzle that will take years to complete.

On the way out, Don, Pat, and I detoured to finish off a side lead that meandered for 200 meters through a dry maze area. As Don paused to work on his sketch at the end of the maze, I investigated an alcove above and to one side of the final survey point. In the tiny chamber was a sand floor covered with transparent gypsum crystals the size and shape of No. 2 pencils. They were not so large or unusual as to be worth photographing, or even worth noting on the map, so I did not bother to call the other two into the alcove. Yet they were exquisite in their geometric perfection.

These delicate bits of gypsum had been growing, I realized, far longer than I. I stared at them for several minutes, the first and only living creature ever to do so. The light hit them well. It was a moment of great *feng shui*. I considered the slow processes by which crystals grow and people live, by which seabeds lift and caves collapse, by which civilizations evolve and governments change.

The moment passed. I followed the dragon's breath to the surface, thinking about our supper bubbling in the wok.

Most of the caves we had mapped thus far opened as insurgences, entrances that swallowed streams or rivers. Dou Bing Dong, Hiding Soldiers Cave, was a resurgence, a slit in a cliff which spewed a river. The topographic map we carried suggested that the source of this river could be one or more of several vanishing streams located on the opposite side of a mountain. All were over five miles away, as the crow flies. As the cave winds, that could mean twenty miles or more of passage. If we could follow the cave upstream without being stopped by impassable sumps, the river should branch into a number of lengthy tributaries.

The name of the cave, we learned, came from an army that had hidden in it during the Taiping Rebellion of 1850–65.

The stream that had carved Dou Bing Dong had established a series of parallel courses over the aeons, each riverbed deeper than the preceding one. This meant that several distinct levels intersected the main tunnel. One could avoid the river by traversing a higher level, but the higher passages often opened to abrupt pits.

At the base of one such pit, on a muddy boulder alongside the river, Don found the shattered skull of a long-lost soldier. We decided to name him George. Most of the skeleton had been carried away by previous torrents. Don put the bits that were left into his pack. Putting George together again became a sort of macabre jigsaw puzzle, something to entertain cavers in the field house between increasingly lengthy survey trips to Dou Bing Dong.

Mike, Ian, and Tom had made a productive trip to the nearest village market, buying sufficient lengths of stovepipe to install a homemade coal stove in one room of our frigid field house. Mike had also wired up a primitive adapter and battery charger which kept the room in rock and roll, and he and Pat had hung large colorful batik work done by local Miao women. Each night, after a long wet trip into Dou Bing Dong, cavers would sit around the improvised crash pad and assemble George with Super Glue, while Pat crunched numbers in a handheld calculator and plotted new passages onto the growing draft of the map, which hung down either side of a small wooden desk.

Dou Bing Dong kept going. Each time the main passage would end in a sump, a team member would climb the walls and find an upper-level bypass that led back into the main passage, beyond the sump. After three days of upstream survey had mapped as many kilometers, small teams began traveling the surface to check out the possible insurgences, while two separate survey teams worked each day in the main cave. All of the potential connections were located at higher elevation, so these scouting teams carried several ropes for the pits they were sure to encounter.

There is a sort of Murphy's Law of international caving,

and it goes like this: The most promising find will appear on the last day of any expedition. Dou Bing Dong continued to extend upstream, pushed in survey trips of ever increasing length and difficulty. But most of the insurgent streams—each of which consumed a day's exploration and mapping—would end in flooded sumps in a kilometer or less. As time for the expedition was running out, the insurgent team of Tom, Ian, and Chris hiked two miles beyond a village at the end of a dirt road to rig a rope beside a vanishing waterfall.

The smooth white walls were scalloped from the force of falling water; it was clear that this insurgence drained a large surface area. After a rappel of over 30 feet in a pounding waterfall, the three followed the frothing stream around the corner to the top of a second drop. They rappelled to the bottom of this, then carried their last remaining rope down the slick passage, free-climbing a series of short waterfalls to reach the top of the third pit.

The third rope they had carried that day was about 50 feet long—ten feet shorter than the third drop. But by anchoring his feet on a short ledge, Ian was able to release the rope and climb to the bottom of the pit, and see where the stream followed a series of short cascades into the dark. The problem was that whereas sliding *down* the slick cascades would be relatively easy, coming back *up* without any more rope, against the force of the water, could prove impossible. The three emptied their packs and found several lengths of webbing, which they tied together to make a 20-foot handline.

While Tom secured the upper end of the handline, Chris and Ian worked their way to its end, from which they were just able to step to a dry ledge and see . . . the top of the fourth pit. If Dou Bing Dong was indeed the lower entrance to the system we had sought, this cave, named Xiao Lu Dong, had proved itself an upper access. Provided, of course, that the map showed the twisting waterway heading in the right direction, something the three could only guess at from where they stood. Reluctantly, they turned around and fought their way back up the short cascade. Even assisted by the handline, they couldn't climb back until Tom blocked some of the heavy flow by wedging his lower body into the shape of a temporary dam.

The expedition was over.

We had mapped more than 12 kilometers of the many passages winding beneath rural Guizhou Province, and the exploration of the first of many great Chinese cave systems had only just begun. The team brought back sufficient maps and leads to entice expert cavers to return to the same field house on expeditions in the spring of 1994 and the fall of 1995. I had brought back a few hundred slides, some Miao handicrafts, a hacking cough, and memories of the largest cave passages I had ever explored. And I had gained one other item, which I carried in my pocket as I walked into a classroom to start the spring 1992 semester, just six hours after the last leg of a grueling transpacific flight: a small black pebble from the base of the pit in Dragon Cave.

Even now I can pull it from my desk drawer and slip backward in time.

22

GRASS

On a breezy afternoon in the fall of 1990, I lay down in a field of tall grass in the mountains of Ru Yuan County, Guangdong Province, the People's Republic of China. Pencil-like stalks poked into my back. I bent several stems at ground level in order to get comfortable. My pack made a fine, if slightly lumpy, pillow. After a bit of arranging, I reclined and chewed on a dusty green blade. I stared at a hazy sky framed by pines and spruce.

Tom Stockert, Ian Baren, and I had been searching—with the help of some local farmers—for a cave that we knew contained a deep unexplored pit. None of the Chinese geologists who had told us of the find had been there in many years. The main passage had been roughly surveyed by a group of architects in the early 1980s, with an eye toward possible development as a tourist attraction, but they had lacked equipment to descend the shaft. Ultimately, they had given up on the tourism plan: The entrance was miles from any road. One of our local guides swore that a rock thrown into the pit took five *minutes* to hit bottom. Although this was quite impossible, we hoped that the shaft might prove to be a few hundred feet deep.

We knew that the rounded peak which hid the entrance had once been farmed. For over an hour we had crossed ancient terraces, now overgrown with brush and saplings. With each fallow field we struggled into, our guides would tell us that this was the last before the cave. Hauling climbing gear from sinkhole to ridge had proved hard work. We needed a break. Tom, Ian, and I had dropped our packs in the first grassy clearing and collapsed. Our embarrassed guides continued beating the bush while we stretched out.

Somewhere among the leafy shadows a circle of blackness led to the mountain's limestone heart. Our chances of finding the proper shadow in the remaining hour of daylight seemed remote. We had mapped several other caves that week, including a sporting overnight jaunt into Swallow Cave— which Ian and I had first begun mapping with the 1988 expedition—that had netted more than a kilometer of virgin passage. We were in no hurry.

My own fatigue came from more than the steep hike. The night before, two local policemen had insisted on a four-hour drinking contest with "strong foreign friend." I had lost. Badly. One policeman, a homicide detective, had told us he was a fan of *Hawaii Five-O* and had been flattered when we began referring to him as McGarrett.

At some point Ian had admired McGarrett's four-wheel-drive police jeep, and had been encouraged to try it out, which he gladly did, weaving through the woods and landing in a fair-sized stream. Sometime later, I thought we might be in danger of arrest, such was McGarrett's disappointment at our lack of interest in visiting the local madam, who was clearly his friend and was perhaps his business associate. They had taken no for an answer only on the condition that I drink copious amounts of a foul-smelling ginseng brandy. A hairy root floated in the bottle.

I recalled meeting Ian on the first official American caving expedition to China in 1988. "Official," I had learned, meant endless dinners with party functionaries, cave "events" staged for the Chinese press, run-ins with professional handlers who tried to keep us at arm's length from ordinary people, and a rigid schedule that invariably stopped a cave trip just as it became interesting. Now the three of us were on our own, pushing leads and delving into local culture as we pleased. Ostensibly, we were scouting locations for a possible Smithsonian expedition the following year. Mostly, we were having the time of our lives. Now that the steep path had sweated out the remnants of McGarrett's ginseng poison, I was happy just to lie on the ground and know that I was in China.

The overhead pines wouldn't have looked out of place in Alabama. Clouds scudded above the limestone ridge. A smell of rain hung in the air. In all probability, we would soon be wet and we would accomplish no caving that day. Still, we lay in the grass, none of us talking. It felt good. A pregnant breeze rattled the leaves and stirred the treetops. When you travel without an itinerary, I had learned, it is sometimes permissible to commit philosophy.

The soft and slightly itchy bed brought back a dozen campsites past. It reminded me of my favorite study ground at Florida State, a quiet Civil War–era cemetery down the road from the Tallahassee boardinghouse where I lived. I did more than study amid the burial ground's black-streaked stones: Something about the gentle turf and the hint of death had made it an ideal place to bring dates.

Two weeks earlier, I had relaxed with a book in another grassy cemetery, one that overlooked Lake Baikal, a few kilometers north of the tiny village of Listvyanka. Baikal was almost painfully beautiful, the day cloudless and warm. I had been delighted to discover that the Russians celebrated the dead by placing picnic tables and even barbecue grills in their family plots. On holidays, friends and relations would visit the deceased and make a day of it. But no celebratory mourners were present as I reclined against a tombstone that was adorned with a hand-painted, ceramic-backed photograph of a woman who looked exactly like Aunt Bea. The book I pulled from my duffel was one of the all-time great travel narratives, Peter Matthiessen's *The Snow Leopard*.

This was no accident: I was reading travel books during my three-day break at Baikal because I was in the midst of reporting on a ten-thousand-mile rail trip. What was an accident was that I had found Matthiessen's name on the registry of the cramped and moldy Listvyanka hotel where I was staying.

He had been through ten days earlier, researching a conservation piece which I would eventually read in *The New York Review of Books*. He arrived, I realized with a few seconds of mental subtraction, at about the same time I met Tom in Budapest.

Tom had been caving and hiking in Eastern Europe, following a trip with his fiancée, Odarkka, to meet her parents in Ukraine. Tom and I had agreed to meet at 6 P.M. on the day Matthiessen arrived at Baikal, at the base of the funicular to the Buda Hills. But I had missed a connecting flight in Belgrade and wound up taking the train through Czechoslovakia, which brought me into Budapest at midnight. Tom had also been running late, returning from a week in Prague.

His cab and mine, departing from separate Budapest train stations, pulled up to the hotel where I'd told him I would stay at exactly the same time, 12:40 A.M. After a few days spent touring the city, I had departed for Beijing by way of the Trans-Siberia Express, on assignment for *Student Traveler*. I planned to hook up with Tom again in China (he had bought tickets for a later train), and we would travel together to find Ian in Guangzhou.

During all the time I had carried Matthiessen's book through Warsaw, Moscow, and assorted Soviet sleeping compartments, the author was boating over Lake Baikal with biologists. But, I was willing to bet, not even Matthiessen himself had reclined with a good book in a grassy plot, on a sunny, breezy day, surrounded by birdsong, within sight of the clear deep trench that held one-fifth of the planet's fresh water. So there.

Lounging on the grass, I realized as I lay philosophizing in China, is one of the greatest rewards of time spent outdoors, no matter where you go.

I remembered the expansive yard in front of my grandfather's farmhouse in Illinois, the exotic destination of my childhood. The sod dropped steeply toward a gravel drive, forming a hill that my cousins and I would roll down on hot summer nights. Adults would take wooden chairs from the porch and rock under the trees, swatting mosquitoes, sipping iced tea, and telling stories. Sometimes an uncle would walk over to say, "You know, Uncle Ernie spit a big greasy chaw right where you kids are playing," or, "I saw Prince lift his hind leg in that spot not five minutes ago."

I'd inspect my jeans and T-shirt with concern, picking at each smudge and stain, until laughter from under the trees let me know I was the butt of a joke. At which point I would dive for the legs of the offending uncle, and down the hill we'd go. This may have been the point. Adults on an Illinois farm generally needed an excuse to enjoy the languorous pleasure of grass.

Years later, I went to live with my cousin Dennis, the Kentucky doctor with the rambling farmhouse, while I tried to become a writer. One of Dennis' younger brothers was a fellow freeloader, trying to establish himself as a joiner by crafting cherry and walnut cabinetwork in Dennis' well-equipped shop. I remember that James Allen liked to lie in the lawn after eating a big meal, which is to say frequently. To know James Allen at twenty was to define the word "strapping." More than once, I saw him introduce himself to strangers with the line "Bet ah can lift your car." He could.

James Allen ate with the same passion he applied to hoisting vehicles and routing flawless dadoes. After a few slabs of home-cured ham or half a backyard chicken, three or four roasting ears (pronounced "row-sneers"), a dozen biscuits, greens, three pieces of pie or cobbler, and a gallon of tea, James Allen would stand at the table and announce solemnly, "Ah gots to go out in the yard and roll around some." And he would. There James Allen would be, wallowing in bluegrass, belly poking from beneath the confines of a torn work shirt. His arms stretched wide, he'd grin like a blue China pig.

I always admired James Allen's unequivocal enthusiasm for the feel of grass, and in his honor I turned a couple of revolutions across this small patch of China. For a moment, sun pierced the clouds. I stretched to soak the warmth. It occurred to me that any nearby snake might wish to do likewise, but I wasn't concerned enough to look for one. For at least two thousand years, snakes have been a prized delicacy in rural Guangdong. Natural selection has made the few surviving species extraordinarily shy.

While I saw no snakes, I did notice a couple of rust-colored pinheads on my hand. Closer inspection revealed tiny red chiggers. Relatives of grass dwellers I'd fed in the Cockpit bottoms, at the Zacatón campsite, and on my grandfather's lawn, they indicated a typical grass ecology, involving periodic contact with grazing or foraging mammals. I could see spiders, caterpillars, and small birds working the forest of tall blades. This could have been a meadow in the Smokies or on a high Arizona plateau.

It certainly didn't look like China.

Neat ranks of hand-tilled crops covered most of the open land I'd seen in Guangdong. The few pockets of wilderness we had tramped through in search of caves—atop high mountains, at the bottom of steep sinkholes—had presented lush tangles of vegetation, appropriate to a region crossed by the Tropic of Cancer. Nor had I found grass in the cities and towns. Raked dirt invariably covered whatever open space lay between the ranks of concrete apartment buildings and rows of mud-brick houses. I'd seen virtually no lawns.

Like so many of life's niceties, grass was politically suspect in China. In the dark days of the Cultural Revolution, Mao had casually repeated a Chinese wives' tale: Grass near the home breeds disease. Immediately, fervent brigades of Red Guards set about eradicating turf wherever they found it. Twenty years later, casual utterances of the Chairman were no longer held inviolate. Yet replanting lost grass seemed a low priority. As Ian put it: "People here have more important things to worry about than landscaping."

From what I'd seen, the Chinese attitude toward grass extended to much of the natural world. I'd observed all manner of litter tossed from the windows of trains and buses, the decks of riverboats. No amount of argument seemed to convince Chinese cavers not to dump spent carbide or candy wrappers underground. In the Ru Yuan market, one could buy trapped (and in many cases endangered) wildlife ranging from snakes and bats to exotic wildcats. Whole villages channeled trash and sewage directly into the water supply. I doubted a catalytic converter existed within a thousand miles of Guangzhou.

Yet grass, like all of nature, is also a traditional element of *feng shui*. It is a sign of rebirth and family in ancient paintings; it is a reminder of the power of small things in ancient poetry. Consider the mention it receives in this passage, dated 1642, translated from the wall of a cave Ian and I explored near Guilin on the 1988 expedition: "In the sixth year of Yung Li, on the twenty-eighth day of the eleventh month, all the soldiers and officials of the city of Guilin, in the prefecture of Guangxi, left in a panic, riding on horseback. The city was empty, with no rule, for several months. People of four villages were strangled. From the capital at Nanking, the upper classes returned with hired guards.

"In the second month of the year, soldiers set about capturing those hiding in towns, villages, and caves. Young and old, men and women alike, were led on leashes and held for ransom. In Huitian, Sidu, and Dongxiang, countless people were put to death. The peasantry feared for their lives. We fled to this cave to hide, and now the names of all of us are worth no more than grass."

The inscription was signed "representing the masses," by Liang Jinyu, Yu Sishan, and others. I sometimes wonder whether the names of all humanity are worth no more than grass.

I was awakened by raindrops hitting my face. I must have dozed off. As I blinked the water away, I recalled Old Lodgeskins, the character played by Chief Dan George in *Little Big Man*. At the end of the movie Lodgeskins, blind and saddened by the loss of his people, by the cruelty of all he has seen, hikes to a high meadow in order to die. Despite Dustin Hoffman's efforts to talk him out of it, the old chief challenges Death to fight him face-to-face. When Death will not come, Lodgeskins reclines nobly in the grass and closes his eyes. Rain hits him in the face. He opens his eyes, sighs heavily, and says, "Sometimes the magic works, sometimes it doesn't."

Which was my comment to Ian and Tom, who answered me with confused looks. They were also blinking themselves awake. We decided, at last, to call in our roving guides, to stumble down the mountain to a county highway where we could catch a ride to our guesthouse. We stood and stretched. The rain stopped—it had been only a sprinkle.

As I pulled on my pack, I heard a shout in Chinese from the next ridge. Ian walked toward the voice, speaking Mandarin as he disappeared into the bush. A few minutes later, he returned to announce, "They say they've found the cave. It's back this way."

Tom and I shrugged, yawned, and followed.

A short hike later, we stood inside a stalactite-bejeweled chamber, lit by a magical shaft from the setting sun. We took photos of each other posing like noble explorers in the laserlike path of light. In a nearby cave passage, we found and rappelled into a virgin pit, 170 feet deep. We photographed beautiful mineral formations, untouched by the hand of man, in the room at its base. We sang Monty Python songs. I lifted a pebble from a ledge and stuck it in my pack. Hours later, we emerged to a full moon rising over the ridge, bathing the valley below in white.

The farmers had gone home, and when we finally worked our way back to the mountain highway, the van which was supposed to be waiting for us was nowhere to be found. The ancient carved footpath we had followed continued downhill from the highway, toward a village of stone buildings that lay several kilometers below. While Ian and I waited by the road for the van, Tom decided to hike to the village for some food and beer.

Tom spoke no Chinese, and even if he had the local dialect was quite different from Mandarin. But Ian taught him to say "san ping pijou," which means "three bottles of beer." He carried several dollars' worth of the "People's Currency," which, although it was illegal for foreigners to hold at the time, was the only money readily accepted in the countryside.

There were neither roads nor electricity in the remote valley, and we knew that it was unlikely that another foreigner had entered the village within the lifetime of anyone who lived there. As Tom set off, Ian said, "Enjoy the sixteenth century."

Sitting on our packs, talking about the cave we had just seen and possible areas to target the next day, Ian and I could follow Tom's progress. Although his cap lamp had quickly faded from sight, we could hear the gradual increase of barking dogs as he neared the edge of town. We heard the distant squeals of delighted children, for whom we always carried small gifts. By the time Tom and his growing entourage—two hundred people, he estimated later—reached the center of town, they sounded like a full-blown festival. Firecrackers, raucous laughter, and cheering echoed through the valley.

After a half hour or so, we could make out a cluster of lanterns and torches moving away from the central square. We heard the crowd gradually quiet down, thinning finally to children and then only dogs. Twenty minutes later, Tom strolled up the path alone. In his pack were three liters of beer, oranges, and a half dozen boiled eggs. No more than an hour after we ate, the van from the guesthouse arrived; the driver had been fixing a flat.

I returned to the United States two weeks later, armed with the text of my travel article and sufficient objectives to justify planning a major caving expedition for 1991. I made it home just in time to start Lamaze class with Kathy, who was pregnant with our first child. We had agreed that after the baby was born I would set up this last expedition, and then give up longer trips, at least for a few years.

As I began describing for her all that had happened in my eight-week ride around the world, I recalled that fall day in China. What I remembered most vividly wasn't the perfect moonrise over an ancient mountain town, sunlight beaming into the cave, or the thrill of being the first person to descend a well-decorated virgin pit. What I remembered was the soft and slightly itchy feel of thick green blades poking through my shirt, the smell of impending rain, the sound of wind rustling the trees.

I remembered lying in that patch of grass.

Like the writing on cave walls or the passage that stays with you after a good book, the tall grass that you lie in, the stuff that grows out there, far beyond the suburbs, carries a message. People have been here and gone, the grass says. This is border ground, a truce between civilization and forest. The land was too rocky, too far away, too polluted, too bloody, too something, and the grass was waiting. It grows green at Shiloh and the Little Bighorn, on the banks of Love Canal, in the leveled blocks of the Bronx. It grows green in the slashed-and-burned rain forests of Borneo. It grows green in a quiet country churchyard atop my buried grandfather.

The lawns of my childhood offered a physical hint of the vast world that existed beyond my suburban home, beyond even the wilderness I imagined my grandfather's farm to be. Alexander Ray Taylor was born on December 5, 1990, and he's a great kid. In 1991, I published my train article, persuaded the Smithsonian to fund a winter expedition, assembled a team, landed a teaching job, and kept my promise.

Kenneth Daniel and Christopher Dale, identical twins, arrived February 28, 1994, and they're great kids too. A month after they were born, Kathy's mother flew in from Florida to help with the babies for a week, so that I could take a short trip to Mexico. I wanted to watch Sheck Exley and Jim Bowden set a world scuba depth record. That sad journey and China were the last caving expeditions of any sort that I have joined.

It's Tuesday, September 26, 1995, and I'm sitting at my desk in Arkadelphia, Arkansas, thumbing through the mail. Here's the October issue of *National Geographic*, another Nick Nichols photo on the cover. Here's the *NSS News*. My computer beeps to signal an incoming E-mail.

It's from Ian: "Mike, I got your message, but cannot accept

the fact that a mere matter of money and family and work commitments would even cause you to hesitate to buy a ticket to China. So talk to the dean, talk to Kathy, rob a liquor store, whatever it takes. You NEED to be in Guadou this November. You NEED to spend three or four days at a time underground, mapping and scooping and blasting and too bad in what could very well be the longest cave in China, soon. You NEED to be alongside me, puking snake bile at the dogs below from the railing of the guesthouse."

I may need these things, but Ian and I both know I won't have them. So I sit here typing at a computer. I sit here, a writer, a teacher, a father, a husband, a former caver who sometimes longs for the time to cave again. I sit here representing the masses, waiting for the magic to work. I sit here, and sometimes I get up to look out of my window at the grass.

GLOSSARY
OF CAVING TERMS

Ascender Any device designed to keep a climbing caver attached to the rope. The most basic ascenders are "prusik knots"—short lengths of rope, attached to a caver's feet or harness, that are slid up the main line by means of a special knot that seizes the rope when weighted. "Mechanical" ascenders include several commercial devices that attach to a rope by means of metallic cams, such as Gibbs, Jumars, Petzl Croll, Petzl Jammers, and Troll.

Ballistic Nylon A thick, rot-resistant cloth, originally designed for bulletproof vests, now commonly used to make caving coveralls, packs, kneepads, etc.

Bolt Kit In the exploration of virgin pits, cavers must often secure ropes to rock walls by means of three or more specialized bolts. A typical bolt kit contains some type of drilling device, hardened climbing bolts, a wrench, and metal hangers for carabiner-to-bolt attachment.

Carabiner A stainless steel or aluminum device resembling a large link of chain with a hinged, spring-loaded gate, used to rig climbing ropes and harnesses. "Locking" carabiners contain a threaded tube that may be screwed shut to prevent the gate from accidentally opening during use.

Carbide Lamp A brass or occasionally plastic device that produces light by the following process: Water drips from an upper reservoir into a lower chamber, hitting gravel-sized chunks of calcium carbide, an inexpensive chemical that releases acetylene gas when wet. The gas is piped through a nozzle mounted in the center of a metallic reflector and ignited. The small flame produces a yellowish light that lasts between one and four hours, depending on lamp type and compartment size. Most cavers who use carbide prefer antique lamps manufactured earlier in the century for the mining industry, regarding as inferior those produced after American coal mines switched to electric light in the 1950s. In the 1980s, some cavers abandoned carbide for new, sophisticated electric caving lamps, which offer a much longer battery life than ordinary flashlights. However, many still prefer carbide, for several reasons: It generally costs less than batteries for light of similar duration. Carbide lamps, unlike electrics, double as a heat source during periods of inactivity. And in rare cases the sudden extinguishing of carbide lamps has alerted cavers to a lack of oxygen from "bad" or "dead" air.

On the other hand, spent carbide, a noisome gray powder, is a toxic pollutant that must be carefully removed from caves in either a "dump bag"—two or three layers of heavy-duty plastic storage bags—or a "dump bottle"—often a baby bottle with a tight-fitting lid. Poorly sealed dump bags have been known explode, especially after immersion in a cave pool or waterfall, sometimes with force sufficient to cause injury. There have been a few recorded cases of carbide lamps igniting subterranean pockets of methane or other flammable gases. Inattentive carbide cavers have on occasion burned the rope to which they were attached, their own hair, or the person in front of them in a cramped crawlway.

Caving Helmet Essential to protect cavers from low ceilings and dislodged falling pebbles. In horizontal caves that require no climbing, cavers often use an ordinary construction cap that has been modifed to include a lamp bracket and a secure chin strap. For vertical work, commercial climbing or caving helmets are preferred.

Column A cave formation that occurs when a stalactite meets a stalagmite.

Figure Eight A simple rappel device, usually made of aluminum and usually used only on rappels of 100 feet or less.

Flowstone A bulbous formation caused by the gradual buildup of calcite over a mud slope, cave wall or floor, or loose rock. A "flowstone shield" occurs when the original mud is washed away, leaving a curved hollow of calcite that rings like a bell when struck.

Formation Any secondary mineral deposit in a cave, such as stalactites, stalagmites, flowstone, rimstone, gypsum flowers, etc.

Helictite A delicate calcite formation that displays twiglike branching.

Horizontal Gear The minimum equipment required for safely traversing a cave that will require no rope work or difficult climbing: a helmet with chin strap (to protect the head from low ceilings); a helmet-mounted primary lamp (to keep hands free for climbing and crawling); extra batteries or carbide and water; at least two backup light sources (flashlight, candles, chemical lightsticks, etc.); gloves; sturdy boots; heavy-duty, long-sleeved clothes or coveralls; food and water sufficient for the anticipated time underground; a small first-aid kit; dump bags for carbide; a folded large trash bag or "space blanket" to be used for warmth during periods of inaction; paper and pencils; kneepads (optional); and a sturdy side- or back-mounted cave pack.

Karst The type of limestone landscape in which caves are most often found, characterized by frequent sinkholes, disappearing or emerging streams, ridges of exposed limestone, and pits.

Mapping Gear A nylon measuring tape at least 50 feet (or, for metric surveys, 10 meters) long; heavy-duty compass; inclinometer; survey flagging tape or other point markers; a waterproof book for recording survey data and sketches; and several pencils.

Pit A sheer or undercut vertical cave shaft. A drop that begins at the surface and that allows daylight to enter is called an "open air" pit; a drop that may be rappelled without the rope coming into contact with a wall is called a "free" pit.

Rappel Rack   A U-shaped metal rod used to descend pits. The legs of the "U" are bridged by four to six aluminum, steel, or titanium "brake bars." The main rope is threaded through the brake bars, which the caver then adds or removes, spreads apart or presses together, in order to precisely control the speed of descent down the rope.

Rimstone   A formation caused by the gradual buildup of calcite at the edge of a cave pool. Rimstone "dams" may enclose several adjoining pools of water, each perched at a different level. Some rimstone cascades are larger than any man-made fountain, with each dam wall several feet high; others are tiny details observed in the corners of tight crawlways.

Soda Straw   A thin, hollow stalactite typically measuring one-quarter inch in diameter, with a length ranging from a few inches to ten feet.

Stalactite   Any formation that hangs from a cave ceiling.

Stalagmite   Any formation that grows from a cave floor.

Vertical Gear or V-Gear   The kit of technical devices by which cavers descend and ascend pits, usually carried in a "vertical pack." A minimal set typically includes: leather gloves, a nylon seat harness, a rappel rack with brake bars (or other descent device), two mechanical ascenders such as Gibbs or Petzls, a third ascender (often a Jumar) to be used as a "safety," four to six carabiners, several lengths of tubular webbing, a chest harness with a Simmons or other chest roller, and a signal whistle.

IF YOU WANT
TO GO CAVING . . .

The *only* safe way to begin caving is to go with someone experienced. An excellent introduction to the underground wilderness is to take one of the "wild" or "spelunking" tours offered at many of the national parks, national monuments, and state parks that feature tour caves. You can also meet an experienced cave guide by contacting the National Speleological Society. Most NSS-affiliated clubs (called "grottoes") offer instruction for beginners and plan several guided novice trips annually. You can obtain the address and phone number of the grotto nearest you by calling the NSS at (205) 852-1300, or writing the NSS at 2813 Cave Avenue, Huntsville, AL 35810–4431 (you can find the NSS on the Internet at http://speleology.cs.yale.edu/nss.html).

Although most grottoes and park spelunking tours will lend you a helmet, primary lamp, and other necessary gear for your first trip, you should bring sturdy but flexible clothing (long sleeves are important) and lug-soled boots that provide some ankle support. You should carry your own small backup flashlight and extra batteries. Also bring a complete change of clothing (including underwear) for after the cave trip, as well as a garbage bag for your muddy clothes. Expect everything you wear into the cave to be permanently stained a mud-brown color. It's a good idea to take along a canteen and granola, candy bars, or other quick-energy food.

Keep in mind that most caves are on private land, and that many landowners have closed their caves to all exploration because of the inconsiderate actions of a single caver. **Always** obtain permission from the landowner before setting foot on private property, and **always** thank the landowner when such permission is granted. If a landowner or guide requests that you sign a liability waiver, be willing do so without hesitation—or don't go caving. Leave farm gates as you find them, whether open or closed. Never camp on cave property without permission, and never disturb a locked cave gate. (Many gated caves may be entered legally by going through proper channels; often a contact telephone number for a particular cave is posted within sight of the entrance. Simply call the number and follow established procedure.)

Recommended background books include *Caving Basics* and *On Rope*, both published by the NSS and available through bookstores, outdoor retailers, and by contacting the NSS directly. For a catalog of other cave-related reading, write to Speleobooks, P.O. Box 10, Schoharie, NY 12157.

About cave diving: Never enter an underwater cave without cave training and certification, no matter how thorough your open-water experience. If you do so, you will probably die. Certified cave divers will risk their own lives to remove your body, and all cavers will suffer for the bad publicity your avoidable death generates.

A final note about the cavers you meet: They may seem a bit wary at first, even cold. At the very least they may seem strange. Don't worry. It's only natural that cavers use caution in introducing new practitioners to their special places. Even if you are an experienced climber or hiker, your guides will (or should) spend a great deal of time talking to you about safety and conservation *before* they take you underground. They will want to see a certain determination and self-reliance in your thinking, to be sure that you won't get weird in a tight spot. Indulge them. Even after you join a grotto, it may take a year or more before you are taken to any of a group's biggest or best caves (often kept secret). Be patient. Every caver I know who has taken the time to learn with an experienced group has made friends for life and has found a truly life-changing way of looking at the world.

INDEX

DATE